Preface: Departure and Arrival

This is a book about many things. Originally, it appears as a c... discourses about the past, and yet it unfolds as an ethnography of pastness that deals with the contemporary city, geographies of affect, generational change and materiality. The work interweaves a number of topics related to how physical and cultural wasting are rarely synchronised, accounting for diverse ways of treating inheritances and the different intensities of urban memory that they generate. By studying the material and social afterlife of the Soviet world in Estonia, I attempt to show the dialectical relation between construction and demolition, and how the need to build something new entails the disinvestment and neglect of the legacies from the old regime. With a fringy anthropology, I explore how the vanquishing over the Soviet world happened on a different time scale from the decay of its legacy, allowing for new availabilities, intricate reappropriations and unforeseen opportunities for recuperation.

The research cultivates transdisciplinary intellectual work and appears as deeply contemporary; for five years, my work has been accompanying actual transformations in a proactive way, insisting that reparative practices have a larger political resonance by reconstituting social fabrics that have been neglected or bruised. The ethnographic fieldwork argues for the intimate connection between postsocialist reforms and negative representations of the Soviet world; yet, by reflecting on how Estonian youth are not following the expectations and values of the previous generations due to their distinct life experience, it also shows how we can understand generational change and affective processes of transmission in terms of materiality, since change is made through the repetition of the different.

The focus on iterations places an emphasis on process and dialogic co-creation, thus showing the multiscalar registers, trajectories and intensities that forge social transformations. Changing notions of legacy and waste in Estonia have been used to define what value is and to provide new accounts for social transformations, generational change, and the interconnections between time and community. Then, the focus on wasted legacies, their nondeaths, afterlives, shifts of value and dissonance helps us to understand affective transmissions, shifting temporalities and the underside of social transformations. Moreover, the research is part of the contemporary preoccupation with waste and the obsolete, and contributes to discussions about how material things represent attributes and convey complex meanings and affects.

While designing my ethnographic fieldwork, I faced the challenge of how to compare different historical eras with their own temporal regimes, legacies and urban memories. I finally decided to articulate a narrative through a positionality model of departure and arrival, taken here as a narrative exercise to exposing the complex ways in which continuities interact with changes. Changing happens in reaction to something and for some purpose. Past, present and future are better understood in terms of each other by differentiating experiences and expectations (Koselleck [1979] 2004). Thus, any process of change has to be interrogated not only by examining the distinctions between past and present, but also the relationships that mutually constitute the aspects between them (Verdery 1996). Therein resides the dialectic of 'the Old' and 'the New', and therefore, my attempt to expose how things are remembered and forgotten through the tropes of departure and arrival.

Instead of a synchronic contextualisation of what happened to the Soviet remains, I rather approach the acceptance or rejection of past things as a process; acknowledging, nonetheless, that social changes do not necessarily happen as a string, one after another, but rather occur through an interweaving of knots, as a field of place-occasions and plural intersecting temporalities. In light of this, we also have to ask what happened in between and how the choices were made, as a condensation that is simultaneously synchronic and diachronic.

An example of a synchronic analysis would be to compare the destinations of Tallinn airport in the Soviet era and nowadays (figure 0.1), and then explain the changes in Estonia based on similarities and differences:

1979: Almata, Arhangelsk, Bakuu, Vilnius, Viljandi, Gorki, Dnepropetrovsk, Donetsk, Jerevan, Zaporozje, Kiiev, Kisinjov, Krasnodar,

Remains of the Soviet Past in Estonia

FRINGE

Series Editors
Alena Ledeneva and Peter Zusi, School of Slavonic and
East European Studies, UCL

The FRINGE series explores the roles that complexity, ambivalence and immeasurability play in social and cultural phenomena. A cross-disciplinary initiative bringing together researchers from the humanities, social sciences and area studies, the series examines how seemingly opposed notions such as centrality and marginality, clarity and ambiguity, can shift and converge when embedded in everyday practices.

Alena Ledeneva is Professor of Politics and Society at the School of Slavonic and East European Studies of UCL.

Peter Zusi is Lecturer at the School of Slavonic and East European Studies of UCL.

By adopting the tropes of 'repair' and 'waste', this book innovatively manages to link various material registers from architecture, intergenerational relations, affect and museums with ways of making the past present. Through a rigorous yet transdisciplinary method, Martínez brings together different scales and contexts that would often be segregated out. In this respect, the ethnography unfolds a deep and nuanced analysis, providing a useful comparative and insightful account of the processes of repair and waste making in all their material, social and ontological dimensions.

Victor Buchli,
Professor of Material Culture at UCL

This book comprises an endearingly transdisciplinary ethnography of postsocialist material culture and social change in Estonia. Martínez creatively draws on a number of critical and cultural theorists, together with additional research on memory and political studies scholarship and the classics of anthropology. Grappling concurrently with time and space, the book offers a delightfully thick description of the material effects generated by the accelerated post-Soviet transformation in Estonia, inquiring into the generational specificities in experiencing and relating to the postsocialist condition through the conceptual anchors of wasted legacies and repair. This book defies disciplinary boundaries and shows how an attention to material relations and affective infrastructures might reinvigorate political theory.

Maria Mälksoo, Senior Lecturer, Brussels School of International Studies at the University of Kent

Remains of the Soviet Past in Estonia

An Anthropology of Forgetting,
Repair and Urban Traces

Francisco Martínez

First published in 2018 by
UCL Press
University College London
Gower Street
London WC1E 6BT

Available to download free: www.ucl.ac.uk/ucl-press

A CIP catalogue record for this book is available from The British Library.

ISBN: 9781787353558 (Hbk.)
ISBN: 9781787353541 (Pbk.)
ISBN: 9781787353534 (PDF)
ISBN: 9781787353565 (epub)
ISBN: 9781787353572 (mobi)
ISBN: 9781787353589 (html)
DOI: https://doi.org/10.14324/111.9781787353534

The future is but the obsolete in reverse.

Nabokov (1952, 22)

People will be born – generation after generation – live a happy life, age gradually, but the Palace of the Soviets, familiar to them from their dear childhood books, will stand exactly the same as you and I will see it in the next few years. Centuries will not leave their mark on it; we will build it so that it will stand without ageing, forever.

Atarov (1940, 15; cf. Paperny 2002, 17)

The city of Leonia refashions itself every day: every morning the people wake between fresh sheets, wash with just-unwrapped cakes of soap, wear brand-new clothing, take from the latest model refrigerator still unopened tins, listening to the last-minute jingles from the most up-to-date radio.

On the sidewalks, encased in spotless plastic bags, the remains of yesterday's Leonia await the garbage truck. Not only squeezed tubes of toothpaste, blown-out light bulbs, newspapers, containers, wrappings, but also boilers, encyclopedias, pianos, porcelain dinner services. It is not so much by the things that each day are manufactured, sold, bought, that you can measure Leonia's opulence, but rather by the things that each day are thrown out to make room for the new. So you begin to wonder if Leonia's true passion is really, as they say, the enjoyment of new and different things, and not, instead the joy of expelling, discarding, cleansing itself of a recurrent impurity.

Calvino (1974, 114–15)

Kingissepp, Kärdla, Kaliningrad, Leningrad, Lvov, Minsk, Mineralnaya Voda, Murmansk, Odessa, Sotsi, Palanga, Petrozavodsk, Pärnu, Riia, Rostov, Sverdlovsk, Simferopol, Tbilisi, Tartu, Harkov.[1]

2015: Brussels, Riga, Oslo, Warsaw, Antalya, Helsinki, Istanbul, London, Berlin-Tegel, Kiev, Copenhagen, Stockholm, Frankfurt am Main, St. Petersburg.

A diachronic analysis would rather focus on historical dynamics and features over time. For instance, it was only in 1989 that Scandinavian Airlines (SAS) began operating in Estonia (the first foreign airline since World War II) and a couple of times airplanes were taken over by hijackers demanding to be taken 'to the West'. However, in 2016, 2.2 million passengers used Tallinn airport and 4.25 million tourists visited Tallinn (three times more than the whole population of Estonia, which is 1.3 million). In addition, it is noteworthy to mention the renaming of the aerial gateway to honour Lennart Meri (first president after Estonia's regained independence) and how Estonian Air was established in 1991 based on the scarce assets of the local airline Aeroflot; and how only 25 years later, Estonian Air entered into bankruptcy once the European Commission ruled that the financial support given by the Estonian government

Fig. 0.1 Kaia restoring the panel of Tallinn airport, 1979.
Source: Marika Agu, 2013.

Fig. 0.2 Tallinn airport, 1981. Source: Pavel Kuznetsov, Rahvusarhiivi filmiarhiiv.

Fig. 0.3 Interior of Tallinn airport, 1980. Source: Pavel Kuznetsov, Rahvusarhiivi filmiarhiiv.

was not in line with the European Union regulations of free-market competency.[2]

Further on, the actual Tallinn airport is not simply a place of technology and transport offering the transitory occupant the illusion of being part of a global scheme of flows, business and mobility; this site is also a national showcase and a sanitised version of a public space. On the one hand, the airport accelerates future expectations by materialising security and the selected multiplication of cosmopolitan strangers; on the other, it crafts a sense of pastness by framing what it means to be Estonian, contributing to national identity through design (figures 0.2 and 0.3).[3] And even so, airports are rarely considered historical or monumental but rather purposeful nonplaces that leave behind no legacy (Augé 1995). Thus, the evolution of Tallinn airport cannot be simply explained by the break-up of the USSR, since issues such as globalisation and new modes of tourism also played a crucial role. Overall, the study of social transformations is not as easy as putting facts taken from the past on the same plane as present events or by listing a chain of relevant events about a place; rather we have to examine trajectories of change, situated iterations, bygone futures and alternatives that were considered yet not taken, bearing in mind that we might learn more on detours than on any direct route (Schlögel 2003).

Acknowledgements

To Ray, because children are not responsible for their parents.

I would like to thank Marika, my companion, and my family in Spain for their unconditional support. I would also like to thank Luule and Silver for their generous hospitality and trust. I have been fortunate to study with wonderful mentors who have fostered a love of learning and a multidisciplinary approach to material culture and memory. With their generous feedback and inspiring work, Patrick Laviolette and Siobhan Kattago have played a crucial role in improving this book. Also, I would like to thank Victor Buchli and Maria Mälksoo for their encouragement and for sharing their sharp ideas, comments and suggestions, as well as the two anonymous reviewers who provided a thorough constructive criticism, and the UCL Press team for their fantastic work.

Several colleagues have contributed to the development of this book by making time to discuss much of the content in both formal and informal settings; namely, Marcos Farias Ferreira and Pablo Zerm while eating *khachapuri* in Tbilisi; also, I am particularly grateful to Andra Aaloe, Karsten Brüggemann, Max Dade, Laura Hirvi, Raiko Jäärats, Liisa Kaljula, Keiti Kljavin, Tiina Kirss, Franz Krause, Andres Kurg, Daniele Monticelli, Raili Nugin, Tarmo Pikner, Siim Preiman, Liina Siib, Klemen Slabina, Hanna Snellman, Helen Sooväli-Sepping, Elnara Taidre, Marek Tamm, Kirill Tulin and Aimar Ventsel, as well as to my anthropology fellows from Murcia, Klaus, Salva and Damián. Many friends are also warmly present in this work. The voices of Ksenia Berner, Alex Bieth, Bruno Gomes, Ott Kagovere, Pille Kruus, Merly Mändla, Madli Maruste, Märt Miljan, Lilli-Krõõt Repnau, Alessandro Testa and Pablo Veyrat are latent in the work.

Last but not least, my appreciation extends to Anne Vatén, Jerry Waters, Peeter Mägi, Maren Poel, Liina Luhats, Riina Varol, Risto Kozer, Sirla, Tanel Rander, Kristina, Kristiina and Anette, Andres Siim, Tõnu Tunnel and Rahvusarhiivi filmiarhiiv for sharing their photographs, and all the informants and participants who kindly took part in this endeavour.

ACKNOWLEDGEMENTS

Contents

List of figures

Introduction: The politics of the old

Youth is supposed to mean future, but in some cases it also represents a new opportunity for the neglected legacies of a troubled past. Drawing on the assumption that a new generation that does not remember the socialist time and is particularly open to global influences has grown up in Estonia, the research makes evident that the impact of the Soviet memory on people's conventional values is losing its effective power in the course of generational change, thereby transforming the conditions for gaining knowledge about the socialist past. The ethnographic fieldwork traces relational imaginaries to the recent past, telling stories about the degradation of the Soviet world, despite the inheritance of its practices, material constructions and ideas. However, this book is not about the nostalgia of the socialist experience or its material culture, but instead it deals with how forgetting is inscribed on built and historical landscapes in various ways. Through a critical engagement with contemporary material culture in Estonia, the research demonstrates that postsocialist processes have meant a negative renarrativisation of the Soviet world. Any new political regime inevitably involves a high degree of active forgetting as a consequence of a novel articulation of collective memory. In that sense, we can argue that not only forgetting but also memory itself involves a neglect of material evidence that recalls a past that is now considered undesirable; yet, getting rid of something is never a simple act that ends with disposal. What has been discarded is not necessarily forgotten or vanished; the neglected may later affect social organisation with both persistent presences and haunting absences. Also, the destruction or negligence of the built environment generates an interpretative excess, as if it were a form of iconoclasm (Forty 1999; Harris 1999; Yampolsky 1995).

By studying the afterlife of those things that did not achieve a full usefulness after the Soviet time, this ethnography reveals the day-to-day representations of the inherited, taking the question of the treatment of legacies as key to understand how material structures might refuse to die but instead instigate particular patterns of behaviour, use and repair, and also how these acts of classification, maintenance or negligence of the inherited influence contemporary social processes. One of the novelties of this research has been the development of a theoretical framework and a cross-disciplinary methodological approach for analysing the materiality and immateriality of the inherited, addressing the dynamic ways in which national identity and historical representations are constructed in relation to waste and by dematerialising the old. I start my research with an uncomfortable question posed in the present – What has happened to the Soviet legacies and why? – and then expose how what remains might not be cherished or maintained (thus determining abandonment, concealment, separation or negligence) as part of an effort to dematerialise past identities and temporal regimes (as an enforced forgetting).

Through kaleidoscopic impressions and a dialogic immersion into urban memories between generations, this work intends to contribute to the acknowledgement of social and material heritage, advance the mutual understanding of different generations, show the raking workings of disrepair, and finally, move beyond the current literature on postsocialism. In postcommunist studies, it has become commonplace to view the remains of the Soviet world as having excremental value; that it is a hangover of the previous period or 'a political phantom that persisted rather than developed' (Oushakine 2009, 27). Thus, this research contributes to understanding the affective aspects of people's engagement with past things and the social effects of disrepair, thereby placing the focus on what has been historically given yet which did not achieve its life expectancy or the utmost usefulness.

There is an increasing fascination with the remains of the past, translated into vintage beauty, souvenirs, retro-utopias, nostalgia, stranger things, the museification of everyday life, as well as a growing interest in what has gone out of fashion and an obsession with not forgetting (Huyssen 2003). Yet, what happens to the inheritances that did not find any continuation – those that were 'wasted'? As something from the past, a legacy is passed down and transmitted to the present; it is in this sense that a legacy is inherently generational – always recalibrated by those coming after. Legacies appear to be visible and lifted to significance only if they can be written by the subsequent generation within a heritage, cultural memory, national identity or in ruined stories. And yet, wasted legacies coexist with us in a state of potentiality and resonance, thus showing a tendency to return, claiming for recognition of their significance.

Ethnographic dispatches from the periphery

This book has an ethnographic aspect without aspiring to be an ethnography in the conventional sense, and it has also a historical aspect without aiming to provide a history of Estonia. The work makes connections across supposed disciplinary boundaries, engaging with a wide range of authors and informants to examine how young people, who came of age after the dissolution of the Soviet Union, differ from their parents. Methodologically, it combines a commitment to long-term fieldwork with an emphasis on macropolitical and aesthetic analysis expressed in experimental techniques and flexible writing. Such a combination serves to broaden the interpretative scope of our mode of research and appears as a fringy anthropology at the contact zone of different disciplines – one that pushes us into conceptual borderlands constituting an outer boundary in itself.

The research is laid out as a series of comparative micro cases and thinking places that tangentially resembles a multisited ethnography (Marcus 1995), here conducted in three cities of one country. The connections between these sites and the distributedness of the anthropological objects were partially constructed as a meta-assembly, following the aim at achieving a comparative potential between them and with other case studies too. The succession of snapshots with scenes of ordinary life sourced through diversified voices is aimed at giving to the book an empathic quality. Then, terms such as waste, suture, active negligence, preserved disrepair and amalgamation appear as microturning points located to conceptualise the presence and significance of the past within the everyday and the conflicted accommodation of the unwanted.

Willing to be historically sensitive, multiscalar and multivocal, this research has been organised as a cultural gleaning, making visible what society has chosen to disregard by accounting for the dropped, capturing heterogeneity and mapping trajectories of change. The sites of my fieldwork were originally chosen in relation to my main problematisation – that the past can be positively or negatively highlighted depending on various factors, including generational change and repair practices. However, I also followed lateral moves, since there were sites and questions that emerged unexpectedly in the pursuit of the clues that fieldwork throws up.

The argument builds upon a polyphony of vignettes that raises original questions about the temporality of communities, how individuals of different generations position themselves in regards to the past and its remnants, and the ways in which value is also founded on historical representations. That being said, there is also a premeditated personal tone in this work that allows my own history and research experience to become part of the study. I believe anthropologists are at their best when the object of study and the problems surrounding fieldwork relate to their inner lives; hence, this belief encompasses my effort to show thoughts in the making and to weave flexible writing that floats among ethnography, cultural critique, reportage, a collection of profiles and a poetic personal memoir. The angle chosen for social research is an act that is inherently political in the way we engage with people and in the questions we ask. Within the array of approaches and innovative data collection methods, my work has been a proactive anthropology: thinking-doing, change-oriented, looking into all corners of reality and creating opportunities for informed political action.

I have aimed to turn this work into a decentred (temporally, spatially and culturally) artefact, theorising from the periphery as a zone of engagement, practising anthropology in the interstices, handmade, with a DIY character (Estalella and Sánchez Criado forthcoming; Martínez forthcoming). The work has been written from a deeply embedded personal perspective in the attempt to understand the ongoing processes both around me and within, thinking from the ground as well as including subjective reactions of affinity and disagreement with the people whom I encountered and with the urban processes I was studying. Questions such as, 'When am I not an anthropologist?', 'Do people recognise me as such?' and 'Shall I intervene as an activist?' often enter my mind. At times, it was hard to define problems within the boundaries of one single discipline and clear-cut categories. At other times, I saw myself questioning the local value framework, touching the nerve of the hegemonic discourse, or becoming unexpectedly involved in the defence of certain spaces and people.

My fieldwork in Estonia occurred within a cross-disciplinary rubric, as I participated in the lifeworlds of disparate groups of informants and research units to explore questions such as: What has happened to the Soviet 'nonheritage'? In what way has the past been infused with present suspicions? How is generational change relevant to this matter? What values and experiences are activated by repairing past things? How should we designate things that are officially pronounced as not being 'worthy' of remembrance, even if they resist, by being remembered? (Vukov 2008). Then, by including comparative references to particular cases in Russia, Finland, Spain and Georgia, the research has aimed to appeal to a wide audience and contribute to the debates about how identities, temporality and legacies are renegotiated and reconfigured in the age of globalisation.

The study of the emergent material culture and changing temporalities underlines the importance of inventive approaches, as if it were a process of building (analytical scaffolding) and art making (performative, crafted). This method is meant to set the path for new studies on the complex registers that affect the transmission of inheritances and their different modes of being taking place in the present, thus showing the intricate interrelation among society, temporal regimes and the built environment. Ironically, an anthropology of waste and repair might turn into a source of innovation, thus providing new methods for studying how people experience time, negotiate changes and construct a sense of belonging. My claims are constructed across disciplinary borders by making use of a diverse range of material evidence gathered through participant observation, interviews, auto-ethnographic insights and artistic experiments. The research was designed to account for the material presence of the past in contemporary life by seeking out what the past worlds around us can tell us about ourselves and why they might represent a refusal or rejection to be integrated into a new community and temporal regime. This assumption inevitably forced me to create multiple working hypotheses, enlarge my disciplinary repertoire, and engage with the political dimension of inquiry: namely, how the relationship between time and power is generated.

The Russian and the Estonian time

'You in Spain are willing to vote for a communist party because you have never experienced what communism is for real', Luule once told me while watching the news in 2015. At the time, I was in another room having dinner, yet she repeated the comment to make sure that I came to see the news. The TV was reporting a meeting organised in Madrid by the new left-wing party Podemos, which gathered momentum after the *Indignados* protests for the regeneration of public institutions in Spain. So there I was, standing in front of the TV and under the gaze of Luule, doubting what to answer, while also knowing that my reaction would be assessed by my mother-in-law.

People of my age are leading Podemos and I feel sympathy for this political party. They are questioning the functionality of the political system that had been established in the Spanish *Transición*. And even though I sense some vertigo because they are willing to change too many things at once, they do not aim to become the plumbers of the system; they want to be the architects of a new political frame. Most importantly, I am aware that my Estonian 'mother-in-law' would not be pleased to have a 'communist' in her family. Luule's comment highlights how communism remains so politically infected in Estonia today. It also shows a common pattern of interfamilial and intergenerational communication of the past. Furthermore, it brings to the fore one of the main themes of this work: generational change and the enduring power of the absent presence of the past: communism was not simply invoked through leftovers, but also as a way of assessing the present.

In Spain the shift of the political paradigm has been preceded by a generational change: only when those born in the late 70s (right after Franco's death) had ascended to the front row of Spanish politics could the values and status quo of the transition be criticised and eventually adjusted. In Estonia, members of a similar generation (the 'Children of Freedom') have yet to make room for themselves. Another striking example of the particularities of postsocialist change is the way Luule refers to the old days; not divided in раньше and сечас (before and now), as in other post-Soviet countries, but as 'the Russian' and 'the Estonian' time. Without being aware of it, Luule agrees with L. P. Hartley's (1953) and David Lowenthal's (1985) maxim of the past being a foreign country, due to how pastness speaks to us in the present.

The Spanish transition was very different from the Estonian one, since the legitimacy of the new democracy in Spain came directly from the institutions and politicians of the dictatorial regime. By the mercy of a *Pacto de silencio* in La Moncloa, all Spaniards were equalised towards the past, in a collective effort of forgetfulness. In Estonia, however, the discursive rupture with the recent past was abrupt, entailing a multidimensional judgement and new historic narratives. Likewise, the legitimacy of the new democracy was relying on a distant past – the first independence experience in the inter-war period – while in Spain the previous democratic attempts were ignored to avoid debates about the Civil War.

For Luule, I am the Spanish partner of her daughter, the one who does not speak Estonian, but instead Russian, and forms a multiculti family. Already in our first 'family' dinner, she asked – half jokingly, half serious – about my opinion of Russia. Luule's spontaneous comments illustrate the postsocialist way of approaching the Soviet past (as an unnatural experience), but also touch upon the discrediting of socialist ideas and things in Estonia, and the paradoxical instrumentalisation of the communist experience and Soviet exposure – as symbolic capital. This made me recall that in my last visit to Madrid I found several bookcases and shelves with books musing about Marxist theories in a popular mall near Puerta del Sol. I picked up one of them (*Marx: Rereading the Capital* by Franck Fishbach), and when buying it I asked the cashier about the sudden popularity of the topic. He replied that the interest in Marxism was not that surprising considering the global financial crisis. On the way out, I found Thomas Piketty's *Capital in the Twenty-First Century* among the bestsellers.[1]

We are shaped by relationships we enter into, as social beings and as ethnographers. The final revision of this book has been done with me living under the same roof as Luule, as Marika had a child and spent the first months of recovery with her parents. These months living together provided indeed more knowledge about generational differences in Estonia, as for instance matters of taste, consumption, enjoyment, self-realisation and ideals, but also, about the force of the family as a community of memory and a mutuality of being, in the form of biological linkage and shared residence and names, but also as a participation in one another's existence without keeping track of give-and-take (Sahlins 2013).

This vignette shows how complicated it was for me to manage matters of confidentiality and definition of the field; also to cope with the ambiguities, uncertainties and contradictions of being a family. I was surrounded by the topic of research, having breakfast with it, contesting it, asking favours from it. Fieldwork at home involves processes of both familiarisation and defamiliarisation (Strathern 1987), casting the findings in terms of ethnographic objectives but also making sure that those 'at home' do not feel exploited. The accountability to those I have studied is more pressing as I have to continue living among them, so I had to be particularly delicate in matters of representation, ethics, the in-group knowledge to be shared and what I could give in return. This collaborative experience has also been part of the challenge of writing about contemporary affairs, and has tended to change and affect my research in their unfolding.

Conducting fieldwork at home requires an exercise of unlearning, double vision and a sort of dismantled identity (Okely 1996). The exercise of reflecting upon my own personal dilemmas has enabled me to recognise the constraints under which I wrote up this book, as well as to be attentive to the unexpected. Several local colleagues have intriguingly told me: 'you can say this because you are not Estonian, so you are not afraid of making enemies here'. But this was not exactly the case, since once I completed my research I had to be able to continue to live there, embedded within the described world of family relationships. Otherwise, by

being present I also refigured the experience of those whom I was researching, facilitating certain narratives and not others, bringing discontinuity
into the lives of the people I was studying; in some cases, impelling them
to change the language they usually speak. The stranger plays an important reflexive role in any community, appearing simultaneously inside and
outside a group, altering social relations through a particular configuration
of nearness and distance, attachment and detachment (Simmel 1997).
As the ethnographer, the stranger has to be skilled to establish the right
distance and master its strangeness, even if we no longer live in societies
in which it is easy to distinguish the stranger – the foreigner, the migrant,
the tourist.

A vanishing object of study

This book is a research on the ways in which the present materialises in
Estonia and a personal ethnographic journey within a society I acciden-
tally started to belong to. Based on empirical fieldwork carried out among
people who are my contemporaries and upon the material remains of the
recent past, the research shows a critical inquiry into the present, engaging with the here and now, rendering the familiar unfamiliar and dealing
with the past as living memory instead of assuming it as history. My fieldwork compelled me to be open to a varied set of research practices to confront the complication of the temporal and scalar heterogeneity of the
now, since people coexist within increasingly different temporal regimes
and irregular scales, and some of the places I was studying appeared in a
radical 'in transition' condition. As a result, the sites and traces of the
events under study vanished too quickly, showing a temporal edge. Indeed,
one of the key features of postsocialism was the erasure of temporal
banisters.

    The ethnography starts from the present and works backwards in
time to show the role that material culture played in the social ordering
and historical classifications after socialism. I was there in a time of intensive change, both forwards and backwards, and the fleetingness of my
description is due, to a great extent, to the inherent temporality of
my anthropological object. The gap between the past and the present was
constantly contested, thus posing a considerable challenge that often led
to collapse. It is in this sense that this work can be considered an anthropology of a vanishing object in that it studies the places, people and
events that relate to living memory and concerns the notion of disappearance, while simultaneously being aware that the disappearance of

places and material things affects our own sense of identity. This challenge also caused me to turn the method back onto myself, to be implicated in a more immediate way than in other kinds of research, often transgressing the traditional separation established between the object and subject of study.

The research queries into the delineations and discontinuities that accompanied the year 1991 as a new beginning, to study how past things bounce around through different generations. Hence, it is important to distinguish between what is contemporaneous and coetaneous, between the coexisting and those who share the same sensibility in the present. By temporal regime I mean not simply the way time is experienced (as pace or rhythm), but also how past things are conceptualised, narrated and inhabited. The book provides a reflection during a period of rapid change, and it does so by engaging the unresolved aspects of the recent experience of radical social transformation and by accounting the things that did not fit into the present. There is something therapeutic in this respect, working through negative affects and emphasising repair as a productive force to integrate different temporal regimes within the society.

I agree with Melissa Caldwell that one of the distinctions of doing fieldwork in postsocialist countries is the challenge to study changes as they are being produced. In light of this, ethnography thus becomes a witness to a 'history in the process', in which the fieldworker is affected by the same gain and loss that s/he tries to analyse. Caldwell gives the example of her fieldwork, carried out in Moscow between 1997 and 2004, which left her with a sense of personal loss and impermanence. She recalls the friendships and opportunities that vanished, and observes how the very object of study has a fleeting interim character which made her engagement highly unpredictable. Indeed, the trigger of her article was the closing of a food aid programme when she was ready to return and do fieldwork. Caldwell foregrounds that when studying these dynamics, the ethnographer has to be aware of the magnitude of change, but also of its pace and its not always progressive character. She notes, for instance, how the very categories of past and present became crucial in her research as defining moments that underscore the notion of change:

> distinctions between 'then' and 'now' continue to creep into the very frameworks used to identify similarities, differences, continuities and even regressions between socialist and postsocialist moments. . . . These temporal distinctions are not simply markers of past and present, but are also narratives of endings and beginnings. (Caldwell 2005, 3)

The impermanence of the object of study, vanishing, likely to disappear (Boyer and Yurchak 2008), complicates the fieldwork in postsocialist societies, but also makes it more exciting and intense. In my research, this concedes to a particular form of embeddedness within the society in focus, posing a challenge to avoid findings expire, or at least to account for their ephemerality. In this sense, the field is to be understood not solely as a spatial concept but also as a temporal and lived one. We can talk of a distinct variety of tempos comprising my field of study: the old and the new, experience and expectation, departure and arrival, generational shifts, vanishing objects and past things that came down to us transformed over time.

Employing empirical data, I critically examine multiple places in the making and the increasing irregularity of spatial and temporal scales. The work thereby draws attention to how accelerated transformations can be understood materially and generationally, examining which affects emerge from the collision of multiple temporalities and the correspondence between small-scale materiality and the pace of social change and collective abstractions. This correlation is becoming more complex, in the sense that the emerging material culture entails multiple temporalities and makes the correspondence between everyday phenomena and actual outcomes more transversal and indirect. Moreover, not only are temporalities accelerated, but the scales have also multiplied, thus making the collision between materiality and the social world even more problematic.

Both the material remains and the ethnographic fieldwork were approached without the shelter of distance. I believe this is what makes this research intriguing and relevant. Whilst the emphasis on material evidence foregrounds an archaeological perspective on the present, the work gives attention to the ethnographic context of the research and its ambitions to be contemporary by combining both proximity to and distance from the present. The contemporary appears, therefore, as being composed of old and new elements and their interactions (Rabinow 2007), as well as an experience of dissonance and disjunction (Agamben 2009). The set of concepts and tools applied in my research are related to the time in which they are made, they do not simply describe it, taking up to the contemporary with modes of inquiry that help to make sense of the non- and counterlinearities of social change (Ferguson 1999). Multi-methodological and multiscalar designs have been applied in order to reflect how the interplay of different factors confirms the process of transformation; as a result, I have recurrently circumvented disciplinary constraints and crossed borders in representational terms.

The case studies examined in this work offer insights into the material and discursive makeup of postsocialist transformations and how the neglect of dissonant legacies reveals cultural and social entanglements. Some of these sites, people and buildings were found and analysed in the very moment of becoming, or, in some cases, at the edge of disappearing. The empirically based analysis puts the focus on shifts in the classification of buildings, people, ideas and professions through dealing with the living memory recorded in past remains, the materialisation of ongoing events, and what is being lost in our increasingly ephemeral materialisations (Buchli 2002). The study of material evidence gave me access to various perspectives of analysis, since materiality and its use are visible, tangible and approachable. Yet, physical things are also known for their transience, seeing as they are affected by sociality, entropic time and semantic distortion. Indeed, the buildings, monuments and arrangements constructed to reinforce certain cultural messages are often perceived differently from expected and reinterpreted by others than those originally intended.

In our case, the Soviet regime has long since broken up, but the material culture associated with its ideology and social practices remains, thus presenting a haunted world. Materiality has provided a revealing site from which to understand the effects of the fall of state socialism on quotidian practices, subjectivities and the generation of value (Collier 2011; Drazin 2002; Fehérváry 2014). The socialist-built environment might not have produced a new kind of communist subjectivity as expected, though the remains still refer to a different ideology of dwelling and a collective idea, since the Soviet architecture was transformed into an instrument of social reform to facilitate a particular project of modernisation (Buchli 1999; Crowley and Reid 2002; Molnár 2013). These remains often appear as 'restless items' (Bach 2017), thus pointing at temporal oppositions with their indirect ways of telling us stories (Hetherington 2001). Furthermore, material culture cannot be separated from the study of what remains and persists beyond the notions of usefulness and profit. This is the reason why the study of the materiality of social life is underlined by loss, in a melancholic, receding view that recurrently triggers nonverbal associations (Buchli 2002).

Not a happy genre

One by one, decade after decade, the passing years since the break-up of the Soviet Union have been noted in dozens of books and hundreds of articles. The dates 1989 and 1991 are most often referred to with a celebratory charge that seems to imply 'one year less of postsocialism'. And here we are. Trying to answer to what 'the old' really is, and what characterises 'the new'; musing whether we can separate these categories so easily, and wondering to what extent postsocialism is a process of deconstruction, construction or the experience of both simultaneously. Like any other 'post-', it hides an a priori anti-assessment. In this regard, studies of postsocialism have tended to reflect a regrettable lack of forward-looking imagination, obsessed with renarrating what happened in the past and paying little attention to the present and the future, which seems not even to deserve a name (Hirt, Ferenčuhová and Tuvikene 2016). Pragmatically, geographer Tauri Tuvikene (2016) proposes to distinguish between three competing uses of the term 'postsocialism' – a spatiotemporal container, a condition and a deterritorialised concept – arguing for focusing more on the relations at stake, instead of reducing the validity of postsocialism to delimited territories.

Postsocialism emerged as an anthropological comparative term coined in the West to study what followed the break-up of the Soviet Union, namely the privatisation of the means of production and public goods, the discrediting of critics of capitalism, the dismantling of the Cold War geopolitical barriers and the reduction to zero value of the remnants from the past world. But even if the concept was first of all associated with East Central Europe, the experience has had several collateral effects on the world as whole as, for instance, an increase of labour and economic inequality, a growing vulnerability for individuals (discrediting of collective thought), a rise in the transnational circulation of capital (a technological shift which accelerates everyday life), an escalation of production (correlated by one of consumption), the incapability to verbalise political alternatives, and an extensive desynchronisation of temporalities.

It is in this sense that Alison Stenning and Kathrin Hörschelmann (2008; also Stenning 2010; and Gille 2010) argue that we are all postsocialist now, that is, as a boomerang effect, in the same way postcolonialism was not external to the societies of the imperial metropolis, but was instead inscribed within. Processes of privatisation and dispossession were not simply contemporaneous in different parts of the world but also justified by parallel arguments and ideologies, pursued by interrelated groups of elites, personally and corporately linked to each other. In this light, we might argue that postsocialist changes have not been an interim step but a long-distance run, in turn generating their own material culture, waste and sites of disrepair.

'Postsocialist studies is not a happy genre', writes David Kideckel (2008, 7). Also, Marju Lauristin (1997) notes that the postsocialist 'transition' cannot be reduced to 'a sum of positive changes', inspired by the West and free of contradictions, being rather characterised by a situation of uncertainty, ambiguity and inconsistency (Berdahl 2000; Humphrey 2002). The study of postsocialist becomings and iterations allows us to reflect on the existence of contradictions and sources of tension, as well as to dig into the relationship among legacies, global processes and political decisions. The outcome of transformation policies has been shaped not only by the design of the policies and the opening to the international market and finance capital, but also by the inherited conditions and expectations, as well as by unforeseen events and contingencies.

The examination of various trajectories of change in Estonia shows how post-Soviet transformations were not simply shaped by market logic, globalisation and Western values, but rather translated according to local legacies and reactions against the recent past. One of the reasons for the complex character of these dynamics was the dialectical relation between radical changes and persistent continuities, as well as by the constant looping of scales and temporalities. Postsocialism encapsulates therefore not simply what comes 'after socialism, but also against it, reflected through it' (Stenning and Hörschelmann 2008, 325). These changes happen and were lived as a highly contingent experience, some by inertia, and others because of calculative reasoning, characterised by a simultaneous process of construction and deconstruction. In many cases, post-Soviet processes were 'a painful struggle to preserve existing mechanisms of need fulfilment' (Collier 2011, 133), rather than a radical rupture and a rapid adjustment to new circumstances.

The Soviet disintegration was a critical juncture that opened a window for expanded social choices, yet the possibilities of change were nonetheless bounded, conditioned by different interests and factors (Johnson 2001). Transformations occurred according to a repertoire of possibilities, partly shaped by active choices and agencies, partly conditioned by legacies, structures and social persistence. This research accounts for these ambivalences, the contingency of the process and its trajectories of becoming. Even if postsocialist societies have increasingly adjusted their lifestyles to the market economy, people have still to confront nondemocratic agreements, antimarket reasoning and side effects; these changes have rather followed a trajectory of 'backing up, fast-forwarding, simultaneously cancelling itself out, slowing down and then speeding up again in completely renewed and reassembled cycles of development' (Materka 2012, 141).

Edyta Materka has shown the hybridisation of postsocialist trajectories by analysing the expectations and side effects produced by the proposed creation of a US antiballistic base on Rędzikowo – a post-industrial village which suddenly became 'the most strategic location in

Poland' (Materka 2012, 150). Multifarious processes started after the missile base announcement: on the one hand, the US militarisation of this rural area froze local activities in the name of global security, subverting the very principles of democracy, transparency and market economy; on the other, international contractors rushed into Słupsk (a city next to Rędzikowo) with Western-style malls, fast-food restaurants, music halls, hotels and public squares. Likewise, Rędzikowians started to need to seek permission from the US military for refurbishing their own city. The bitter irony of the story does not stop there. While the initial plan for the missile base had been cancelled, the Western stores diverted their catering to a different clientele – the Polish migrants working temporarily in Western European countries, who are familiar with those brands and have the currency to purchase Western goods.

Something similar is starting to happen in the town of Tapa, Estonia. In 2016, the US military invested $11.2 million in upgrading a NATO military base next to the Russian border, where a thousand British and French soldiers are deployed. Changes in Tapa are now contextualised in the framework of international security, and the everyday life of its inhabitants has entered unexpectedly into a totally new scale, making more complex the dynamics and trajectories of change of Soviet remains. By approaching postsocialist processes as an organic interplay between different scales, tempos, localities and legacies, this research explores how the global connects to the local and the way past materialities take a particular shape in specific contexts. The described changes have been driven by the give-and-take of multidimensional ruptures and legacies (physical, cultural and social), and a specific kind of governmental reasoning (shaped by the geopolitical context; combining incentive-oriented reforms, neoliberal ideology and active negligence). These aspects are contextualised in this work by connecting seemingly small things with larger questions; also by querying what things say about social relationships and problematising order and discourse.[2] Thus, the research invites us to think these processes through connections and comparisons, presenting Estonia as partaking of global flows of images and ideas, people and policies.

Overview

This book is intentionally provocative in aiming to trouble and stimulate broader engagement with debates about the interaction between material culture and generational change through conversations among anthropology, archaeology, contemporary art and urban studies. The research explores the distinction between what is given historically and what the subsequent society, as well as the new generation, actually makes of what is inherited. I studied generational change, material culture and temporal regimes after socialism, but not Estonian culture or history as such. Rather, the research brings to light the unresolved aspects of recent experiences of change and of what lays behind, or below, official representation. Hence, it is meant to function as an account of what has been wasted or made superfluous, participating in the process of social inclusion, as well as the synchronisation and visualisation of other political sensibilities.

The notions of 'wasted legacies', 'suture', 'preserved disrepair' and 'active negligence' are invoked to make sense of the various mismatches between the postsocialist predicament and the material and social legacies of the previous era. Therefore, research foregrounds that cultural transformations do not take place at the same speed at which political regimes are established. My reason for focusing on the iteration of legacies and tracing the relation between histories and material remnants is that they illustrate how the past is being reengendered and allow us to describe the inherited as neither fixed nor definitive.

Wasted legacies can be out of use but not circulation, which means that they are available to be used by different ones than those originally intended and in diverse ways. The concept of waste refers to a conscious act of neglect and disinvestment, as well as to what it is to expend carelessly (yet not ahistorically). Thus, waste possesses some kind of supplemental value beyond its immediate use and it locates itself in the intersection of other concepts such as sacrifice, equivalence, use, discard, loss, failure and persistence, which most often appear unarticulated (Martínez 2017d). In contrast, repair is presented as a generative experience of care and potentiality, a form of 'preservation without permission' (Brand 2012) which transmits affects of belonging, care and commitment. The value of repair goes beyond market measurements, as this practice helps to sustain a sense of duration and reconnects personal biographies to public and private materiality. To repair is therefore also to connect – times, people, things; a way of creating encounters, making possible a longue durée of relations.

Sutures are here presented as interstices, incomplete, ephemeral, yet located and palpable, as spaces of compossibility in which heterogeneous parts coexist in their contradiction or even antagonism (see chapter 5). In turn, the concept of amalgamation indicates a precarious and elusive live composition made of microhistorical fragments. Their study describes the affective transmissions that occur between material objects, spatial assemblages and social actors, making visible unfinished beginnings and the uneven durabilities of past formations. Both suturing and amalgamation emphasise the relationships and attachments of people and places, which thus help us to understand short-term adaptations and long-term conversions. These phenomena remind us that change is contingent, multidirectional and cathartic, altering our relation to the things and ideas of the past in their unfolding.

The monograph comprises a preface, an introduction, eight chapters, a conclusion and an epilogue. I start by developing the main concepts of the research and methodologies. Also, the introduction reflects on how the categories of the 'old' and the 'new' are mutually constitutive in an ongoing dialectic, turning on the depiction of Soviet remains as waste, which has been one of the sensitive factors upon which the actual society is built. In the first chapter, I discuss the way the Soviet world was reduced to waste after the break-up of the Soviet Union, standing as a negative model from which other classificatory schemes are derived (generating a system of meaning and value). Based on Douglas's assumption that the account of what is considered as 'wasted' permits an understanding of the principles that order the social system, the affect-informed research questions narratives that present postsocialism as driven only by convergence and innovation, instead presenting a series of case studies in which transformations followed a political logic of dismantlement and disinvestment.

In chapter 2, I draw on a number of ethnographic examples of symbolic fixing that helped to redeem implied inequalities and discontinuities. In doing this, I place an emphasis on 'repair' and 'suture' as an analytical means to comprehend the continuities and discontinuities within Estonian society. Acts of repair simultaneously transcend the material reuse of items and devices while also recovering social attachments and meanings. This sutured understanding of repair practices updates the Western idea that reconciliation and empowerment can happen only through verbal recounting. Repair and suture can be part of a changing common sense, fixing different expressions of brokenness, recovering social and material heritage, and binding and synchronising societies.

Chapter 3 shows how both global capitalism and Soviet legacies have been negotiated in a street market of Tallinn. At the Jaama turg, Western concepts such as 'market' and 'employment' took on distinctly different meanings from those applied by policymakers. The excluded economy present at the open-air market was often informal and sometimes illegal; even so, it proved to reduce social inequality in Tallinn, as well as the distance between the centre and the outskirts. The study of this bazaar also shows how Soviet material and cultural legacies are still relevant to understanding the way people make sense of their lives to the point that once the market has disappeared, the access of some groups to public space and participation in social life became more difficult, thereby decreasing urban diversity.

Chapter 4 puts the emphasis in the correlation between the materiality of built forms, maintenance and duration over time. The research explores the way people might extend themselves outwards into the built environment by paying attention to the multiple meanings and maturing of Linnahall arena in Tallinn. This building comes to have a unique history, yet the consideration of this building as 'Soviet' poses the problem of how to present the biography of the site in specific terms and how to study the simultaneous maturing of people and buildings overall. Linnahall is an iconic place in Tallinn and illustrates the dramatic identity of the city. This palace stands as both scatological and monumental, giving to the site an effectual energy. I thus advocate for treating the building as a curated ruin, establishing a set of measures that do not obliterate the offences of time and acknowledge the traces of the past.

Chapter 5 presents an examination of the material traces and gaps in Tallinn's cityscape to expose how built forms connect opposed categories and index further transformations. The urban ethnography articulates a portrait of the city, as a synthetic image of Tallinn and the (spatial and temporal) scale shifting going on there in a particular period of time. Taken as a chronotope, the Estonian capital is examined as a whole characterised by the cumulative effect of ruptures and obduracies, and not simply shown as a postsocialist city. Then, the study of amalgamations brings to light both slow morphologies and spatiotemporal horizons, thereby outlining the way materiality remains from the pasts and how historical breaks feed the material culture and gravitas of this city.

Based on 15 informal interviews, auto-ethnographic insights, two round tables, and repeated visits to the maquette master Fjodor Šantsõn, chapter 6 investigates the ways in which notions of repair and brokenness might have implications in the narrative politics of belonging in Narva. Also, how the frontier is embodied by the local inhabitants, and the affective constellations that the border generates. This Estonian city marks the border between the Russian Federation, NATO and the European Union, situated on the periphery of all of them, standing as a place of continuous negotiation and a translation of bigger forms and wider processes. A careful study of everyday life in Narva makes evident the polycentricity of the Estonian society, and presents the construction of national identity as both incomplete and continuously differentiating, entailing also a strong performative character.

Chapter 7 studies the problematic construction of collective memory in post-Soviet Estonia by analysing the conceptualisation and architectural design of the new Estonian National Museum as a 'Memory Field' in Raadi – an area on the outskirts of Tartu which condenses historical narratives and unfinished projects of modernisation (recognisable in the form of scars and its patchwork landscape). Hence, I claim that the reconsideration of multiple modernities in Estonia – including the Soviet one – could also be a task for the museum.

From collective memory, chapter 8 shifts the focus to politics of coevality to expose how young people who had come of age after the dissolution of the Soviet Union differ from their parents and fit into the actual temporal belonging. Ethnographically, it engages with the term 'Children of Freedom' as coined by Lauristin (2003) to categorise those born just before or after independence was regained. The discussion shows the limits of this term to conceptualise the way social bonds have shifted over the last few decades due to both national and global processes. Due to their distinct life experience, young people are reshaping the traditional understanding of identity, location and representations of the past, reconfiguring the tired notions of postsocialism and Eastern Europe too.

The conclusion revisits the book's central set of questions and closes the monograph by reflecting on the outcomes of the research and its comparative potential. The exercise of summarising focuses on two key points in particular: (1) how the postsocialist renarrativisation of the Soviet experience brought about a deliberate negligence of past symbols, generated new exclusions and produced misrepresentations, thus requiring the extra work of suturing and repair; and (2) how Eastern Europe and postsocialism might have become zombie concepts, being deterritorialised by a young generation that brings with them new approaches towards the recent past and hegemonic categories.

1
The past as a rotting place

Waste and forgetting

There was no war, but countless ruins, waste and brokenness were produced. Abandoned industries, rusting machinery, obsolete power plants, decaying buildings, chemically polluted zones, environmental catastrophes and debris have, for decades, symbolised the collapse of the USSR, displaying the break-up of the regime in its more literary and material sense. This gives the impression that communism, toxicity and the production of waste cannot be separated, and produces a physical abjection towards that era and all that it meant. Soon after its breakdown, the Soviet world was described as wasteful, symbolically polluted and economically out of order, the consequences of the 'collapse' being inseparable from the sociomaterial effects of the Soviet regime. As a rotting reality (Stoler 2013), the socialist inheritance was automatically associated with inefficient practices, hazardous products, empty spaces and a sense of ending, activating an imaginary elimination.

Anthropologist James Ferguson (1999) defines this kind of adjustment as an 'infrastructural abjection', which designates certain aspects of social life as residual, beyond institutional care, expulsed, thrown down and humiliated. The 'abject' refers to something that simultaneously generates a somatic and symbolic reaction, appearing in a state of cast-off, violating the clean and proper, and perceived as an external menace from which one would like to keep a distance, which is a seemingly impossible task (Kristeva 1997). Mary Douglas (1966) explained how waste and dirt might be connected with the processes of ordering. Hence, the concept of waste is part physical, part social, and involves classification and separation – reinforcing the positioning within and outside a systemic organisation. As described by Douglas, the constitution of waste has two phases: first, the categorisation of what does not fit and rejection due to its being 'out of place'; and second, a process of dissolving any characterisation (rotting), which utterly leads to its disintegration and loss of identity.

Waste is therefore categorised within a frame of value that relates to temporal regimes and the constitution of cycles – profit and loss, use and abandonment, and life and death. Any valuation and generation of waste is the result of contested human decisions, whether in the form of social relations (Gregson 2007) or as a reminder of the processes of modernisation – when the good, useful and valuable have been already taken (Scanlan 2005). Designations of waste are enmeshed in relations of power and domination, as people are incited to make moral and political judgements based on associations with dirt (Alexander and Reno 2012; Martínez 2017c; McKee 2015). The term refers to whatever needs to be expelled so the system continues to function, to all that is meant to be concealed and hidden, lying in a transitional state, ready for disappearance and yet ripe for reinvestment, reinterpretation or revaluation (Thompson 1979).

The Latin etymology of the word goes back to *vastus* – meaning deserted, unoccupied or desolate, a space that is void and appears uncultivated. However, waste also has other meanings, such as missed opportunities and dilapidated time and resources, being part of a process of disqualification as well as a trigger for self-assessment (Pardo 2010). Waste and society are mutually constitutive through 'waste regimes' (Gille 2007), being part of a larger set of epistemological assumptions, norms and social conventions. Different relations to waste indicate different relations to profit, thus revealing shifting cultural values and processes of world making. Still, waste always occupies the negative side in dichotomies such as efficiency and inefficiency, usefulness and uselessness, order and disorder and alive and dead (Gille 2007, 20). Waste has been also taken as a remainder of withdrawals and extractions, propelling the mind backwards when an object was in full usefulness. An example of this is the Garbology project (1996), whereby William Rathje investigated fresh garbage as if it were archaeological evidence, studying consumer behaviours from the material realities they leave behind rather than from self-reports.

A study of the discarded and the dissipated reveals gaps in the prevailing narrative of evolution and progress. As pointed out by Benjamin (1968), debris calls out to be recognised in the present, moving into the future while looking backwards – with a reverse gaze. Disposal has also been described as simply a way of 'moving things along' (Gregson, Metcalfe and Crewe 2007), a dynamic which can lead to unexpected afterlives, revalorisations and reappropriations by different people. Even if legacies become waste, they might retain the potential for redemption through social, economic or political change, reminding us that anything occupying the site of disgust at one moment in history is not necessarily disgusting at the preceding or subsequent ones (Laporte 2000, 32).

Damnatio memoriae

To understand the articulation of collective memory, it is important to pay attention to what one forgets; not simply to what is erased, but also to what is made inaccessible, silenced or reduced to waste. Past things are forgotten not simply by erasure, but also by excluding them from the agenda. Further, they are made invisible by situating both the remnants and the related narratives out of place and with no possible circulation, thus constituting a refusal to let someone enter into the past and preventing new generations from establishing direct contact with its remnants. As pointed out by local art historian Andres Kurg (2006a), attempts to forget the fifty-year-long Soviet period in Estonia as though it never existed have inadvertently denied people's personal memories. Also, anthropologist Sigrid Rausing identified three aspects of the 'social amnesia' about the Soviet world: the intentional lack of transmission of memories between the generations, the suppression of practices to which social memories are intricately linked, and an 'organised oblivion' of the state – promulgating a fallacious version of history (2004, 93).

My research draws attention to anomalies in the actual classification of past experiences and things. This compelled me to be sensitive to the way that the past intervenes in the present and is still resonant in the built environment and local people. During the last decades, Estonian society experienced the dismantlement and destruction of the recent old (the Soviet past), invoked by a nonrecent old – the first Republic in the interwar period on which the state bases its legitimacy and builds institutions. The long historical episodes when foreign forces occupied the country were thus presented as exceptions, instead articulating narratives that highlighted the short experience of independence and downplayed the foreign domination. To a great extent, this narrative was articulated through an active dismissal of all that was inherited from the previous regime (as if the Soviet organisation of society could be simply dismantled and replaced), a mnemonic silence and retrieval-induced forgetting meant to influence how individuals and groups remember the past (Anderson, Bjork and Bjork 1994).

The past is not simply there: it has to be collected, articulated and maintained to become memory (Young 1993). Hence, the past may be activated, forgotten, embodied or neglected depending on political goals, such as rebuilding the new Estonian state. The construction of new exclusions and separations is specific to any regime change (in the attempt to establish a new hegemony); yet, the degree of vengeance or the narrowness in the purity may vary. It is the labour of the negative, the oscillation between the old and the new, between presence and absence, that constitutes the memory space of postsocialism (Bach 2017).

As Inge Melchior notes in her dissertation (2015), the official history of Estonia was built on family life stories, while countermemories were perceived as threatening the homogeneity of the society and the independence of the state. Further on, in her study of the 'threshold generation', sociologist Raili Nugin agrees that the delegitimisation of the Soviet era was 'needed' in the 1990s. Nugin adds that the 'black-and-white version' of the past changed in the 2000s when an alternative narrative emerged, indulging in details without challenging the hegemonic treatment of the Soviet time: 'Yet the already established dominant narrative was too strong to be questioned, as that would have meant questioning the political base structures of the entire society' (Nugin 2015, 126). In a similar vein, historian Marek Tamm describes this articulation of memory politics as an 'ideology of restoration', according to which all measures (in their legal, institutional, commemorative and monumental dimensions) were dedicated to restoring prewar traditions, institutions and national romanticist models. Eventually, such reactivation of the patterns of nineteenth-century historiography led to 'the massive restoration of monuments to the War of Independence, the reinstating of prewar place, town, street and house names, the re-institution of old anniversaries, or the reinterment of politicians in their homeland from the interwar independence period' (Tamm 2013, 654).

Postsocialist transformations in Estonia have been driven in reference to the past, with 1991 marking the inaugural, teleologically constructed event. These changes involved the revival of the imaginary of the interwar Republic, relegating memories and visions of Soviet modernity to removal or oblivion. Indeed, the Estonian state is officially presented as a legal continuity with the first independence period (1918–1940). The subsequent process of the restitution of properties to the prewar owners was thus fundamental for the legitimisation of the new state, correcting the *errors* of history and symbolically meaning the negation of the Soviet past. The new was therefore reconstituted with reference to history and preoccupation with the past, using terms such as 'cleaning' and 'leaving behind' socialist remains. As a result, the Soviet past has been reduced by the current political power to a one-dimensional stigmatised experience that has been institutionally displayed as a 'prolonged rupture' (Kõresaar 2005), 'culturally alien' and unnatural (Feldman 2001). Yet, using the Soviet period as a constitutive outside led to the demonisation of all elements connected to the recent past, presenting it as Russian and brutal in contraposition to the harmonic and familiar first Republic (Kattago 2009).

The Soviet world, with its visions, expectations, tempos, skills and material culture, suddenly *became* something obsolete, excremental and wasteful, and soon turned into a toxic prelude to what came after. Accordingly, the ideas, people and materialities associated with it were considered dispensable, in need of recycling, or even of exorcism.[1] Postsocialist processes were mostly driven by negative retrospective assessments and destruction under the assumption of 'what the past does to us' (Olick 2007). The Soviet past was thus classified in anomalous ways by a historical revisionism based on the postsocialist moral and political agenda. It is even possible to make a parallel between postsocialism and a therapy of psychoanalysis in which the past appears as something that threatens – in terms of a burden.[2]

In Estonia, memories and representations of the past have been reconstructed in the light of subsequent events, often showing an 'arrogant and disgusting attitude towards things emanating from the socialist era' (Lobjakas and Paulus 2000, 9). The Soviet past might have suffered a *damnatio memoriae*, a group of processes of destruction, erasure and silence that were applied in the Roman Empire to assault the memory of a fallen enemy. When a *damnatio memoriae* was issued, an array of official and unofficial sanctions was practised to erase all historical references to that person; monuments were defaced and the name of the damned was scratched from the history books. Yet, the 'condemnation of memory' was a complex exercise beyond erasure, allowing people to see the supposedly removed name on the stone, drawing attention to acts of removal and creating a stigma that might last through generations through a preserved disrepair (Flower 2006; Varner 2004).[3]

Active negligence

Often things fail partially, but the Soviet Union collapsed completely in one fell swoop, with 1991 appearing as a year of massive and sudden obsolescence. A major cultural and civilisational break was supposed to happen then, and many things and life stories were consigned to oblivion, unworthy of maintenance or recollection; some others remained, yet were recontextualised as improper and impure, as a wrecked entity living in another time (Fabian 1983). The Soviet Union was a great producer of premature ruins, derelict factories, bunkers, and redundant mining and military towns; all that was transformed into a testimony of modern debris with the arrival of postsocialism and late modernity.

Negligence is not a natural process but rather part of a strategy of disqualifying something. On the one hand, abandonment and negligence are the products of particular decisions, of attentions and inattentions, subjected to practices of maintenance and use, or disinvestment. On the other, disrepair has working effects that not only supports state legibility (Chu 2014; Scott 1998), but also conditions broader political sensibilities (Rancière 2006). Drawing on the assumption that discourses have also a material life, I foreground how postsocialist processes have relied on specific strategies of value creation and degradation. Such processes generate 'orders of worth' (Boltanski and Thévenot 2006) that contribute to creating and maintaining the legitimacy of institutions and sustain the arrangement of things. When we engage with our surroundings and participate in society, we already carry an order of seeing, which conditions who can take part and in which way people can participate. Jacques Rancière (2006) conceptualised this order as 'forms of visibility' and the 'distribution of the sensible', referring to a legitimisation of certain ways of seeing, acting, speaking and being in public.[4]

The way legacies are treated makes evident how a society engages with difference. The framing of legacies appears as a sociocultural process of identity formation and belonging, often presented as a family affair and directly influenced by those who are related to and surrounding us. Frames and delineations emplace things in the present; however, the assessment is always circumstantial, made by people in a given context and based on particular trajectories of appropriation and discard. Any classification of waste and heritage is a dynamic process, not a static system, and is thus subject to changes and movements between categories. They both establish a particular continuity with the past, however, while a legacy is there (to be acknowledged or disregarded), heritage has to be 'made up' out of heterogeneous layers and changing regimes.

The categorisation of something as heritage is entangled in multiple factors and qualified by a present system of values. In this vein, Kevin Hetherington (2004) observes that disposal and inheritance are not as far apart as might initially be imagined; they both produce a trace effect that is passed on. A legacy functions as a link between past, present and future, compelling one to negotiate persistent ontologies and learn historical lessons (Kattago 2009a). However, legacies can be interpreted as both negative and positive – either as an inheritance or as residual, a mercy or a burden (Kattago 2012). Legacies are not always wasted because of being unsuitable for functioning and lacking a role in the system; further, the wasting of the inherited is not necessarily produced through its use, but rather, by neglect. Thus, wasting is also a judgement (not simply a process), and as such, it is prone to vary culturally and generationally.

In Latin, the verb *legare* (to send) serves as the origin of two different nouns: *legatus*, which means a delegation or an authorised representative, and *legatum*, which refers to anything that is left behind by a predecessor (e.g., money, a property, cultural heritage or descendants); hence, *legatum* requires a process of transmission and the existence of an ancestor. Thinking carefully, legitimacy and legacy are not that far from each other, semantically and orthographically. Indeed, one needs a legacy to legitimate power, and one has to have some legitimacy in order to access what has been passed down. It is in this sense that we can also talk of wasted legacies as aborted pathways or purged symbology, thereby referring to situations in which there is presence but no acknowledgement of value, appearing therefore as discontinuity or dissonance instead of a direct correlation between outcome and antecedent. We can also talk of remnants that persist over the duration of people's lives, occupying multiple historical tenses. A remnant refers to the pieces, fragments and scraps that are left unused and whose value is partly lost. Nonetheless, it differs from waste and ruin; whilst waste carries notions of judgement, remnants are stripped of negative connotations, without reaching, however, ruins' ability to tell stories and express the dimension of time (Marini and Corbellini 2016).

In their traces and remnants, wasted legacies appear as a tangible manifestation of how the past has been represented and integrated into the present. The wasting of a legacy exemplifies a strategy orchestrated to turn an inheritance into something useless, strange and uncomfortable. Accordingly, the hardships of building a neoliberal market economy (the so-called transition) have been attributed to Soviet 'wastefulness' and 'intrinsic failure', presented as the cost of decades of communism (Pop-Eleches 2007). This follows a logic of sacrifice, making it 'necessary' for a bigger goal, infusing the destruction of value with other values (Bataille 1998). Sacrifices were thus presented as necessary in order to clean Soviet residuals and move back to the future (through a more distant past, paradoxically: the first interwar Republic). During the last twenty-five years, many postsocialist outcomes have been blamed on communist legacies, whether as an after-effect or as the reason that justifies an actual replacement. In both cases, the past is approached according to present circumstances. The difference relies on its interpretation as something that is or is not still convenient.

Negligence may arise either from acting carelessly or from failing to act when needed; hence, it is a failure to act and to preserve. As legacies often need a linking mechanism (Wittenberg 2015), the wasting of the inherited can be understood as the product of failed relationships and institutional inactivity, dematerialising a given past and turning it invisible in order to materialise a new historical regime (Buchli and Lucas 2002a). Forgetting is a complex process, which affects localities by making things anonymous and invisible (Connerton 2009). In this light, any interpretation of the recent past is a politically engaged act, which requires the inclusion of remains and marginalised actors teetering uncertainly between ruination and renovation (Buchli and Lucas 2002a).

Heritage is selected but legacies are not optional; they do not refer simply to the cared-for past, but also to involuntary transmissions and the unwanted baggage. Wasted legacy refers to something inherited that has not been fully used or developed, implying missed opportunities and neglected potential. This term helps to conceptualise processes, whereby the relationship between the inherited and coeval agency is not resolved, reminding us that the potential or life expectancy of things, buildings and skills is often not fulfilled because of social decisions rather than natural, historic processes. In order to explore the materiality and the stories that reside at the intersection of the present and the absent, the research requires paying special attention to the temporal regimes and traces that survived.

A wasted legacy is not simply something inherited that has very little economic or symbolic value, or that is no longer in use in the present; the wasting of a legacy indicates a shifting memory and a rupture in historical time (Koselleck [1979] 2004). It refers thus to beginnings without proper endings, to premature deaths and abortive effects from an external cause. However, wasted legacies have the ability to resist and to respond to human agency, waiting for a moment of recognition and redemption. I noticed, for instance, that the material inheritance from the Soviet world decays at a different tempo from the evolution of values within Estonian society; this quality and generational changes provide another chance for past things, and demonstrates that wasted legacies do not follow straight trajectories of destruction.

It might be that the USSR was not mature enough for the collapse – a condition that would have enabled a more gracious layering down of its legacies. We might also distinguish between static and dynamic legacies, depending on whether they remain embedded in the past, as carriers of history that emanate lasting effects, or they appear alienated from their past self. The distinct duration of remnants allows us to work on recuperation, remembrance and attachment through the practices of repair, maintenance and curation. Those who come after have to deal with what is left, with the material and social afterlife of structures, sensibilities and things (Stoler 2013). Wasted legacies are those that endured despite having been reduced to zero value, influencing social structures through obduracies and relational effects, residually left over but in a state of unfinished deposition, and standing in potential for multiple forms of reconstitution. Still, something can be repaired only if it is actually available and accessible, even if only in the form of waste or ruin. The physical degradation of Soviet legacies poses a challenge to their preservation and to an in-depth understanding of people's historical experience. Hence, a crucial issue in the study of these legacies is how the subsequent generation accepts, rejects or is indifferent to what is given.

It is not only the act of forgetting, but memory has also been used in the neglecting. Wasted legacies refer to much of the infrastructure and many of the buildings that, despite remaining perfectly functional, were either demolished, recycled or left to decay, in the sense of an active negligence supported by official narratives. For Nietzsche, the need to forget is a mandatory complement to remembering. That approach takes forgetting not as a failure of memory but as an affirmation, a way to fix up our hauntings. Forgetting can also be approached as a faculty and as a symbolic expenditure, liberating negativism, accessing other ways to knowledge (Forty and Küchler 1999). A precedent for this was the first postwar Europe, built upon forgetting as a way of life. However, since 1989, Europe has been constructed upon a compensatory surplus of memory (Judt 2005). Otherwise, empowerment through historic grievance is a source of division and confrontation, as well as a reluctant sign to search for compromises (Black 2008).

Official vandalism

At the Tallinn Architectural Biennale of 2013 ('Recycling Socialism'), the architects in attendance spoke of prefab panel construction housing as a problem, not simply presenting modernist structures of the 1970s and 1980s as having lower status but also discussing whether it was necessary, in order for society to move on, to demolish structures and buildings that represented the Soviet ideology, thereby assessing the material inheritance from this regime as residual. Destruction precedes most construction. The making of the new always implies that the old is to be torn apart, not simply because building is dependent on the demolition or dismantling of something else, but also because it is the destruction of the predecessor that allows for the realisation of a new state or plan, affirming the power of the victor 'to the same extent as the erection of a monument to victory' (Yampolsky 1995, 100).

These interdependent processes of construction and demolition are constitutive of a particular urban materiality, whereby the object of memory politics is both spatial and temporal (Schwenkel 2013). For instance, in the attempt to construct new historical narratives, several Soviet landmarks have been sacrificed, or dissected, in Tallinn, so that we have seen impressive buildings torn down to make space for shopping malls (e.g., Sakala keskus) or privatised to undergo an experiment in architectural taxidermy (Postimaja, Teenindusmaja, and so on). Some others linger on as remnants, since international heritage organisations did not allow their demolition against the wishes of the city hall (e.g., Linnahall). Around them, trash often accumulates as a result of official disregard, a situation which is later used by real estate companies as an excuse for a speculative type of redevelopment or privatisation, along with discourses of 'having potential' and 'wasted space' (Martínez 2017c).

The most recent sacrifice has been the Ministry of Finance, built in 1978 by the architect Ülo Ilves to host the planning committee for computing. The building is regarded as bearing the first work of public abstract art created on a façade, made by the artist Edgar Viies. The officials' original idea was to renovate the existing building; however, claims were made about the low quality of the construction materials, which led the real estate company to propose demolishing the building to rebuild it again. In the end, a competition for a new 'super ministry' office complex (a site of 14,420 square metres, hosting four ministries) was organised, the project chosen being a glass building topped with the three lions that symbolise the power of the new state (figure 1.1). The decision to demolish the old building ignored the architects' union advice to preserve the historical building as 'an architecturally valuable monument of its era'. Reflecting on how the obsolescence of buildings is neither inevitable nor natural, local artist Leonhard Lapin (2015) notes that functional buildings can hardly last more than three decades in the centre of Tallinn, adding that 'the fact that the house was built during the Soviet occupation does not mean it is worthless'.

The previous case of 'vandalism' against the modernist legacy was the Central Post Office, which was nonetheless subjected to a different sort of sacrifice (or afterlife?). The Central Post Office (Postimaja) was built

Fig. 1.1   Façade of the 'super ministerium' in Tallinn. Source: Tõnu Tunnel, 2017.

between 1977 and 1980 on the eve of the Moscow Olympic Games, for which a regatta was scheduled on the outskirts of the Estonian capital. The main function of the building was to host mail processing and local telephone services, while long-distance calls were also available through an operator on the first floor of the building (figures 1.2 and 1.3). A distinctive, three-storey limestone construction replaced an old gas station, symbolically connecting the Rottermann quarter with the old town and the Narva highway.

Fig. 1.2 Postimaja, 1985. Source: Harald Leppikson, Rahvusarhiivi filmiarhiiv.

Fig. 1.3 Postimaja interior, 1985. Source: Harald Leppikson, Rahvusarhiivi filmiarhiiv.

Fig. 1.4 Silver Agu showing a drawing of Postimaja. Source: Author, 2015.

The Central Post Office had the first escalator in Estonia, and people came from all over the country to see it and experience the ride. However, the escalator soon broke down, and was definitively replaced by a conventional staircase in 1988. While researching the nuances of the Postimaja, I discovered that my father-in-law, Silver Agu, was the person in charge of its repair and maintenance between 1990 and 2001, fixing problems in the building's health like a surgeon (figure 1.4). Indeed,

Silver was very glad to recall details of the everyday maintenance of the building, showing photographs and confiding the personal affection he had developed for the Central Post Office. For him, to work there was something to be proud of. When asked if the building was designed to accommodate obsolescence and allow adaptive reuse, Silver replied by dwelling not only on the architecture's temporality but also on its financial utility:

> In its time, in the 80s, it was an elegant building. But now, surrounded by other buildings, such as the hotel and the cinema, it loses its presence. Back then it had sufficient space around it; however, the director of Postimaja had to sell part of the territory because of the constant need for money. By selling the surrounding area, they made the building dysfunctional. . . . In its original context the building was majestic, but being surrounded, it lost the perspective from where to look at it.

Looking back, Silver correlates the restoration of Estonian independence with the invisible hand of the market economy and an increase of building technology, in contrast with the 'sloppy finish of the Soviet era and the Communist system'. Furthermore, he found a tension between the preservation and rehabilitation of functioning buildings, arguing that it is not as simple as retrofitting Postimaja using some new technology, but that it would have required extending the life of an economic system, spatial structure and society at large that are already dead. When asked if the right maintenance would have been sufficient to keep the building in a suitable state nowadays, Silver answered:

> Yes. However, the building was made with bad materials and a weak foundation. The concrete pillars and beams had to be reinforced to gain bearing capacity. . . . Postimaja made sense in the context of its function; for the current cityscape, the building is better now.

Many of the architectural and industrial ruins of Tallinn are not simply Soviet but also material signifiers of the decline of Fordism and neoliberal policies. For instance, the innovations brought by information technologies led to structural changes in mail and communication industries during recent decades, gradually reducing the volume of traditional mail.[5] But it was the privatisation process and the need for self-financing that forced the Estonian Post to sell practically all the real estate properties they owned, keeping just four of ninety they had in the 1990s.[6] Since 2005, the building has been under heritage protection, so its demolition is formally forbidden. However, the new owners started a complete 'building surgery' (Harris 1999) that changed the façade, interior and use of the Postimaja, and it is now transformed into a shopping mall with a glossy crystal façade and numerous advertisements: 'It is not the same building', argues Silver, 'only the form and size were preserved'.

In March 2015, I conducted twelve informal interviews next to the building, asking random passers-by: 'What do you think about the current shape and use of the Postimaja?' The answers could be divided into four groups. The first group criticised it, complaining that there were enough shopping malls and *Rimis* (supermarkets), with too many Soviet buildings of Tallinn lost in recent years. The second group comprised those who were favourable to the changes, because there was 'finally an affordable supermarket in the city centre' (most of them were elderly people who would come by tram, take a walk in the old town and then buy something in the Rimi). The third group was composed of those who were indifferent, with the fourth group forming the majority of participants who were glad that something had been done with the building. For instance, Toni stated, 'It looked bad. Now it is very good again. You know, fresh, renovated. The façade is preserved as it was in the Russian time'. Or Eve, who commented, 'It was unique, but in a very bad shape; terrible shape. I guess something had to be done and there was no chance to keep it how it was. About the shopping mall . . . perhaps a shopping mall was not the best, but at least it was not demolished as the Sakala Keskus was. Shopping malls are the spirit of the time!' There is nonetheless a fifth group of opinion that I did not reach in my interviews: those who believe that the H&M now in the old post office allows them to dress like the rest of the world.[7]

Architectural taxidermy

There is a tradition of skilled taxidermists in Eastern Europe, yet architectural taxidermy is also a unique phenomenon in the region, showing not simply the fate of modernist architecture and industrial heritage, but also the ongoing relational and processual materialisation of urban settings and life. The term 'taxidermy' itself derives from the Greek: *taxi* meaning 'movement' and *derma* meaning 'skin'. If they were not considered to embody Soviet ideology, modernist buildings would be hunting trophies, specimens which, through the act of dissecting and freezing from the effects of time, could achieve an outward look of the past and an authenticity, an organic appearance attractive for touristification and investors. However, the political infection of past things leads to a deeper degree of emptying and dissecting, beyond design logics of redressing what is raw or naked.

As with displays, the emptying of buildings allows new forms of representation of the past, redefinitions in the present, and alternative visions for the future (Marcoux 2001). However, the emptying projects and architectural taxidermy seek less and less to render buildings as lifelike, or to imitate reality; rather, new projects show a preference for enhancement and for a perfected nature (van Dijck 2001), making buildings look as if they were not made but born (Haraway 1984). Besides sending the social world that they represented into oblivion, an important feature of the architectural taxidermy practised in postsocialist cities is that the buildings-creatures were often not dead before the taxidermy, but functioned well even if they were lacking sustained investment and maintenance (i.e., Kreenholm).

Buildings can give and receive; they are performative, they also *happen*. The opposite of architectural taxidermy, which removes the human voice and warmth from the architectural skin, is to honour maturing buildings with occupation, repair and maintenance work, a form of warming them up, as physical, historical, political and financial bodies. An example of this is the rediscovery of the Tallinn energy plant, next to Linnahall, or more precisely the creation of the Contemporary Art Museum of Estonia (EKKM) and its organic development, which has now gone on for more than ten years. The EKKM is a nonprofit exhibition venue established in late 2006, when artists looking for studio space started squatting in the office building of the former boiler plant. The museum gained convenient institutional stability in 2011, as a consequence of the increase in the number of visitors to the shoreline that the programme of the European Capital of Culture brought. Yet as a side effect, a detailed plan has been prepared by the city hall to privatise all the area surrounding the museum, because of the gentrification of the neighbourhood and allegedly the need to pay for KultuuriKatel (the so-called Creative Hub), the big iconic project of the European Capital of Culture (opened three years after the event), whose costs put the survival of the museum directly at risk.

In November 2017, artist Kirill Tulin presented in EKKM *Help for the Stoker of the Central Heating Boiler*, an installation-performance inviting the audience 'to imagine together what public spaces we want in winter and how we could claim and maintain them' (figures 1.5 and 1.6). For a period of one month, and organised into seven separate shifts (a 24-hour

Fig. 1.5 Help for the Stoker of the Central Heating Boiler, project, 2017. Source: Kirill Tulin.

Fig. 1.6 Help for the Stoker of the Central Heating Boiler, project, 2017. Source: Author.

workday followed by a three-day break, 'сутки через трое'), the museum was kept open and warm, day and night, by the stoker-artist and his successive helpers. I had the pleasure of acting as a helper, warming the building and acting as a host for discussions among the nearly 50 people who came to visit the space during my shift. The project created a thermal communicative condition (Robinson 2015), transforming the museum into a platform for thought-making. In a way, this project echoes Mierle Ukeles's *Maintenance Art*, which involved shaking hands with each of the 8,500 sanitation workers of New York, expressing words of gratitude to them, or inviting people to perform their regular duties as art. 'My working will be the work', declared Ukeles.

The bench-like structure built by Kirill in the entrance room was a reflection onto the floor of the shape of the load-bearing ceiling. This bench worked as a giant radiator, with hot water tubes inside, transforming the exhibition into a *tepidarium* by hidden pipes from an adjacent boiler-room (a design which restores the premuseum plan, locating a shower box in the corners where it once was). The heating fuel came from the wood material left from the museum's previous exhibitions. Besides functioning as a form of research on its own, the exhibition had several layers of cultural and material archaeology. For instance, *Help for the Stoker of the Central Heating Boiler* borrows its title from a book found in what would later become EKKM, when the building was 'rediscovered' in 2006 (figure 1.7). That manual was written in the early seventies to provide the technical instructions to heat the Tallinn power plant. Otherwise, the figure of the stoker has particular connotations in the former Soviet Union – as the embodiment of idleness, lack of ambition and inappropriate behaviour, a redundant drunk wasting time (although many were highly educated), the lowest social position in official accounts; and yet, the freest possible job for young artists, poets and musicians, allowing for a space of autonomy, a chosen peripherality, being simultaneously inside and outside the system.[8]

Another important layer of the exhibition is that Kirill provided a space where visitors could spend time and exchange thoughts, a simple *service* which, however, appears critical and subversive due to the fact that physical public spaces are shrinking in Tallinn while the privatised commercial ones are overwhelmingly rising. We can relate this to the phenomenon of architectural taxidermy, as well as to the decreasing lives of buildings for speculation purposes, the actual politics of memory and revanchist urban planning, which has resulted in recent buildings being rapidly devalued, thought unworthy of investment and finally made expendable. Hence the question of which buildings are 'worth' preserving

Fig. 1.7   Museum of Contemporary Art of Estonia (EKKM). Source: Author, 2017.

and which are architecturally, historically and culturally 'worthless' strongly echoes social considerations and values.

The above-mentioned urban plan also intends to demolish the building and privatise the plot adjacent to EKKM – pertaining to the same energy complex. Due to the negligence of the building (a storage room and infrastructure supplying coal for the surrounding plant), artists, scholars and students worked together for months in 2013 repairing the ceiling, paving the floor and reinstalling electricity in the space. Then they opened an exhibition space called Gallery of the Installation, Photography and Sculpture Departments of the Estonian Academy of Arts (ISFAG) (figure 1.8), where young artists and curators can organise alternative shows.

In October 2014, I co-curated a site-specific meta-exhibition in ISFAG, *I Looked into the Walls and Saw . . .* , which refrained from physical intervention in the gallery. The curatorial act consisted of inviting 20 participants to identify and interpret diverse physical qualities of the space, reflecting on the space as if it were a sculpture, an installation or a painting in its own right. The artworks of the show were the patina of the former energy plant precariously transformed into a gallery, making entropy visible and enabling the building to respond to physical and social

Fig. 1.8   Entrance to Gallery of the Installation, Photography and
Sculpture Departments of the Estonian Academy of Arts (ISFAG).
Source: Author, 2014.

time. Artworks themselves were found as leftovers and subject to disintegration: limestone bricks from different eras, mushrooms incrusted within
rocks, pipes, insulation foam, holes, water puddles, walled-in windows,
metal remains, codes written on the walls and changing weather conditions were some of the main exhibits on show, as signs of age that accumulate on both the surface and the intestines of the space (figure 1.9).

The exhibition concept built upon curators' experience of visiting
previous shows at the ISFAG, when they were unable to distinguish
between exhibited art objects and the walls and floors of the gallery. For
the show, anthropologist Patrick Laviolette chose to write about a dark
corner situated at the very end of the exhibition area. To observe this
space, visitors had to open a door to a musty, dank black room, which had
a hole at the bottom of a fake wall that blocked their sight and passage
into the very end of the coal loading tunnel. Architect Toomas Tammis
made a list of all the loose stuff present in the gallery, the detached
things that appear as changeable and that lie outside regulations (two
brooms, for example, the telescopic tube of a vacuum cleaner or a folda-
ble ladder). Other contributions approached material decay as an act of

Fig. 1.9 One of the many scars present at the exhibition space, ISFAG. Source: Author, 2014.

communication similar to graffiti, as shown by street artist MinaJaLydia. Architecture historian Ingrid Ruudi reflected on how the labour of art workers is to sustain zones of unconventional critical thinking, which also includes Sisyphean tasks such as drying the floor of the gallery or repairing holes in the roof. Ruudi brought to the debate Ukeles's *Maintenance Art* and the original meaning of the term 'curating' – to take care of – concluding: 'A non-profit gallery as a commerce-free zone of exchanging ideas is made possible by someone initiating it, maintaining it, taking care of it. Sweeping up the water from the floor. Doing it voluntarily, out of enthusiasm, largely unpaid'.

Also we can refer to the choice of anthropologist Franz Krause, who wrote: 'These pipes are not supposed to be here. They are just passing through. They are hidden, where possible, behind a makeshift plywood facade. And they are insulated with thick sheets of material, so as not to reveal any of the riches they carry, on the way from somewhere to elsewhere. Much like this room itself, they are not made for loitering, but as corridors – spaces to hurry through on the road to a proper destination. They connect points, a point of origin and a target point; and this connection has to be as smooth, fast, as frictionless as possible and to deliver all the content in its original state, unadulterated by the journey'.

Topographies of political cleansing

The transformation of cityscapes has provided the ground for former Soviet republics to reestablish themselves as nation-states, mobilising architecture and urban planning in the service of social change, constructing pasts and futures through the built environment (Boym 1994; Khalvashi 2015; Laszczkowski 2016; Molnár 2013; Ojari 2012). On a symbolic level, a historical rush appeared to erase any physical representations of the Soviet era from the city centres; new monuments, street names, museums and historical narratives quickly emerged and the old *stigmatised* ones were forced out from the urban landscape. Such extensive reorchestration of official memory through the redesign of urban surfaces and newly commissioned monuments followed a spatial pursuit of legitimacy (Buchli 2007), turning postsocialist cities into an overwritten palimpsest in which the hidden was as meaningful as the exposed (Oushakine 2009). Indeed, to *clean* the old iconography and symbolically reappropriate the space within the city centres was just the first stage of a wider process driven by the removal, rediscovery and recreation. As an important part of this phenomenon, the past was reconsidered and history reinvented, not simply to create a new community or legitimise the new government, but also to attract investors, customers and tourists.

Probably the best example of the discursive reappropriation of Tallinn is Vabaduse Väljak (Freedom Square). This plaza was reconstructed in 2008 to function as a stitching point of Estonian national identity, yet the site has had several manifestations during its history, hosting a 5 metre monument to Peter the Great under the Russian empire, and then being called Victory Square (Võidu Väljak) (figure 1.10) during the Soviet time and used as a parking lot. Recently, it has been rebuilt and packed with memory symbols (the Liberty Cross and the Memory Column), hence turned into a *lieu de mémoire* (Nora 1989). In the framework of the 90th anniversary of the Republic of Estonia, the Ministry of Defence decided to erect a 23.5 metre glass pillar reproducing the 'Cross of Liberty'

Fig. 1.10 Victory Square (Võidu Väljak), 1961. Source: Karl Oras, Rahvusarhiivi filmiarhiiv.

(a military award of 1919) in a prominent site of the plaza (figure 1.11). The monument was proposed not to address the idea of democratic liberties but to promote freedom as the outcome of a war, and it gained the opposition of many locals, especially architects and artists. For instance, architect Karli Luik argues that 'aesthetically, the monument definitely does not belong to the 21st, or even to the 20th century, but rather to the 19th century . . . it is out of proportion and leads to misunderstandings'; while Daniel Raudsepp, head of the nearby Art Hall, shares that 'this official monument is hard to explain when we receive foreign visitors'.[9]

Unexpectedly, an attempt to fix this misconception emerged in the Estonian capital when the final decision was taken. Then, hundreds of white posters with the text 'VABADUS' (Freedom) appeared in the public space of Tallinn overnight, inviting the passers-by to share their understanding of freedom and to express their opinion about the design of the new square. The posters were announcing a contest to find out the best solution to the public debate concerning 'Freedom'. The intention of this anonymous poster action was not entirely obvious, with the media's first speculation being that this was some kind of advertisement campaign. In the empty space of the posters some people used the opportunity to express their opinion about the Cross of Liberty, while some others just

Fig. 1.11 Cross of Liberty at Freedom Square (Vabaduse Väljak).
Source: Author, 2017.

wrote dirty words. Authorities, however, immediately criminalised the freedom posters.

In October 2017, another polemical debate emerged around the use and design of Freedom Square, after the decision of the state to prevent young people from skating on the site, blaming them for making noise, breaking the city furniture and not respecting the past. Yet, as Hannes Praks, professor of Interior Architecture pointed out, the unwelcoming of young people in Freedom Square was a serious strategic mistake by the government, distancing the youth from the rest of the society and generating negative affects.[10] I agree with him that the key problem is not that claims against skaters are false, since the intense traffic nearby and repeated commercial and patriotic events taking place in the square might be more disturbing to local inhabitants; worse is that young people are to be prevented from reappropriating public spaces and the past in their own way.

The strategy of rearticulating the public space of Tallinn through a selective erasure of architectural and monumental legacies and the erection of new historic references also became evident with the removal of the Soviet Bronze Soldier (also called *Alyosha*), originally placed in the city centre (figure 1.12) and since 2007 standing in a military cemetery. *Alyosha* became a 'symbolic abject' (Mälksoo 2009), gaining a contesting power with regard to the conceived centrality of the city and the corresponding constitution of normative cultural margins, since the presence of *Alyosha*

Fig. 1.12 The Bronze Soldier in its original location, 1967. Source: Oskar Juhani, Rahvusarhiivi filmiarhiiv.

in the centre materialised different understandings of national identity, collective memory and centripetal relations. In turn, the removal of the statue commemorating the 'Soviet liberation of Estonia' enforced the new zone of symbolic restoration of the first Estonian Republic, drawn from the Parliament to the Museum of Occupations and Freedom Square.

Henri Lefebvre ([1974] 1991) noted that monumental space constitutes a collective mirror, offering each member of a society an image of that membership, a social visage. Since 1991, the Bronze Soldier has become the gathering point for both celebrations that honoured socialist traditions and Estonian nationalists who protested against honouring the Soviet regime. Aptly, Andres Kurg (2009) points out that the monument's removal from its site undermined Tallinn's public space (in the widest political sense), since the Bronze Soldier filled the gap in representational politics for the Russian-speaking counterpublic, but also served as an entry point to the city centre for those living in the suburbs (especially elderly people). After being displaced from the city centre, the Soviet Bronze Soldier rests in a military cemetery behind the bus station. The removal could be understood therefore as a disruption of the dialogue between the marginal and hegemonic parts of the society, ostracising minorities even more. Accordingly, the riots that broke out during the removal of the Soviet monument were not merely about how to interpret the past, and the engagement was not as simple as 'Estonians fighting against the Russian minority' (Norman 2009), but they were a Bakhtinian carnival in which hierarchical distinctions and norms were suspended (Mälksoo 2009) or, even more, a radical attempt to subvert the new relationship between the centre and margins of Tallinn and Estonian society at large.

Monuments can also be understood as visible reparations in the public space, answering to some damage, occultation, loss . . . conjuring a void and establishing a new correlation of presences and absences. A monument is simultaneously a material and symbolic operation, retrodictive inasmuch as the past re-presents itself differently to shed a new light on history (Attia 2014). Demolitions and removals have turned Tallinn into a city of unintentional memorialisations beyond the major monumental sites. The demolition of monuments entails a strong symbolic capacity, the act being monumental in itself. Mikhail Yampolsky (1995) and Adrian Forty (1999) have shown how the destruction of monuments in the context of post-Soviet iconoclasm and exorcism created voids in the urban environment, as certain sites gained significance because of the sense of absence generated.

In this context, the destruction of the Bronze Soldier affirmed the power of the victor to the same extent as the erection of a new monument. Raising new monuments and tearing down the socialist ones was thus part of a process of giving new values and resignifying the space (Verdery 1999). As Yampolsky pointed out (1995), monuments have a unique impact on temporal regimes, almost magical; they create a 'chronometer of history', a sort of sacral zone that affects the course of time. The aim of reconfiguring temporal regimes was thus accomplished by constructing a metanarrative for and through the space, generating an alignment between ideas pertaining to urban planning and those pertaining to politics.

Interestingly, the physical erasure of the Bronze Soldier does not mean that its existence is forgotten (Kattago 2009b). The absent presence of *Alyosha* still lingers in Tallinn as a 'countermonument' (Michalski 1998) and as organic evidence of absence (Buchli and Lucas 2001b), registering disagreement and encapsulating a process of reflection in motion.[11] The discussion around the monument serves as a reminder that Estonia is faced with the difficult question of what to do with its Soviet heritage, an uncomfortable issue often mingled with ideological confrontations, power relations and marginalisation, which is transferred onto space and has an echo in representational politics. 'It is easier to erect a monument and freeze an image of the past, than to acknowledge the complexity of historical events', notes Kattago (2012, 124), emphasising that monuments, museums and commemorations do not monopolise the interpretation of historical traces, and reminding us that tensions cannot simply be solved by the placement or removal of monuments.

And yet, monuments represent the past in the present, and their removal provides the means of rewriting historical narratives. In Estonia, for instance, we can see this in the statues of Lenin, turned into a symbol of toxicity that had to be made invisible, moved out of place. Between 1952 and 1990 there was a statue of Lenin at the intersection of Riia and Võru streets in Tartu, beside a building which is currently occupied by the NATO Baltic Defence College. As urbanist Raina Lillepõld investigated, this was the first statue of Lenin made by Estonian sculptors and architects.[12] In 1972, the monument was listed as a national heritage site. After its dismantling (23 August 1990), the statue was taken to Tartu's central square, where a placard was hung on it, stating 'Socialism equals Fascism'. In the 1990s, the local government tried to abolish the heritage status and sell the sculpture at an auction; however, the plan failed. Meanwhile, the statue was moved swiftly to various warehouses, its last location being the site of a waste company (108 Tähe Street). In 2005, Lenin was transported to the backyard of the Museum of History, where he has been lying on the ground alongside 14 statues and sculptures of other comrades. On the website of the museum, they were defined as 'homeless monuments', 'ideological' and 'a forgotten heritage' (figure 1.13).[13] In February 2018, the situation changed, however, since the 15 monuments were reerected and displayed in the backyard of the museum, nowadays transformed into a garden. Also, the official description of the monuments has changed, and one can read on the website of the museum that these sculptures deserve to be preserved 'from a historical point of view' because of their 'high artistic quality' . . . and in spite of recalling painful events.[14]

With its veneration-depreciation trajectory, the statue of Lenin confirms Mayakovsky's words, which assert that the Soviet leader is more alive than the living, at least in his absent-presence, acquiring an Other value. Now resting in the backyard of the History Museum, the statue shows the transient value of Soviet things, which may regain their value after passing through a period of being been regarded as waste. Yet does it also point at a latent change in the public memory discourse? And shall fallen monuments be exhibited, recycled, inventoried or just buried? In the central square, in a junkyard (figure 1.14), or in the backdoor of the history museum, the statue of Lenin remains as an obdurate reminder of the Soviet time and its pretended ahistorical condition. Through the

Fig. 1.13 A statue of Lenin in the backyard of the Museum of History. Source: Alex Bieth, 2014.

Fig. 1.14 Jäätmekeskus (Junkyard in Tartu). Source: Jerry Waters, 2005.

demolition or neglect of statues of Lenin, the past started to be not only revenged but also distorted, becoming partly dematerialised and concealed. Decades after the break-up of the Soviet Union, some of the remains are still here but the narratives have disappeared, demonstrating that things have a longer duration than people and political regimes. It is in this sense that materiality allows us to access (and preserve) cultural meanings and vanishing worlds.

Residual histories

One of the aims of this book is to offer an insight into the significance of waste for the creation of temporal regimes and representations of social identity. To be categorised as waste implies that something no longer has a use or purpose, lacks cultural distinction and has zero worth (Bauman 2004). Those things considered as 'superfluous' or 'dispensable' appear in contemporary society as a matter out of place, excluded from the normative, rejected from the system and thus potentially dangerous. In the case of Estonia, 'wasted humans' are not the traditional migrants or asylum seekers (as in former empires, such as Britain and France), but those who entered into such conditions by the collapse of the previous order. The constitution of waste also refers to broken knowledge and obsolescence, to what no longer fits, to a mark between the old (what has ended) and the new (what has begun). And yet, the act of separation is neither that neutral, nor free of after-effects, since the destruction or neglect of the recent past erodes an individual's sense of belonging.

Socialism was over but the people are still here, reveals Svetlana Aleksievich (2015) in her oral history of the post-Soviet world. Many of those who grew up in the USSR are living on 'second-hand time', an era of disenchantment, in which they did not find the freedom that was expected, but rather a borrowed time and others' life.[15] These are people out of history, a remnant of the twentieth century and a question mark against temporal linearity, cast aside without anything durable to counter surrounding societal changes. And yet we coexist with them; those who do not take part in success discourses intrude into our scheme of things from time to time, 'polluting' linear narratives and our sense of order. This is precisely complexity brought by waste and the obsolete – it does not vanish, it lingers on, shaping contemporary notions of the subject, of time, and of the world (Tischleder and Wasserman 2015).

In the summer season, more than a hundred youngsters gather in the esplanade Roheline Turg, in the heart of the old town. Every evening

Fig. 1.15   Urmas. Source: Author, 2012.

they play ping-pong, sing, flirt and drink alcohol. This space of fun is also a working place for a few people. Besides the waitresses of Hell Hunt, we may meet Urmas (figure 1.15), who earns around €20 a day picking up cans and bottles. On Fridays and Saturdays, he might get over €50. Early in the morning, he goes to the recycling machine situated in a parking lot nearby Rimi supermarket to deliver the cans and bottles in order to receive *his salary* (26 cans amounts to €2). During several nights in July 2012, I brought him beers. We then sat on a bench and he told me stories, repeating himself a bit. 'I'm the king of this place. People know me and respect me. At the end, this is not a job; it helps me to forget my pains and sadness', he confessed. At the time, there were more than 300 can collectors in Tallinn, most of them working at night and only during the summer. Urmas acquired the best area because his son is a popular Estonian rapper: Lennart Lundve, though everyone knows him as 'Abraham'. The youngsters look for Urmas, bringing the bottles to him: 'They respect me because of my son'.[16]

   In the autumn of 2011, Urmas ended up in prison after getting into a fight for the territory with another can collector. Urmas spent four months and four days behind bars. Last time we met, in August 2012, he told me that he had already saved more than €2,000 to leave the country.

He did not want to ask for money from his son, even if he supposes that Abraham is earning well. 'People should know how difficult life is', says Urmas, who fought for four years in Afghanistan (1982–1987), in the Red Army. In the 1990s, he worked as a mechanic, repairing boats, but he lost his sight and had to choose between the job and a medical operation. 'I also fought for the independence of this Republic, Estonia was not fair with me', he claimed. Forgetting is a tough place, often without a shelter. In the present context, Urmas appears as a social leftover who survives by gathering economic and material leftovers, experiencing abandonment by the state, standing as a human ruin. In a way, he lives in a temporal marginality (Frederiksen 2013), since his opinion is cast aside, and his projections towards the future are different from those envisioned by the official discourse.

Lija, owner of the Georgian restaurant Argo in Tallinn, managed to go through different temporal regimes after a hard time (figure 1.16). Originally based in the Kadriorg quarter, Argo had a loyal clientele composed of neighbours, construction workers and people from the suburbs. The lingua franca in Argo was Russian but I heard Lija, the owner and waitress, speaking in Finnish, Estonian and English. Intrigued, I asked her how many languages she spoke. Unexpectedly, Lija told me that she's trilingual, but not in any of those three languages. Her native languages

Fig. 1.16   Lija in the new Argo. Source: Author, 2015.

are Armenian, Georgian and Russian, languages that she learned in her childhood in the Caucasus. Lija graduated with a degree in law from the University of Tbilisi. She married a German man and moved with him to Estonia. Having divorced in the 1990s, and with her university BA unrecognised, she took over the restaurant from an Armenian entrepreneur.

Transitions can be hard, especially when you're old and frail. After fifteen years with Argo, Lija was told to move out as the new owner of the land had a plan to build an apartment building. Since 1980, there has been a bar at this site. Just before the Moscow Olympic Games, a canteen called White Bears was opened, serving cheap beer for seamen and construction workers. 'Sure, there were many things forbidden in the Soviet period, but we enjoyed stability and social differences weren't that huge. People say that the Soviet system was alienating, but I have the impression that the current system doesn't need humans; or at least, it doesn't need people like me', laments Lija, who has lived the first half of her life in the Soviet Union and the second half in independent Estonia. 'In the name of freedom and democracy there have also been injustices', she complains. After a year in a limbo, searching for a new place for Argo, helping out her sister, Lija found a spot next to the Kristiine shopping mall, and is actually doing well (they even plan to open a second Argo in Helsinki).

Another place that has had a hard time adapting to recent changes is Ariran. This Russo-Korean locale was the first exotic restaurant opened in Tallinn (1991) and, at the time, the street of Telliskivi was a location away from the centre. The owners are a couple and they live at the rear of the house. Sergei was born in Korea, and moved to the Soviet Union when he was 17 years old to study marine engineering. Vera is Russian, works as the chef of the bistro and managed to marry Sergei in spite of the opposition of his mother (figure 1.17). They both moved to Estonia in 1970. He worked in the harbour of Tallinn until the collapse of the USSR, and has been the Baltic billiard champion for 20 years in a row, yet neither of them knows the Estonian language well. They have a son living in the United States, and they liked Florida when they visited him some years ago. The style of the restaurant is somewhat eclectic: real Russian objects and manners coexist with some imported Korean products. They have Russian TV channels playing, but when clients other than regulars enter the restaurant they switch to Korean TV. In the 1990s, the clientele was composed of professors, politicians, metal entrepreneurs, mafia bosses, and so on, but nowadays few adventurers dare to give it a try. The offer of exotic restaurants grew exponentially in the town in recent years, but the couple blames the neighbour, Jüri Liim (an Estonian nationalist figure), for the decline, as he undermined the image of the restaurant in the media.

Fig. 1.17   Sergei and Vera. Source: Anne Vatén, 2013.

History and personal biographies intersect in dramatic ways in post-socialist societies, showing not simply in institutional transitions but also as a crisis of values and knowledge (Humphrey 2002, 43), as well as dyssynchrony, a soul delay, an experience of the body being in one time and the mind in another, pointing at a collision of temporalities in the individual and social selves. Further on, the system that sprung from the so-called transition has been rendering those unable to adapt increasingly invisible, irrelevant and superfluous, as depreciated individuals. While young people could manage and better adapt to sudden changes and precariousness (responding with competitiveness and developing a crisis mindset), the elderly came to understand themselves as not merely displaced into the informal economy, but rendered redundant, outdated, endlessly unable to realise their goals (Bauman 2004; Shevchenko 2009).

East European societies were disciplined and remade in order to fit 'capitalist normality' (Buchowski 2006); those who were 'inept' were accused of obstructing progress and undermining the process of becoming 'normal'. Facing rapid social and economic change, many people found themselves inexperienced and compelled to reassemble their (inter)subjectivities and simultaneously reinvent their moral personhoods in multifaceted ways (Humphrey 2008). We can even speak of a lack of pragmatic or 'civilisational' competence, as Piotr Sztompka suggests (1996), pointing at the discrepancy between the speed of institutional reforms and the slowness of cultural changes, which becomes an obstacle for development. We can also note an ideological construction of time, adding that dominant ideas of time in society raise the question of whether certain groups and individuals believe themselves to be part of these times (Frederiksen 2013).

Indeed, the distinctiveness of postsocialism rests not only on the influential legacies of socialism, but also on the personal skills that were required afterwards, as well as the acceleration and urgency of the process. As Liviu Chelcea shows in his ethnography of bank workers in Romania, postsocialist transformations also meant an acceleration in the experience of time – accompanied by the installation of new routines, disciplines and standards, a sharper separation of work and life (yet with the colonisation of personal time by the corporation), and a diffused long-term future where meaningful plans appear as fantasy or daydreaming. This has led to significant changes in the organisation of economy, culture, space and time, manifested in discourses of flexibility, the demand for 'self-regulating selves' and the creation of a new category – the 'old timers' (Chelcea 2015, 350). Furthermore, each new employee was supposed to master and perform operations previously assigned to different employees. This is what David Harvey called the 'accelerated destruction' of prior skills (1990, 230) in relation to processes of deindustrialization in the West.

In her ethnography of an Estonian oil shale mine, Eeva Keskäla (2016) notes that the introduction of new technology was as significant to the history of the miners as the year 1991. The introduction of computers contributed to making previous jobs obsolete and intensifying time planning, yet which are the postsocialist nuances in this process of making the past order and skills obsolete? Reflecting the capitalist understanding of 'time wasted' as profit lost, rather than the logic of the socialist economy, in which time was made of short-circuiting interruptions, Katherine Verdery remarks that changes in the experience of time have been crucial for the economic and political organisation of these societies, since individuals developed certain responses to the irregular socialist time that affected their daily lives (e.g., hoarding), and with the introduction of standardised yet unequal capitalist time people had to create new responses, living through a transformation of the experience of temporality itself.

Also, Svetlana Boym (1994) notes that temporal regimes were a constitutive dimension of the postsocialist life, in the form of an altered perception of time in response to radical changes and snowballing transformations. It was not simply that people started to live in a deep fleeing present, but also that they assumed as normal a vast production of excess and obsolescence, which led to the incompatibility of the old and new orders, besides rendering the socialist experience inaccessible, both socially and symbolically (Oushakine 2010). Hence, it was not only that the Soviet political system broke up, but also that the collective memory of the period collapsed in the exercise of eliminating and undoing through negation the cultural myths and representations of the regime (Aarelaid-Tart 2016; Ries 1997).

Concluding considerations

The depiction of socialist legacies as 'waste' and 'residual' has to do with the remaking of historical representations and temporal orders around which the society is organised: on the one hand, by presenting the USSR as a toxic regime leaving behind only waste and ruin, and on the other hand, by treating people who embody the old personal skills as disposable and superfluous. The break-up of state socialism has been thus a decisive factor in generating a new perspective on the Soviet remnants, depicted after 1991 as a strange and useless inheritance, rather than as a legacy. The efficacy of past representations as waste relies on the framing effect that they deliver. These social constructions function as indexing templates, influencing cultural frameworks and possibilities of becoming. They are easily recognisable and generate affect while not suggesting any obvious ideological agenda.

In this chapter, the phenomenon of waste came into focus not merely as a by-product of manufacturing processes, but rather as an integral element in cultural systems and social structuring, which also has influence in representations of the past. The wasting of things is thus a way of making some things important, by making other things unimportant, taken away, disposed of or sacrificed. Collective memories are always intertwined with selection, discarding and replacement, showing that a particular value, significance and cohesion also emerge through practices of discarding. Yet, the old, the obsolete and the neglected may be seen to oscillate between a derelict condition and precious recognition, depending on the sociocultural context.

2

Reframing the Soviet inheritance through repair

The production of the self through repair

In this chapter, I shift the emphasis from brokenness and waste to repair, recognising the importance of this intervention for social synchronisation and also to reaffirm a person's identity. The efficacy of repairing interventions resides somewhere other than in their relation to material value per se, relying rather on cognitive and affective processes. In repair, we can recognise anthropological density and affective investment. This activity brings devalued things to light, extending the duration of things, attaching cultural meanings, and permeating new kinds of affects to circulate in public. Thus, repair does not refer simply to the practice of completing things that stand in a stage of in-betweenness, but also to an empowering experience entangled in the ordinary, played out in quotidian material and affective registers, which are part of an overarching process of recuperating.

The recuperation response is already implicit in the words naming the condition ('in a state of repair') – as an act of reactivating what has been wasted and amending what has been lost. A state of repair refers to a form of damage due to exhaustion, effects of time, disinvestment or simply because something went wrong. The failure of maintenance is disintegrative, perceived as a threat to memory and to historical preservation and making negative affects contagious. Contrarily, the reappropriation of abandoned stuff helps to recover identities, histories and relations (Laviolette 2006), pairing together again what was separated (re-pair) and allowing a second opportunity.

Hence, repair is about investing in believing that the end has not come yet, and it has also a critical and subversive dimension. As an antidote to forgetting or wasting, repair might acquire the quality of a recuperative value, a sort of practical sovereignty, making social attachments and intimacy endure. Repair contrasts therefore with other types of intervention more fixated on relieving and mitigating, which point at a slow death instead of recuperation (Berlant 2007). This argument may seem counterintuitive though, since the imperative to mend imposed under the Soviet regime, the later availability of cheap mass-produced goods, and postsocialist practices of consumer citizenship seemed to signal the decline of repair (König 2013; Rausing 2004). Yet as this research shows, disrepair and negligence distribute destructive agency across time and space (see also Laszczkowski 2015), and it is enmeshed with other forms of power such as the routinisation of state-sanctioned narratives of failure (Ssorin-Chaikov 2016).

Further on, the anchoring of memory needs material stability, and the act of remembering occurs with an attitude of care about something from the past, whether in the form of repair or maintenance, shaping along the affective texture of familiar places. Memories are external processes too, extending outward into things, affecting social relations, performing what is worth remembering and what is not. Notions of urban memory, remembering and forgetting, are actively transmitted through perceived material worlds, materialising identities and functioning also as a medium through which those identities and temporalities are transmitted (Tilley 2011, 348). People actively contribute to the continuous reconstruction of the past, articulating accounts which get transmitted intergenerationally, contributing to the creation and definition of value and constituting a tangible part of local affective history (Navaro-Yashin 2012). This is a highly political process, materialising new social forms, historical regimes and political ideologies (Humphrey 2005; Verdery 2003).

Buildings and monuments should be seen therefore as forms of political action, capable of shaping subjectivities, cognition and legitimacy, embedding normative ideas in the material order of cities (Buchli 1999; Grant 2001; Molnár 2013). The built environment mediates past experiences and recalls by being tangled up with our individual and collective memories (Buchli 2002). In this context, ruination, demolition and brokenness appear as a reminder of forgetting, an estrangement of people from their past. The debate about wasted legacies is thus crucial after socialism due to different and competing valuations, claims and uses of the past, as well as the obduracies that remain within social transformations.

Processes of sociopolitical change can be understood by examining the afterlives of what remains, by the study of how things that have left their time and have not yet found a resting condition continue to work and linger in an altered form (Stoler 2013). This phenomenon has its own physical dynamics too; in their obduracy, the remains might generate tensions and dissonance, as well as being there to be reappropriated and revisited by new generations. And yet, the past is bounded by its very duration and visibility; this implies that we have to work with cultural survivals, withdrawn legacies and dissonant remains, interrogating material affection as public and political. Hence, part of my research is dedicated to accounting for those remnants of the past that fit with difficulty into present narratives, accounting for their varied trajectories and fates, attentive to what things have become and to the way their present being has an effect (Pétursdóttir and Olsen 2014). The research does not follow, however, problematic Cold War assumptions which depict socialism as unnatural and inherently failure-bound. As noted by Michał Murawski (2017b), against the background of the ongoing degradation of socialism's built legacy, its architecture and infrastructures have proven more obdurate than the socialist system itself, being still in place and in many cases functioning within market economies.

Putting repair into action

Social things are inherently unstable in both their meaning and their material shape; even so, through the study of the physical and durable we can enter into the less visible, the undertones and the nonverbal. There are traces that endure and traces that disappear, that occur through disruptive layering and singular experiences of deposition. These competing materialities and their social effects are rather contingent, yet they affect subsequent transformations through processes of framing and indexing. We can talk of value circuits and ordinary affects lodged in social life (Stewart 2007), which have significance as 'affective transmissions' (Navaro-Yashin 2012) and are central to the exercise of statecraft as a management of sentiments (Stoler 2004; Thrift 2004).

Discarded as waste or leftover, a remnant can be nonetheless found and valued as a memory object or as an invitation to play, incorporated in the new material order of things, regenerating itself in new encounters and through generational rediscovery. This is a relational phenomenon generated in our encounters with objects, buildings or landscapes and which can be passed on and can generate particular affects (Navaro-Yashin 2012, 2017). The study of affect puts the emphasis on felt intensities and structures of feeling to investigate how our attachments and encounters are conditioned through traces. Thus, affects are related to the registering of life and palpable modes of attending public feelings (Brennan 2004; Stewart 2011; Williams 1977). In this light, brokenness and repair can be considered as part of the engineering of affect (Chu 2014), altering the content of memories and informing how the Soviet past is being remembered in Estonia today. Further on, practices of repair can also help to cope with radical changes and redeem implied discontinuities, failures and exclusions, widening also what is possible to think and do in postsocialist societies, and telling less visible stories about labour, identity and urban politics.

In my fieldwork, it has proven fruitful to approach repair as a spatial and aesthetic practice related to remnants, sutures and modalities of experiencing the past. By examining tangible things from different aspects of social life, we can learn how values are distributed over a range of actors and projected into a system of shared consensual meaning. During the Soviet era, there was a building in the centre of Tallinn entirely dedicated to the repair of things (besides many garages where people dedicated their free time to different sorts of repair activities). Erected in 1974 under the design of the architect Maimu Kaarnaväli, this building was called Teenindusmaja (Дом быта, in Russian) and over one thousand people worked there in the 80s (figure 2.1). However, after the break-up of the USSR, this 'house of services' was not needed anymore, or at least it did not find a place in the new market economy of Estonia and the designed resignification of Tallinn; after several years of uncertainty, the property was sold in an auction to the Soviet Estonian Shipping Company (now Tallink group) and became a hotel.

Leather clothes, jeans, shoes, bags, suitcases and household appliances were readjusted in the Teenindusmaja, extending the life of things that were scarce. It was a true house of services, as photo sessions, dry cleaning and beauty treatments were also offered there.[1] For instance, Luule, my mother-in-law, remembers that, when she turned 18 years old, she went to the Teenindusmaja to get a haircut, and she detested it! In her way of recalling the scene, the failure to get a 'normal' haircut eventually evidenced the negligent treatment of its subjects by the regime, its inability to provide basic needs, and a proof of the forthcoming 'collapse'. In her kitchen, as she prepared lunch, I asked Luule for more details. And even her acknowledgement of the symbolic power of bananas and oranges for

Fig. 2.1 Teenindusmaja, 1975. Source: Photographer unknown, Rahvusarhiivi filmiarhiiv.

the people of her generation implied a negative assessment of the Soviet world, meaning lack of choice and uniformity, making tangible a sort of precollapse obsolescence. A link of causality was thus established between past anecdotal events and the current construction of the nation.

Under the Soviet regime, everyday life was a fundamental site of ideological intervention, instead of opposition to Soviet predicaments (Buchli 1999; Crowley and Reid 2002). Failures of supply and poor-quality goods were likewise understood as problems in the materialisation of the citizen-state relations, a judgement increasingly influenced by an 'imaginary West' and perceptions of more abundant lifestyles elsewhere, but also used as an argument to expose that the state was not strong enough and should be reinforced (Ssorin-Chaikov 2003). Yet in late socialism, everyday life was more and more imagined in relation to capitalism; then Western commodities appeared as sources for dignity and self-value, as well as tangible evidence of the economic inefficiency of the Soviet system. For instance, jeans were not simply a pair of trousers, but also a manifestation of connections and social capital. Likewise, people decorated their homes with packages of Western products, even if empty, because of their symbolic value (Berdahl 2001; Fehérváry 2009; Yurchak 2005).

Nonetheless, the overstocking of commodities and the means of production can be also seen as an indicator of a different relation between people and things (Kiaer 2005; Oushakine 2014). Shortages and storage were critical components of socialist material culture, generating a 'culture of frugality' (Fehérváry 2009) with sensitivity to the long-term value of things and a particular sense of care, as goods not only required frequent repair but also interventions to make them fully functional (Gerasimova and Chuikina 2009). Certain goods were available only in certain places, at certain times and in certain quantities; a peculiar form of economy which led to quotidian practices of hoarding and repair, associated with idiosyncratic types of waiting, transmission and acquisition (through luck, persistence or special contacts).

This created a complex material culture in which people 'flirted' with things and did not simply use them, being drawn into the network of social relations. As Ekaterina Gerasimova and Sophia Chuikina note in their article 'The Repair Society', the difficulty of straightforwardly acquiring an object in the Soviet Union made that thing more desirable, increasing its subjective value and moulding 'proxy' relations between the object and its future owner. Often acquisition was not the final stage in the cycle; people had to work on things to make them fully functional, accommodating the object to their needs and themselves to the object's idiosyncrasies. 'Citizens were forced to "muddle through", becoming experts in research and development and successful inventors' (Gerasimova and Chuikina 2009, 71). Then, in the early 1990s, repair turned into an anticatastrophic part of the post-Soviet *byt'* that superseded the historical break by capillary mechanisms of survival, negotiation and translation. In Russian, the word *byt'* refers to quotidian micropowers and the construction of domesticity, interweaving the private and public dimensions of personal experience (Buchli 1999). These are everyday interventions that go beyond routine and *habitus*, acquiring a shared and performative character and becoming subversive vis-à-vis ideologies and institutions (Boym 1994).

Another example of this idiosyncrasy is the term *remont*, which Walter Benjamin found impossible to translate into German. Originally, it came to Russian from French, and meant the provisioning of horses for the cavalry. In modern Russia, the use was extended, describing all sorts of repair activities and ways of handling losses. During his visit to Asja Lacis in 1926, Benjamin described Moscow as 'the city of remont' (1986, 36). As he observed, nearly ten years after the Bolshevik uprising, the initial revolution led to a massive renovation, converting Soviet society into a mobilised laboratory. Such a profusion of fixing and repairing was due to a simultaneous paucity of items and lasting structures, yet it has been also understood as a particular modality of power, which enabled an expansion of the Soviet governmentality through the pervasive reproduction of uncertainty (Ssorin-Chaikov 2003).

Remont refers to small quotidian material engagements completing mass-produced goods, embedded practices which reached a particular normative set and material culture (Gerasimova and Chuikina 2009). *Remont* can be thus understood as a means of conjoining domesticity and public life, the micro and the macro, margins and centres (Alexander 2012). It differs from actions of repair in two crucial aspects, an exaggerated aspiration to make things look Western and practices of shoddy workmanship expressing a state of permanent unfinishedness (Martínez and Agu 2016). There is a third term, *euroremont*, which emerged not as a way of attenuating shortcomings, but as an engagement to achieve a social status and renovate according to supposedly European standards and values – often done with a postmodern taste and contributing to an actual national identity (Sgibnev 2015). Indeed, *euroremont* appears as a quintessential experience of postsocialism, expressing expectations and imaginaries of Europe, yet conditioned by cultural traditions, material affordances (e.g., the surplus of plastic windows coming from the West), and also geopolitical circumstances. As few could travel to the 'real Europe', people created their own image of Western comfort based on movies and glossy magazines and made reforms to reproduce it in their dwellings accordingly.[2]

I agree with anthropologist Catherine Alexander (2012) that the specificity of *remont* is not that it happens, but the values attached and its aesthetic and moral implications. Repair practices make visible the relationship between 'temporary' and 'permanent' structures, showing care, mindfulness and cultural appreciation of what is inherited. Otherwise, repair is unequivocally relational, a stitch in time (König 2013); it is also a feeling, since it expresses a state of failure as well as an affective response to brokenness. Hence, this concept refers to a practice (of fixing) and a condition (damaged, neglected, in-between), and works also as a metaphor for an active negotiation of processes of change, an act that consists of rethinking ends and beginnings (Jackson 2014) and recuperating what has been wasted and neglected.

Everyday micropowers

Infrastructures and buildings should be constantly maintained to meet new contingencies and emerging breakdowns. This activity demands that we take the effects of time into account, simultaneously retrofitting and foreseeing what comes next. Maintenance is related to planning, appearing as a form of 'repair-before-failure' intending to prevent 'repair-after-failure' (Jacobs and Cairns 2011). Yet it is also a matter of concern in the present, an active practice of monitoring, tracking and intervening to sustain a system and its wider relations over time (Denis and Pontille 2015). The study of these activities sheds light on the invisible relationships between order and disorder, foregrounding a process that makes possible a kind of relative permanence for a given system as a whole.

Maintenance and repair are moments of learning and of politics too, enabling negotiations of new orders and values (Graham and Thrift 2007). We can situate repair as part of everyday micropowers, those which forge the materiality of built forms but also demonstrate that mundane acts contribute to create transcendental narratives through histories of care and personal co-construction, leading to a distribution of the sensible across the political landscape (Rancière 2006). Repair is a form of recuperation, passing through and carrying out, a way of lending continuity to discontinuity, an ongoing rework of differences. This intervention enacts affirmative micropolitics and injects kindness and affects of care (Thrift 2005), making societies more balanced, kind and synchronised. For instance, there is in the old town of Tallinn (next to souvenir shops and fancy restaurants), a modest *remont* business. The very same business has been there in Nunne Street since 1920, and is the oldest of its kind in Estonia. The space is no bigger than 2 m², where a man repairs clocks, radios and photo cameras every working day from 12 to 4 p.m. Toomas Koitmaa has been the owner since 1996. He has an apprentice, Dmitri, who finds it interesting 'to learn different mechanisms and imagine different lives of things' (figures 2.2 and 2.3). They have thought of making a *remont* of the *remont* place, but they don't earn enough money for that. They already struggle to keep it open every day, as both Toomas and Dmitri have other jobs to earn their living.

For them, to repair broken things is a hobby that helps to establish social relations and produces a joyful cultural experience. The result of their work oscillates between gift and commodity; sometimes they have to repair expensive pieces, while at other times they just do some basic *remont* to keep a device working. 'Rich people, middle-class and poor people come here. We attend to them all; often to the poor people around the Railway Station, we do the *remont* for free', explains Dmitri. Observing the variety of people coming to this tiny place, I realise that these clients not only bring different devices and belong to different social classes; they also seem to live in diverse temporalities – with a different configuration of the old and the new.

Fig. 2.2　Dmitri working in the repairing booth. Source: Author, 2015.

Fig. 2.3　Repair appears as a work dealing with the increasing municipality of temporalities in our everyday lives. Source: Author, 2015.

Somewhat, postsocialist societies are like a watch shop; where each clock shows a different time. Eventually, these differential relations over time and temporal representation organise and perpetuate inequalities. Repair practices are especially meaningful when changes extend social dyssynchrony, undermining any experience of duration and complicating a sense of belonging. In this sense, we can talk of repair as a suturing practice that recalibrates synchronicity and generates a sense of commonality through collaborative endurance and definitions of worth.

An atomic city in a state of repair

A few grammes of uranium started the history of Sillamäe in the 1940s, when it was given a code name (R-6685), and thousands of people were relocated to build up the town and work for a nuclear factory. For decades, it hosted a secret uranium-enrichment plant, as well as metal and chemical factories. As a secret town that did not appear on maps, Sillamäe was surrounded by barbed wire and any visitor needed a special *пропуск* (permit) to get in. This also entailed certain privileges: those living there could buy high-quality shoes, perfume, suits, coats and fur articles. Coming to Sillamäe meant getting a room in a communal apartment, a job with a high salary, and prospects for buying a car and getting a separate apartment after a few years. In the early 50s, there were around 11,000 inhabitants, most of them under 25 years old. Sillamäe was something close to a utopia, a no place built all in one style and according to the modernist plan, with state-subsidised corporatism, acceptable salaries and well-stocked stores (Brown 2013); however, this paradise soon turned into a dystopia, when workers were poisoned with radioactivity and unemployment once the system collapsed.

The history of the town is intimately related to industrial development and the Cold War (over 100,000 tons of uranium were produced between 1946 and 1990), but there is also a pre–World War II Sillamäe. The first records of the site date back to 1502, referring to a pirate's tavern called Tor Bruggen located therein. At the end of the nineteenth century, Sillamägi and Tursamäe became popular holiday resort settlements among St Petersburg intellectuals like Igor Stravinsky, Pyotr Tchaikovsky and Ivan Pavlov. Then, in 1928, a shale-oil processing plant, an electric power station and a small port were built by Swedish investors.

But this is also a typical story of Soviet-type modernisation: a one-factory city which lost its purpose. As architect Andres Alver explains it: 'Sillamäe . . . is a broken city and you have to glue the pieces back together' (cf. de Montesquiou 2006, 205). Decades later, Sillamäe lacks basic medical and administrative services. After the disintegration of the USSR, factories were reorganised or closed down. The heightened level of radiation was also publicly detected. Many people left. The population registered in Sillamäe in 1989 was 20,280 people; in 2015, just 13,964 people (90.8 per cent Russian speakers, half of them holding a grey passport). In 1993, the International Atomic Energy Agency labelled the waste depository of the factory a serious radioactive risk, and the clean-up was completed only in 2008. However, people also left because of unemployment, because of not feeling at home and because of feeling stigmatised.

In 2013, journalist Andrew Stuttaford visited Sillamäe and wrote an article that presents the waste dump of the town as 'a Leninist lake, toxic and vile'.[3] The location is certainly dramatic, with great views, but the city has also surfaces resonating with Soviet ornaments (hammers, sickles, stars) and neoclassical decaying façades. Nowadays, Sillamäe has an air of being in a permanent off-season: empty buildings, closed shops, unrepaired roads transmit disaffection and generate a state of disrepair (figure 2.4). For decades, the town was a sort of border area, on the coast, 20 km away from Narva. Nowadays, the town is a free-trade zone and there is a ferry connection with St Petersburg, serving as a bridge between

Fig. 2.4 Sillamäe bus station, 1989. Source: Viktor Rudko, Rahvusarhiivi filmiarhiiv.

the European Union and Russia. As Valentina Repina (an English teacher at a local school) acknowledges: 'Perhaps it is not right, but we consider this land as ours since we are living here. So I don't want to handle Russia and Estonia separately. Despite the fact that they are now different states. Lots of people feel the same' (cf. de Montesquiou 2006, 200).

I have been there three times; always on the way to Narva. The first time I visited Sillamäe was in October 2013, during a road trip with Patrick and Dan. Then, we just strolled around, impressed by the number of abandoned houses and factories. I remember we entered into one of the several atomic bunkers around the town. Also, we visited the main concert hall, which remains intact, as it was built and furbished in 1948. The second visit was in May 2015, when I asked my partner Marika to drive through the town. It was the first time for her, so we stayed there for some hours. We walked around the new harbour and in a park. Hoping to get some food, we entered into a restaurant where a birthday party with loud Russian music was taking place. Looking at the map of the town, near the main concert hall, we learnt there was a museum about the history of Sillamäe and there we went (figure 2.5).

Elena Gorneva, archivist of the museum, kindly agreed to guide our tour (figure 2.6). She spoke only Russian and talked with excitement about the exhibited pieces. On the first floor, the show is overcrowded with Soviet household objects, mostly from the 1950s. There we can see shoes, uniforms, furniture, costumes, flags, portraits and rusty tools alongside

Fig. 2.5 A bust of Lenin in the office of the Sillamäe Museum. Source: Author, 2015.

Fig. 2.6 Elena Gorneva (right). Source: Author, October 2017.

ancient minerals. On the second floor, there were items about the ordinary lives of workers: pictures, factory descriptions, account books, banners . . . a museum made of remnants turned into memorabilia, experienced as a flood of pastness engulfing the present. Indeed, there seems to be a continuity between the former exhibitions organised at the energy plan during the Soviet period and the actual display on the second floor of the museum.

Museums organise temporal categories and sequences, as well as the accounts and understandings of the passage of time. In 2015, the museum published a kind of memoir of the city, with letters and articles that serve as a nostalgic tribute to old workers, comrades and neighbours, remembering the life in the early years of Sillamäe, a city of youth and hope as the book put it, with many sport and cultural activities (Gitt 2015). The Sillamäe Museum was opened in 1995 as an attempt to amend the collapse of the city functioning and its identity crisis. As stated by Elena in my third visit to Sillamäe, from the very beginning the museum has aimed to be a recollection for future generations:

> We created the museum to save history, we felt it was being lost. I remember when the monument of Lenin was toppled, 1 October 1993 . . . [she searches for a newspaper and points at the pictures of the monument being dismantled]. Instructions came from Tallinn, we know that monuments are symbols of power, but they did the same with all the past . . . political technologies changed

very fast then, Estonians did it well, but people here were not taking these reforms, to put it diplomatically . . . these were Russian
people in a Soviet town, and they all loved Sillamäe; for them, the
balance was broken and not only Lenin, but a whole world was dismantled. . . . When they came here they were young, groups of
young boys and girls sent from Moscow to work, but coming from
villages, glad to live in a modern city; they had only future, no past,
they believed themselves as the most privileged proletarians . . . I
call them diaspora but of course they did not feel like that back then,
they did not emigrate abroad but within the same country, or what
it was one country.[4]

Refurbishing and mending are often associated with attempts to re-
create one's home and belonging. The same is true of this museum. The
items displayed confront us, however, with various sets of values, meanings and interpretations, from nostalgia to memory, class, migration,
material culture, labour, industrial development and place making (or the
sense of being from Sillamäe). The fact that the items displayed have been
donated by locals adds another public dimension to the city museum. The
exhibition shows that to care for something affirms a moral relation to it,
beyond instrumental and functional reasoning (Jackson 2014). Otherwise, this reluctance to discard past things can be explained as a way to
resist loss, understanding throwing away as a threat to memory and historical preservation (Cherrier and Ponnor 2010). In contrast, refurbishing, mending and collecting contain emotional states of being attached
to things, which is both defensive (responding to scarcity, facilitating
adaptation to changes), and generative (reconnecting and producing new
kind of affects to circulate in public). These terms refer to a process of recuperation, which can include many heterogeneous elements, chosen by a
variety of actors, and differs from recovery, which generally refers to the
restitution or replacement of whole systems (Guyer 2017).

A work of making present

Polymer is a former rubber toy factory in Tallinn where motorbikers,
mechanics, anarcho-vegans, satanists and artists have coexisted for
over a decade. According to several informants, the building (2,500 m²)
was a squat in the late 1990s. Soon after, illegal band rehearsals, as well
as rave parties, were organised there. In early 2003, Madis Mikkor (later
director of the Estonian Print and Paper Museum in Tartu) founded

Fig. 2.7 The author in Polymer. Source: Maren Poel, 2013.

Kultuuritehas Polymer with his brother Tõnis and Alfred Rosenroth. They first focused on historical preservation and worked to transform the space and renovate the building. Activities officially commenced as a civic initiative, and by 2004, the Polymer Art Factory was registered as a nonprofit organisation. 'This was done in spite of the bitter understanding of the fact that the rental agreement was always extended by three months only, and that the future of the building would most probably be demolition', observes Madis, who adds: 'it was in 2002 when I rented the first spaces in the huge derelict factory for a furniture workshop and a rehearsal space for live-action role players'.

A visit to Polymer offers a chance to drop out of the prevailing rhythm of the city, to enter into a space of alterity and suspension (figure 2.7). This building embodies a dream of an alternative lifestyle. As noted by Madis, Polymer did not correspond to any model, yet it was strongly conditioned by the material forms and uses it had inherited. In his view, Polymer presented a different notion of collectivity and commonality, taking art as a way of life and challenging the dominant production–consumption dichotomy.

In January 2014, the real estate owner cancelled the contract with the NGO that had managed the art residency, thus forcing the art factory to move out. Artists and activists had been working in the building for ten years, yet had been extending the original contract every three months. This impeded any long-term strategy or renovation, with the dwellers mostly focused on survival maintenance.

After the break-up of the USSR, the relation property use radically switched, and property rights were prioritised over the use and maintenance of buildings. The Polymer art factory was developed with recycled and repaired materials and filled with several fascinating leftover objects. The most impressive artefact was the letterpress printing machine that still contained all the typesetting equipment. The core machinery (Victoria 1040–2, see figure 2.8) was produced in the German Democratic Republic in 1979. The machine was used over more than ten years in a printing house located in the city centre of Tallinn. After the break-up of the USSR, the machine ended up in a suburban storehouse, where it was discovered by Madis's gang and brought to Polymer in late 2003. Nowadays, it is located in the Estonian Print and Paper Museum of Tartu.

'Yes, they all were great people [молодцы]. I'm particularly thankful to Madis, who hired me when I most needed a change', admitted Ljuda during one of our interviews. And yet, the change she refers to heralded a step back to the past. Ljuda (a Russian speaker) had studied typography in Riga in 1968, having completed four years of training there. In 1972,

Fig. 2.8 Ljuda using the Victoria 1040–2 typesetting machine. Source: Author, 2013.

she moved to Tallinn in order to work in the Ühiselu printing house, the oldest in Estonia. In 2002, Ühiselu was integrated into Reusner publishers, and the old workers were degraded to mechanical work such as supplying paper to the newly imported machines and producing cheap books. 'I consider typography as an art', Ljuda adds. From a discarded worker, she became a worker of discard. More than 40 years after her first training, Ljuda was still willing to print posters and visiting cards. She had been going to Polymer until the factory was closed. She also had been giving workshops to students of the Estonian Academy of Arts and taught the trade to Lemmit Kaplinski, who points out:

> Ljuda is a phenomenon bigger than herself. In the sense that 40 years ago there were hundreds of Ljudas, and nowadays she's the only compositor, somehow saving a secret knowledge. The case of Ljuda shows that people are affected by the change of technologies in an identitary way. Losing her job in the early 2000s meant losing her identity, being just half a part of herself or something like that. It is important to remember this matter in contemporary societies. I do not mean that changes are bad, just that we have to be aware of the human aspect too.

Ljuda is conscious of that and a couple of times repeated that she remains 'the only person in Estonia who deeply knows this art. My former colleagues left the profession in the 1990s and the new generations don't want to get dirty'. Retirement did not mean Ljuda quit her profession; it is inconceivable for Ljuda to stop doing typography voluntarily (figure 2.9). Printing helps her negotiate changes that elude her comprehension and render her skills obsolete, deploying affective attachments to labour and demonstrating that social and temporal belonging is still related to employment. In the USSR, labour had a strong subjective dimension, as people often built their identities upon their job. In postsocialist societies, however, technological innovation, neoliberal economy and discourses of flexibility and the enterprising self brought a loss of frames, causing many people to lose their means of production and their source of gremial identification, therefore impelling them to assume individually collective risks (Annist 2014). Otherwise, there was a different material attentiveness in Soviet society; repair was especially praised in a context of shortage of mass production. This attentiveness was also related to particular skills, which are not appreciated in an economic system, that rely on planned obsolescence, accelerated cycles of production-consumption-disposal and rapid financial profit. In this light, the death of the old gen-

Fig. 2.9 Ljuda in Polymer. Source: Author, 2013.

eration and the vanishing of material traces bring with them a loss of knowledge never to be replaced.

'This should be considered a museum, as Madis and Lemmit managed to do in Tartu', concluded Ljuda the last time we met. Once Polymer was closed, printing artefacts were brought to Tartu and placed in the Estonian Print and Paper Museum, founded in 2010 as a NGO. Lemmit explains: 'I was originally involved for emotional reasons; I like the shape, sound and smell of these machines. Also, I believe that innovation stems from the understanding of old technologies. From them, we can learn the basic rules and think past dead-end solutions'. Every year, the Estonian Print and Paper Museum invites Ljuda to spend some days teaching and getting dirty with the machines in Tartu. In 2014, the museum was relocated from Kastani Street to the Aparaaditehas, a former military factory that has been recently bought by the group which developed the Telliskivi area in Tallinn (which similarly transformed a military factory into a commercial area with space for cultural events). 'Art has always served other causes and purposes. Before, artists were mothered by the Soviet Union, and nowadays by entrepreneurs who act as medieval Italian patrons', remarks Lemmit.

Lemmit's favourite artefact is the linotype (line casting) machine produced in Leningrad in 1972 (figure 2.10). In the tour through the

Fig. 2.10 Lemmit with a group of Georgian artists in the Estonian Print and Paper Museum. Source: Author, 2015.

museum, I felt a sort of obsolescence vertigo from being surrounded by all kinds of discarded artefacts. In a way, it was like a tour into the intestines of the twentieth century. The obsolete is also a carrier of memory (Hetherington 2001), with an ambivalent presence capable of revealing imagined communities emanating from the past. As Lemmit observes, 'it is possible to see the recent history of this country by observing the changes in printing. For instance, there is a cleavage in World War II. Before that date, all the machines were produced in Germany, and after that, they were produced in the Soviet bloc. As printing was about communicating ideas, the profiles of those learning the profession in the Soviet period were closely checked by the authorities; printing was not simply a magical process, but had strong political effects too'. However, a challenge is that rapid obsolescence blocks our access to the past in that we become unable to use those technologies and even to read old computer files; also, our way of experiencing and thinking increasingly gets shaped by new interactions with media (Kattago 2012). Overall, the material culture associated with the Soviet world is at risk of loss due to the decreasing knowledge of how the most representative materials of this past work as well as its entropic degrading.

The museum has over 240 m² and still conserves the original lamps of the military factory. Seven people are involved with different sorts of works. One-third of the budget comes from the Ministry of Culture and municipality, €2,000 from private donations, and the rest from the sale of products and by providing workshops. The books that the Trükimuu-seum reuses are those discarded by the state libraries, so it gathers tons of books every year for free (figure 2.11). Lemmit, trained as a semiotician and with working experience as a Linux programmer, also manages an art

Fig. 2.11 Decommissioned books arrive at the Estonian Print and Paper Museum. Source: Author, 2014.

residency and plans to organise a book-crossing project. He concludes by reflecting on the changes provoked by the socialist break-up: 'The 1990s affected the printing industry in major ways. Publishers could access modern equipment, if they found the financial means. But changes happened so quickly that that people did not care about preserving industrial heritage. What you see here around are the few things left. They help to preserve memory'.[5]

At the corner of Aparaaditehas, there used to be a café called Soodiak. That space, two metres below street level, used to be the resting room of those officials and ranked officers coming from Moscow to check the production of the factory. Indeed, there is still a secret door connecting the café and the factory. Soodiak used to have a sauna and a swimming pool. There, before he escaped to the United States, artist Mark Kalpin designed a beautiful mural. Even if not well preserved, the mural has survived all the refurbishing of the room. In the early 1990s, Soodiak became the place where the postsocialist entrepreneurs of Tartu gathered. According to unofficial accounts, *metalist* businessmen and various mafiosi used to go there to close business and spend time with prostitutes. 'At that time the café was full, with 35 people here every day', describes Lea, owner of the café. In the late 1990s, a billiards table was located in the 'dark room'; however, the café has never recovered its maximum splendour and occupancy.

Soodiak was opened on 1 August 1995. 'At the time there were only five or six cafés in Tartu', adds Lea. She had previously worked as a waitress in the restaurant Kaunas, which is nowadays called Atlantis. I visited Soodiak for the first time in October 2013, after exploring the then rundown industrial space. In June 2015, I went back to talk to Lea and recalled what she had told me back then (figure 2.12). I ordered a coffee before I saw that there was no device to pay by card in the café. Lea was warming up the coffee machine still, but I told her not to prepare the coffee as I had no cash with me . . . after two seconds of hesitation, she told me that she would give me the coffee anyway for having come back to the café.

The interior of Soodiak was designed with lots of plastic flowers, wooden ornaments and Soviet chairs, complemented by a Marlboro sign welcoming visitors. The special meals of the house are *snitzel* and *pelmeni*. In the dark room, there is still a big cassette stereo – a reminder of a glorious active past. The morning after, I came back to pay for the coffee and ask why the café was called Soodiak. Roland, Lea's husband, was there. He told me they were preparing a birthday party, so they could not prepare a coffee for me that day. Still, Roland dedicated a few minutes to explain the origin of Soodiak; the name of this *cabalistic* café was given by the 12 signs decorating one of the walls. When I was heading out, he

Fig. 2.12 Author at the entrance of Soodiak. Source: Marika Agu, 2015.

suddenly asked me if I went to church; I said no. And then he asked why and I kept silent. Again, Roland inquired about my views on American politics; my silence made him feel uncomfortable, so he insisted on saying that America controls Europe and is trying to control Russia too. I simply replied that it is not that easy and left the place with a taste of sadness on my tongue.

A work of adaptation

In Apparaditehas, we also meet Kaarel Narro, a young carpenter who works in one of the basements of the courtyard (figure 2.13). Kaarel's workshop somehow confirms his kind of marginal status within Estonian society, yet it also gives a cosmological character to the place; all of which is manifested by the physical layout of things. In a way, the intricate relationship between men and ends is expressed through his material domains, by how they are organised in the workshop and by the ability of materials themselves to multiply and to compose other things. This cosmology is related to Kaarel's morale and skills at transforming rubbish and varied scraps into something valuable again.

In the workshop, it is hard to figure out if the scraps were already there before, or are rather offcuts from Kaarel's work. Aggregations of dust, pieces and scraps lay around, forming a sort of repairscape. 'From trash, and with trash, I have produced my little workshop', says Kaarel, who pays a symbolic price for renting the basement. In his working space, the objects are ordered by the needs of the work carried out there. Kaarel has organised the 25 m² into two rooms, arranged according to different skilled work he has to do. Amongst the distinctive characteristics of the work of repair are the use of a complex repertoire of gestures and the gathering of sensual knowledge (Dant 2009); in some cases, the tools that Kaarel uses seem to take part in the forming of his thoughts, in their shape and rhythm. Every day, his body encounters the material world to fix a different kind of brokenness, and Kaarel sometimes has to break things up in order to put them back together differently.

Kaarel's hands are cracked, callused and rough, yet during our conversation, he appears unexpectedly delicate, vulnerable and charismatic; thinking carefully what to say, taking time to answer, measuring every word (later I learn that he makes music too). Kaarel complains that 'Estonia has become a throwaway society . . . people cannot control the instinct of possessing. Nowadays it is excessive, and people possess and consume just for the sake of it. . . . In my view, there is a bit of arrogance with newness. Ha! People may think that used or repaired items hide a ghost inside'.

Most often, repair does not imply the transformation of one material into another or a radical creation; it is rather a contextual engagement of adaptation and refurbishing of what is around. Both the emancipatory potential and the limitations of repair rely on the materiality and situatedness of the action. 'I forced the manager to rent me this basement. Originally, they didn't know what to do with the space, so I insisted and asked Lemmit to mediate. Some dynamism has now started in Aparaaditehas; I guess they could have rented this space for more money; or perhaps I am also working as a catalyst, making this area more attractive', says Kaarel ironically. As has been done before with Telliskivi in Tallinn, Apparaditehas is being presented as a 'creative area' of cultural workers in Tartu. I asked Kaarel if he also considers himself a part of the creative class, to which he allegorically replied: 'I have been reading sci-fi books since I was a child. There I found all sorts of fictitious societies. Most of the authors were Russian, you know, like the Brothers Strugatsky, reflecting on the Soviet society through their novels, of which one of my favourites was *The Adventures of Dunno and his Friends* by Nikolai Nosov; first, it describes the city of the sun, a place where people are equal and happy and have a job, and then the city of the moon, a place inhabited by stupid, capitalist people, who just run after money and have to pay for their every move.

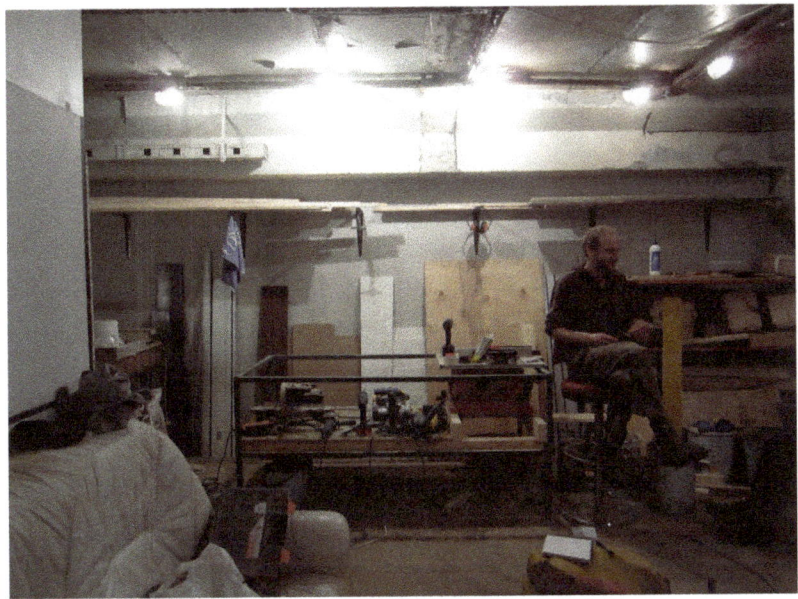

Fig. 2.13   Kaarel Narro in his workshop. Source: Author, 2015.

The creative city is the city of the stupid, the world where we live now, where everything is about money'.

Is money important to you? 'Of course, I would like to have more money, but I like to repair and reuse stuff; I learn to live cheaply, exchanging services, beyond monetary calculations. . . . I am thankful for having the chance to build things with my hands; also for using my own tools and not depending on anybody'. So what is important for you? 'That Estonia gets better and heals the Soviet past; also, the connections within families, which got weaker or broken in many cases'. Kaarel is particularly worried about intergenerational stability in Estonia. In his view, there is not enough communication between generations: 'one of the things I like about the printing museum is that people of different ages gather there', he adds.

Repair activities might foreground attunement and connectivity, binding together different generations, synchronising – bodily and temporally – asynchronous forms of community. As we see in this case, mending might function in a therapeutic way, helping Kaarel to reposition himself, cope with the competing temporalities and negotiate the actual system of values. Here, repair appears part of a work of adaptation that relates the production of the self with efforts at fixing the world.

Kaarel works as a freelancer, repairing stuff and installing art exhibitions in galleries of Tartu. After high school he started a course in pedagogy, but didn't finish it. In the meanwhile, he has been confined three times in a mental institution, 'repairing my brain', explains Kaarel smiling. In the future, he would like to teach arts and crafts in a school.

Objectual microtemporalities

It is through the practices of repair and maintenance that things are defended from social neglect and abandonment. Yet repair can also be generative and constitutive, pulling forces and sensibilities against brokenness, gathering materialities, scratching on the surface of rhythms and temporal regimes, and then making affects of attachment and connection to circulate in public. Thus, these practices are a phenomenon in their own right that follow both a defensive and a regenerative move. In this chapter, repair is proposed as an enactment of care, pulling forces, materialities and sensibilities against brokenness, negligence and waste making. As a human attempt to establish continuity and heal failures, the act of repair draws attention to changes and an involvement in what is around – tinkering, refurbishing, readjusting, attuning – giving the opportunity for the recovery of meaning and for reframing dissembled pieces.

Repair is a process of exchange between the objective material qualities of a thing and the problem-solving capacity of a person. These practices refer to a skilled range of interventions extending the life of things, a healing activity that makes things present, enables dwelling and keeps social constructions alive. Hence, the organisation of these practices does not refer simply to the application of a technical knowhow, but also to a disposition to attend to others, manifesting a social effort and preoccupation. Repair is always relational, constrained by affordances and skills, taking place and involving the passage of time. This is a sociomaterial practice that punctuates and reconstitutes what is out of order, fixing what has been damaged yet also assuming responsibility and taking a moral stand. In a society such as the Estonian, conditioned by multiple disruptions, accelerated changes, inequality and pressure for aimless innovation, repair appears as a practice that asserts continuation, endurance and material sensitivity, valorising affective qualities and intensities.

This process can also be considered as a response to the cult of newness and the increasing desynchronisation between societal and personal time. Accelerating cycles of acquisition and disposal, as well as technological changes, require a deeper attention to repair. These practices are a form of reenactment accompanied by emotional and bodily investment. Not surprisingly, craftsmen take most pride in skills that mature and evolve, approaching them as empowering and enabling imagination (Sennett 2008). Repair can be thus considered as the other side of waste making – it exemplifies a metalevel dimension of care and recognition, and one of mundane revaluation of the surroundings, suturing together infrastructures, different generations and social needs. Rather than restorative, any act of repair is reflexive; aiming to put right something which was damaged and, in the meanwhile, to help us learn about ourselves.

In its Latin etymology, *obsolescere*, obsolescence means 'to grow old' and does not imply neglect or abandonment. Processes of destruction, pathologies of desynchronicity and temporal marginality have intensified with late modernity, eventually questioning ecological survival and social capability of adapting to changes. Yet disposal and abandonment have stopped being merely a product of our own activity, as they have reached a level of extension and intensity that has remarkable effects on our lives. Likewise, social changes are affected by a greater range of materials, thus requiring more sophisticated maintenance and repair. We can observe that breakdowns have an impact on a large number of people simultaneously, while feelings of uselessness have also become an intrinsic aspect of contemporary life. However, looking at the practices of maintenance and repairing illustrates the importance of human labour, experiential skills and infrastructural networks that characterise contemporary societies (Graham and Thrift 2007). The full importance of repair surfaces during moments of crisis, when things cease to function as they used to and the prevailing notion of normality is interrupted. Making amends facilitates adaptation to changes and also helps to reconstitute and heal after wrongdoing.

In Estonia, the study of multiple expressions of repair requires connecting postsocialism to other theorisations of contemporary social change, questioning late modern and postsocialist processes as simultaneous and interrelated. Thomas Hylland Eriksen describes the last 25 years as a period of 'overheating' (2016), calling attention to the accelerated change and the heightened level of activity in the realms of economy and communication, which manifest themselves in a crisis of identity linked with xenophobic tendencies and the reshaping of conceptions of locality. Suddenly, from analogical societies we turned into a turbo world of asymmetrical forces and out-of-sync experiences, resulting in a fragmented coexistence of multiple temporalities. As pointed out by Hartmut Rosa (2013), social acceleration is experienced in three dimensions: technological development, historical changes, and the pace of life. Yet what distinguishes contemporary society from previous ones is the conscious knowledge of obsolescence (Kattago 2014).

The way individuals experience time is diverging (becoming increasingly unequal); also, the cultural tools and world resources do not directly accompany the acceleration, thereby complicating conscious experiences overall. To illustrate the evolution of competing temporal vectors during the last decades, I went to talk to Arno Pihl, who is in charge of the maintenance of technological devices in Tallinn University (figure 2.14). As he says, ten years ago most of the devices were still analogue, whilst nowadays they are almost 100 per cent digital. For Arno, this change has meant more responsibilities: as there are more technologies surrounding us, more repair is needed and the technician has to continuously learn and update himself. Arno earned a certificate in the Soviet time as a mechanic: 'at the time there was not even MS-2 operating system', he ironises. Ten years ago, Arno dedicated his time to making sure that projectors, computers and microphones were working correctly. Nowadays, half of his time goes to repairing broken devices. He is also in charge of multimedia, 'as they call it'; Arno explains: 'I have to multitask, but I would not say I work more than ten years ago. It is just different'.

A bell hanging from the roof repeatedly sounds with the wind of the ventilator. A person passes across the corridor and says 'Hello Arno!' *'No,*

Fig. 2.14 Arno Pihl's office. Source: Author, 2015.

tere tere!', he replies, adding, 'at least this person saw me; for most of the people I'm invisible'. In the 1980s, Arno worked in a bakery; and in the 1990s, in a factory programming milling machines. When prompted about that experience, he simply adds that: 'eventually, there is not much difference between working in a big factory and in a university'. In the last ten years, many things have changed in the institution, observes Arno, people have changed, the institution is more 'European', and the way of life more 'American':

> you know, keep smiling; how are you? Fine, fine . . . not much conversation. Society has changed and the university mirrors that, with some nuances of course. In the Soviet time, people talked more for longer, and about many things. For example, people talked about their everyday struggles. Nowadays, people are ashamed to talk about money and difficulties. . . . I went through three different societies, three eras: the Soviet, the Estonian, and now the European, which is another conglomerate as the Soviet Union was. . . . But I am not nostalgic. I just compare the old and the new. I don't miss any past era. I live with my time. . . . I saw many changes, and more will come. Those who are older than me saw even more changes. Remember: Tsarist Russia, First Republic, German occupation, Russian occupation . . .

On the walls of Arno's atelier there are magnets to hold the tools as well as various obsolete things with potentially valuable components to be ripped out and reused: dozens of mice and dismantled computers; old radios and speakers; and then cables, many cables hanging, lying down and pointing at past futures and objectual microtemporalities that invite foraging, hoarding and tinkering (Pine 2016). 'You can take pictures of the stuff, but if the rector sees what I have here he will ask me to throw all this stuff away'. And why do you keep all this here Arno? 'Because anytime I could be in need of one of these pieces. You know, every year there is more bureaucracy to order anything and I don't have my own budget. If I want to buy a tool, I have to fill half a dozen documents. Ah, euronorms! . . . but I select a lot. I mean I just keep one-third of the stuff that comes to my hands. I think in perspective: what could be of use in the future?'

Any person involved in repair activities embodies a particular position in relation to time. Arno insists on encouraging people to think more in perspective and reflects on the transition from durable goods to disposable ones: 'In the Soviet time, it was all about accumulating stuff; and now it is about throwing away. I'm for a middle way; . . . nowadays, technologies get old very fast, but the skills of a mechanic last longer', he surmises.

According to Arno, there is a hierarchy of qualities among devices: the best are made in Japan, the worst made in China. Even so, nowadays it is more difficult to know where the product has been produced, since there are different pieces produced and assembled in varied places. 'Products from Japan were possible to repair. Nowadays, all have an inbuilt obsolescence and stop working after two years, the minimum to respect the warrant. Once they break up, it is truly better to buy a new one, because the device is not worth repairing'. Arno emphasises that he is not in favour of a society of consumption, but that he observes a regression in the performance of technological devices. Things are not designed for repairability anymore: 'In the European era, the quality of products has decreased, because it is not always clear who is responsible for making the thing'.

During our interview, Arno often checks the control tablet that manages the live functioning of the five buildings of Tallinn University. He lives in Lasnamäe, a neighbourhood mostly populated by Russian speakers ('they live in their own world, apart from the rest'). Arno says he is not afraid of changes, but it is hard for him to imagine what the future will bring. 'Part of my work is to keep up with changes. I have the impression that people know less about the future than ten years ago. It is more difficult to imagine what is going to happen in the next years than it used to be'. Perhaps the future consists in seeing fewer wires around. Arno states that people at the university have asked him to change some devices in the classes not because the items do not function anymore, but because the devices look old: 'There is a strong aesthetic component in technologies', and yet repair and maintenance workers remain always peripheral to networks of design and manufacturing.

Concluding considerations

'Repair' is a polysemic term; it refers to an opportunity for adjustment, to an actual need, and to a mundane assessment of what we have at hand. 'Repair' comes from the Latin *reparare*, which means 'to pay attention to' as well as 'to make ready' something past.[6] This act goes from apologising to recovering and legal recognition. It is thus a sought consequence, and also an attempt to make amends and fix what falls into a state of disrepair. Remembrance and repair entail a similar exercise, creating as they repeat, yet the former refers to a backward movement and the latter is recollected forward.

Repair practices help us to ensure a reasonable amount of continuity in our lives – continuity of meaning, of social relations and of material durability. As shown in this chapter, repair has a recuperative value in Estonia, with a potential to reframe the Soviet inheritance against recent abjections, such as the dismantling of state services, the privatisation of public properties, the neglect of modernist architecture and disinvestment in factories, as well as the invisibility of lives attached to past forms and the loss of frames in the face of changes. These practices can be put into action as a set of processes that involve a dynamic of exchange between the old and the new, able to broaden political sensibilities too.

The recontextualisation of repair as a work of suture honours care over wasting and also turns to materiality as a key to understand synchronisation and placing narratives. Repairing interventions have consequences for how we think about social relations, appearing as a complex balancing act of remembering and forgetting – reconciling conflicting temporalities and helping one to overcome the logic that carries a negative representation of the past. Further on, in attempts to lengthen things' lives, people construct a moral self, create value and connect with others. This understanding of repair updates the Western idea that healing of past wrongs and empowerment can happen basically through verbal recounting, and suggests material repair as permeating synchronisation and recuperation too.

3

Anything works, one just needs the right adaptor

The 'Hot' Railway street market of Tallinn

This chapter sadly works as the epitaph of the old Jaama Turg (Railway market), and as in Gabriel García Márquez's *Chronicle of a Death Foretold*, it announces the decease of my object of study at the very beginning of the narrative. The Baltic street market was active for over 25 years at the centre of Tallinn, each day being frequented by hundreds of people, often coming from the suburbs. The character of the place, constantly in the making, evidenced a survival negotiation of postsocialist changes and elasticity towards neoliberal policies. Not surprisingly, Karl Schlögel described street markets as the paradigmatic form of postsocialist urbanism:

> Everything began on a small scale: with a stall, a booth, a snack bar, a food stand . . . people that allegedly knew nothing of economics learned in no time how to trade. . . . One has to have seen the bazaar cities in order to understand that they are not some exotic, marginal entities, but rather central expressions of life, that a society's strength and will to live are condensed here, not an adventure that one can also ignore . . . they are a socially significant phenomenon. (Schlögel 2012, 26, 31)

This market, as any other site of exchange, was first and foremost a social place, not only a search for profit activity or a purely financial phenomenon. Indeed, in the Jaama Turg commodity transactions often added a symbolic value traditionally attributed to gift exchange. At the market, reciprocity types of social bond were created beyond the aspiration to maximise profit, helping marginalised segments of the society to find their place in the world. To a great extent, users of the Jaama Turg derived their social identities and sense of belonging from their market activities, by means of the social relations they built and their intersubjective awareness. Likewise, relations of reciprocity and language or ethnic identification played an important role in both the provision and the distribution of goods. This informal economy had continued after socialism to be of crucial importance to households in meeting needs that the market could not provide.

As Douglas and Isherwood noted (1979), consumption might also be seen as a performance of belonging, rather than simply as utilitarian individual choice. The Jaama Turg was an example of that, making the public space more diverse, being accessible to anyone and enhancing, through public interactions, feelings of empathy and difference. In this sense, we can say that far from threatening the local economy and neoliberal policies, Jaama Turg was rather threatened by the uncertainty generated by the latter, policies which are explicitly turning the city centre of Tallinn into a commodified and standardised space that is increasingly segregated.

Studies of privatisation and marketisation describe how people's local economies have been often felt as incompatible with the new (global and neoliberal) ways of doing things (Mandel and Humphrey 2002). After the break-up of the USSR, people were suddenly presented with much more choice and a shift of affordances, very different from Soviet distributional methods, in which consumption was limited and closely aligned to allocation. All these simultaneous transformations (e.g., the arrival of a market economy and implementation of neoliberal economic reforms) were often experienced as confusing (Humphrey 2002b); and many people, particularly elderly ones, developed their own strategies of retaining and rearranging, which display surprising continuities in practices and values rather than a one-dimensional rupture or transition. Postsocialist street markets emerged in this context, without being 'introduced' by anybody in particular; they simply appeared during perestroika, 'overnight and almost like an act of nature . . . tolerated because there, at least, some of the pressure caused by the general shortages could be relieved somewhat' (Schlögel 2012, 30).

By paying attention to how users of the Jaama Turg made sense of the always uncertain situation of this site, the ethnography foregrounds the way this site has enabled inclusiveness and accessibility in a city in which half of the population are Russian-speaking, and half

Estonian-speaking. As shown in this chapter, this market functioned as a meeting point and social glue for precariously positioned groups within Estonian society, healing economic and cultural excesses and fostering urban conviviality. Further on, both global capitalism and Soviet legacies were intensively negotiated in this site of exchange, producing a particular material culture that, as came out with the erasure of the market, was unwelcome in the new representations of Tallinn and Estonian society at large. Indeed, the vanishing of the Jaama Turg was part of a wider strategy to get rid of remnants that recalled the Soviet time, yet the closing of this gate to the city centre also affected the way precariously positioned individuals move in urban spaces. The Baltic market could be therefore understood as a centre for class and ethnic marginality, and a periphery within the centre, serving as a point of spatial entry and social reconfiguration.

I visited the site regularly for months, conducting interviews at the market, observing behaviours, buying stuff, talking with friends on the topic, gleaning different impressions of the market, sometimes in the form of a deep hanging out, since I even penetrated into the alarm-guarded space of the Jaama Turg at night. To complement my ethnographic findings, I curated an exhibition displaying objects chosen from the market by 23 'artists', in which I tried to figure out what is the importance of the site for those who come to buy and sell there and what are the affects that this market generates in Tallinn. The exhibition was organised to contrast what was taken for granted in Estonian society, such as claims of the market being dangerous, residual and mostly hosting illegal activities, and because of my feeling of not being entitled to speak authoritatively about the market or its users, as well as my sense that many things that cannot be verbalised could be however captured in a visual way.

Breakdown in practice

'Don't you have to work? I mean, why do you ask these stupid questions? It is early morning, go to your job and let me work, because I am working', was the irritated reply I received from a vendor selling underwear at the Kopli entrance of the market. 'But my job is to ask questions and write an article about the market', I answered back, without sounding very convincing to her. She looked at me with disdain, as if she were seeing a 'European child, with a too full stomach'.[1] The elderly woman refused to give her name, yet she added: 'and who cares about my answers? If the director says that the market closes down we go away and that's all. Это всё! [That's all]. Now go to work'.

Yet not all the people I approached in the 'railway bazaar' reacted in such a way. We are talking about an open-air market that used to have around 200 stands functioning every day. People were varied, in character, origin and background; there were features that most of them share, such as the native language, which was Russian, their ages (over 50 years old) and the suburban areas of Tallinn where they live: Mustamäe, Lasnamäe and Kopli. At the beginning of my fieldwork, I considered it an advantage to be seen as an outsider by the people with whom I had to interact, playing the role of the 'stranger' or game master, as one who does not belong to the community yet is present bringing people together. Yet in a site in which most of the people are treated as outsiders, I soon found myself with all sorts of cross-cutting and contradictory personal commitments (Marcus 1995), which made the sharp line between the natives and the ethnographer, the locals and the foreigner, strikingly blurred (Ferguson 1999).

'With such beautiful eyes I can answer whatever you want', replied Olga in a playful way while looking into my eyes. She has worked at the market for 13 years and shows the skills and self-confidence of those who are used to bargaining and dealing with people. 'I am already tired of the market, I won't mind if it closes down, but at the same time, I like that I can talk to people here. Somehow, the society and the market changed in different directions. Or rather, the market hasn't changed. Only prices got higher', reckoned Olga. She has lived most of her life in the suburb of Lasnamäe[2] and used to come here to get extra income for her family. Unlike the vendor of underwear, Olga became involved in conversation even if it was clear that I would not buy any of her products. She even showed some interest in what my project was about and my origins.

Viktor Alexandrovich is 65 years old and was born in Ukraine (figure 3.1). 'Look there', he said, pointing at the corner, where clothes were piled up. 'This looks like a Tartar market, it is uncivilised [некультурный]. Most of the people here are not good people. They are not honest. I say that to you because you look like a good guy'. Then a person around his age caught his attention by asking 'Does it work?' The client was holding an old shaving machine in his hand and Viktor just answered: 'I don't know, try'. These different conceptions of a breakdown in practice (Rosner and Ames 2014) encompassed something we tried to capture in the exhibition rescuing items from the market. For instance, Eva Dino provided an old mechanic drill describing a similar scene: according to the vendor from whom she had bought the drill – an obviously

Fig. 3.1 Viktor Alexandrovich standing near his shop. Source: Author, 2014.

obsolete and broken piece – all the devices of his stand work if one finds the right adaptor ('работает, только адаптер надо') (figure 3.2).

At the market, one was allowed to try the products before buying them. I had on several occasions experimented with such sampling at different stands of cheese, nuts and fruits. We can see this, for instance, in the Estonian TV report about the project, in the scene when I asked a vendor, Alla, to let me try the candies she sold from her stand. There, we bought products, not brands. The main criteria in the selection of a product were neither the label nor the atmosphere where the goods were displayed, though low prices were behind the decision. A clear example of this is the stand that sold expired goods at half-price, a popular spot in the market that often had a queue in front of it. As long as one was informed about the expired date, such activity was legal. For the poor and marginalised, 'inadequate consumers' (Bauman 1998), to buy expired products is not alien or outside the formal economy, but rather part of the cycles of accelerated production and consumption.

Otherwise, human interactions were crucial to understanding the functioning of the 'Balta' (the nickname of the street market) and the personal links of confidence created between vendors and customers. Both vendors and clients tried to make their lives more livable by locating

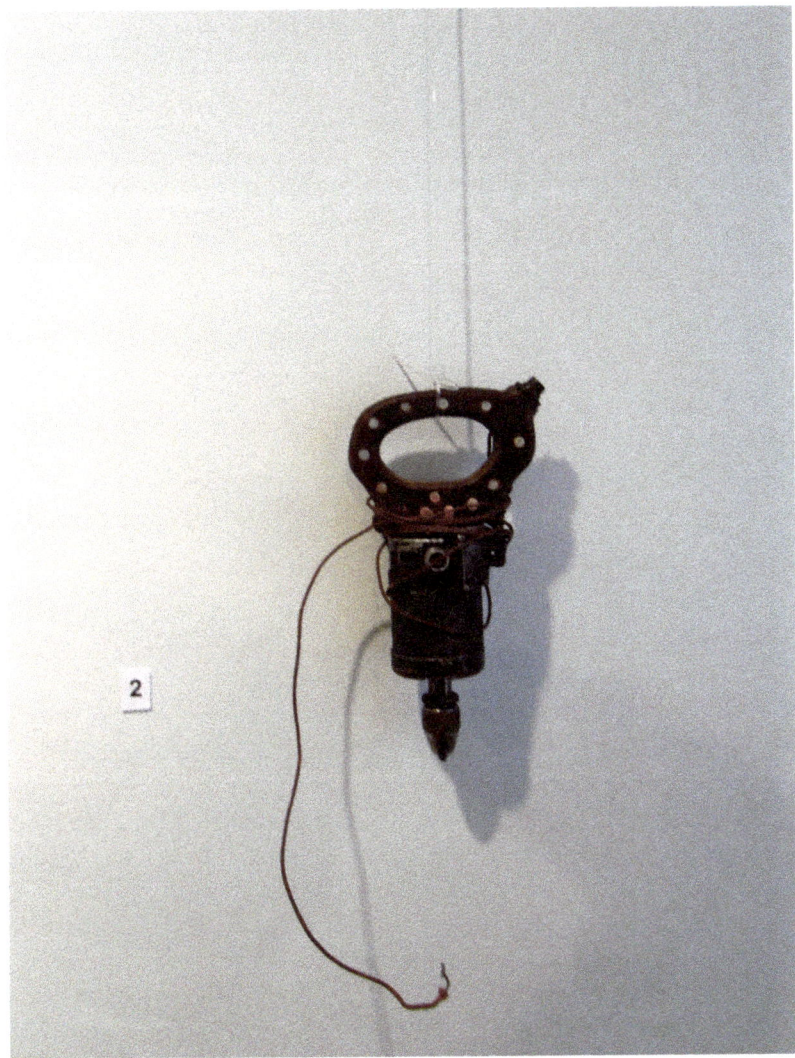

Fig. 3.2 It works, one just needs the right adaptor; ready-made at the exhibition, Jaama Turg. Source: Author, 2014.

themselves within a network of peers, despite the network's being marginal. At the market, many people reinforced their subjectivity (affect, cognition, material strategies, and so on) through economic relations. In other words, this was a site where one could feel reciprocity and camaraderie (Pachenkov 2011), and it was a channel for finding products that were not available elsewhere (for instance Russian medicines or *babushkas'* homemade meals; figure 3.3).

Fig. 3.3   Homemade food in Balta. Source: Author, 2014.

Valentina was one of these babushkas. She supplemented her scarce pension by selling woollen socks and gloves. Valentina confessed that she would get sad ('мне жалко') if the market closed down, but not only due to the loss of income: 'I'm a pensioner and if not for the market, I will just sit at home all week long'. Placed on the unused rails that are in front of the main territory of the market, Zinaida displayed a few items on a white sheet. This old stuff looked familiar and uncanny, as if she had gathered the items from her own flat, turning Jaama Turg into a gate for domestic materiality, a site where household responses to market capitalism were played out (mostly in the form of subsistence). Zinaida lived in the suburb of Mustamäe (25 minutes to the centre by public transport) and reacted with a loud silence to my question about the rumours of the market's closing. Interpreting her glassy gaze as being offended I quickly apologised. Then she whispered with a complicit look: 'I have been coming here for too many years'.

Two years later, I met a similar loud silence in the Mustamäe market, when I found by accident that Alla was working there, now selling fruits and vegetables instead of candies (figure 3.4). She conserves the same seaman's hat, yet avoids talking about the market where she had her own stand. How are you doing these days, Alla? 'потихоньку, потихоньку' (so-so, getting along). As Svetlana Boym (1994) points out, silences, tone

Fig. 3.4 Alla and author in the market. Source: Frame from the report, Estonian TV.

of voice, nuance of intonation and practised indirection contribute to create the rituals and meanings of ordinary life. In Boym's study of the everyday mythologies in post-Soviet Russia, she describes how the non-verbal might be an important aspect of communication that a native to the culture would pick up without difficulty. In this sense, the ethnographer has to be skilled in the art of listening, being able to hear what is absent as much as what is present.

Viktor was always willing to talk: 'All this is caused by the disintegration of the Soviet Union. This is the source of all the problems, of the alcoholism, unemployment . . .' 'Yeah, Viktor, we know that story. But why do people still come to the market these days?' I asked. He looked at me surprised, not just because of my question, but also because of me interrupting his 'prerecorded' speech. Viktor thought of what to say for a few seconds and then concluded: 'Life is getting expensive, don't you see it'. Paradoxically, for some people the market economy brought a reduction in economic freedom, as compared with the state-dominated system of socialist times (Kaneff 2002).

Otherwise, postsocialism cannot be separated from the fracturing of social networks and a sense of disorder in the way changes took place. As the following case of Stass suggests, the actions and inactions of the state have generated new ways of being marginalised, related to the difficulty in creating new forms of inclusion once exclusion and personal misfortunes had occurred. Kathleen Millar has shown something similar in her study

Fig. 3.5 Stass working behind the counter. Source: Author, 2014.

of waste pickers at Rio de Janeiro's municipal landfill (2012), demonstrating that marginality ought not to be understood as a condition of being left out but, rather, as the outcome of specific forms of inclusion in the city, the state and the global. Yet as Millar concludes, people at the economic margins come also to redefine 'resource', 'value' and 'waste', even within markets assumed to be only capitalist.

Stass's position is more nihilistic however. He was born in Ukraine and he is 15 years younger than Viktor. He owned two stands at the 'Balta' – one in front of the other – selling 'relics' and stuff for pets: 'I began to work here because I lost my job. I was working in construction and now I have to sell all these stupid things' (figure 3.5). He gesticulated wildly with his hands and turned his head down and to the other side. 'Write it like that. I don't care if the market closes down. Actually, I don't care about anything. I fought in the war [Afghanistan] and then I fell into a country that is not mine. So I don't care about anything anymore. This is not a life', he added bitterly.

Grey zones

Nadezhda used to sell fruit in the street market, sometimes alone, sometimes with her daughter. She was born in Ukraine and makes fun of me with one of the clients: 'Look what a handsome man. Obviously, he is not Estonian'. 'Why? Because of my accent?' I reply. 'No, because one has to search a lot to find a handsome man here', says a client next to me at the stand. And then Nadezhda adds: 'That's true, but the Armenian who works on that stand is also handsome', pointing at a man a bit younger than me, who sells vegetables with his mother under a newly built tent.

In the middle of the Balta, there used to be a shop selling gravestones; I entered into the crystal booth and took pictures of the marble pieces with inscriptions. Then I asked the vendor about the future. 'There have been rumours about the market being closed down already for five or seven years. Owners come and go, none of them wants to invest money here. If it closes down, I will just move somewhere else', replied the vendor, who wished to remain anonymous. Nearby, Sergei sold plastic flowers and scarfs. He could not come every day since he combined different small jobs to earn his living. 'Closing down? These are rumours, only rumours'. I then asked if a solution would be to attract more tourists to the site. 'Tourists don't come here, they go to Rocca al mare' (a shopping mall in the suburbs), responded Sergei.

Yet I always recommended a visit to the market to foreign friends who came to Tallinn for the first time and this journey was often well loved by them. Actually, I was not the only one advising touristic exploration of the Jaama Turg. For instance, *The Guardian* and *The Mirror* had defined the market as a 'Must-see in Tallinn'. I used to make three routes when 'excavating' the open-air markets. The first one looking at objects and distractedly strolling; the second one looking at people and their performativity; the third one correlating both items and vendors, and engaging with them if it was convenient.

Sociologist Oleg Pachenkov (2011) notes how dialectics of private and public are represented through objects and people in postsocialist bazaars, in a way with a taste of sorrow and regret. The study of these bazaars shows also how Soviet material and cultural legacies are still relevant to understanding the way that people make sense of their lives and convoluted transformations. Goods function as vehicles of communication and frame the perception of the social world. Arjun Appadurai (1986) draws on this assumption to assert that both the object and the mode of exchange create social relations, as well as specific local and global configurations. Anthropologist Janet Hoskins continues this idea (1998) by pointing out that objects both have their own biographies (so they might go through different stages or afterlives) and display others' biographies (along with specific parts of individuals' personalities).

The range of items sold at the Jaama Turg was exceptionally varied: from jewellery to food, art, music, spare technology, expired goods, winter clothes, souvenirs, second-hand clothes, handicrafts, tobacco, lingerie and a great amount of junk. Both diversity and marginality affected the market materially, since different styles and tastes were incorporated in items, manners and displays. In the stands, goods were organised in a tangled arrangement that could not be repeated or recreated even if undone. Moreover, conceptions of authenticity, tradition and uniqueness were contested every day, and we could talk about a particular material culture of fakeness and unexpected hierarchies of value, influenced by the stories told about the products (Craciun 2013; Gregson and Crewe 2003). Such was the case of Lena Grishaeva (figure 3.6), a vendor who had no doubts about promoting her fake 'Bosco' (a popular Russian label) sports clothes as having better quality than other copies 'because they were made in Turkey'.[3]

Even if fake brands represented a tiny part of the trade, it did characterise the market because there was no other site in Tallinn where products of fake brands were so openly exposed. Vendors used to inform clients that this or that good was a fake copy; they even identified a hierarchy of fakes, distinguishing between those items fabricated in China, Russia, 'Europe' and Turkey. Both socialist material culture and globalisation were intensively negotiated in this place, showing how

Fig. 3.6 Lena Grishaeva, a vendor who participated in the roundtable. Source: Author, 2014.

cultural meanings of things and consumer practices formed during the Soviet period survived the construction of national identities as well as a neoliberal market economy. For instance, some of the products sold at the market were part of different global circuits (many of them came from Poland, Russia, China or Latvia), but in some cases, the roots of and routes followed by the items were ambiguous or simply hidden.

We could even describe part of what was going on in this bazaar as 'para-economic': alongside, through and beside established forms of transactions. Concepts such as 'market' and 'economy' took on distinct meanings from those applied by policymakers. The exchanges that used to be present at the Jaama Turg were often informal, sometimes even illegal, yet they helped to suture the effects of social inequality, to reduce the distance between the centre and the outskirts, and to configure the public understanding of diversity. Hence, by acknowledging the value of certain grey zones as an urban suture, we are also rendering visible the kind of social infrastructures that make the city more livable (De Boeck and Baloji 2016).

These sites of exchange have been places in the making, undefined, chaotic and informal; features which paradoxically allowed minor communities and marginal individuals to find not only refuge, but also a sense of belonging and access to the city centre. The combination of low entry barriers and profits meant that marginalised populations could take part in a quotidian act of shopping and meet with peers, bringing together into a public and central area people who might otherwise remain apart. In this sense, street markets help to shape the public meaning of diversity and to configure the social life and identity of a city.

The Jaama Turg had been characterised by its survival functioning already from its origin (in the early 1990s, a period characterised by shortage, as well as economic and political turmoil).[4] Certain places contribute more than others to shape and constitute our sense of belonging to a society; on this matter, Karl Schlögel distinguishes between 'hot' and 'cold' locations (2003, 292), arguing that hot locations of a city (those in the making) demonstrate qualities such as inclusiveness and accessibility, and might also help to suture the broken parts of a given system; yet often, they are qualified as dangerous and dirty, being a source of antistructure and disorder. Hence, cities also need the cold locations, which appear already consolidated, clean and hierarchical.

In my initial fieldwork, it surprised me to discover that the image that neighbours and clients had of the market was far better than the associations given by those who had not been there for an extended period. For instance, articles with the headline 'Would Your Child Dare to Wait for the Bus behind the Balti Jaam?' have been published in the Estonian media.[5] Historically, postsocialist open-air markets have been under attack by formal institutions, urban planners and financial speculators. These bazaars were already viewed with suspicion by socialist regimes, as a site of 'parasites' who do not produce anything 'real' (Silk and Wallace 2009). Mostly based on prejudices, these kinds of street market were often presented as especially dangerous and immoral places (Aidis 2003), or as shameful, almost criminal areas, inhabited by the 'downtrodden who feel that they do not measure up to social standards' (Pachenkov 2011, 191).

Galina was often standing at the entrance of the *kohvik* (café), smoking and observing people with a mixture of curiosity and disdain. She worked there as a waitress and was worried about the rumours spreading: 'if the market closes down, I will lose my job and I won't find another one'. Many people came to this market because they did not have any other choice, to buy very cheap products or because they could not find any other job. As other street markets, the Jaama Turg was located in a communication hub and functioned as a space of inclusion for precariously positioned groups: from elderly residents who strolled to ethnic minorities who wandered without fear (Hüwelmeier 2013). These had been ambivalent spaces of vulnerability, risk and legal transgression, whereby practices of informal exchange took place, hosting interactions that not only had an economic value but also worked as expressions of sympathy and recognition, thus blurring boundaries between sociability and instrumentality (Ledeneva 2018). Vendors navigated there a grey zone between the 'whiteness' of legality, approval and safety and the 'blackness' of eviction and negligence (Yiftachel 2009). Also, Kaneff (2002) suggested uncertainty as a key threat among the users of these bazaars, since they were more exposed to changes, combined a formal and an informal functioning, and their vendors relied only on themselves or on a close community of relatives.

Look at the Tšeburek!

Following my wish to use my ethnography to engage public audiences in conversation with my research topic, I invited 23 individuals to go to the Jaama Turg street market and 'rescue' an item. These objects were displayed for two weeks at the EKA Gallery of Tallinn and the exhibition raised media and popular attention (with a seven-minute report televised on a national network). Different people participated in the project (artists, scholars, punks, advertising managers, civil activists, officials of the ministry of defence and so forth). I chose them intuitively and based on two criteria: I liked the way they looked at things (thus I knew them beforehand) and they were not the expected clients of the market. Below, I include some comments from the participants explaining their rescued object:

Anna-Liisa Unt: A pair of jeans

It was the arrival of jeans to the market that represented the new and promising Western well-being twenty years ago. Balti Jaama Turg gave me these jeans last week for 50 cents.

Andres Kurg: A book in Russian

I wanted to avoid exoticising the market, by buying something that I would not normally buy, and to see the market as an everyday environment where I could find something related to my interests. But at the same time, I wanted my object to represent 'an other' to the dominant networks of production and distribution, where the list of products is controlled either by large corporations or strongly regulated ways of commerce.

Ott Kagovere: A toy (produced in the local polymer factory)

This foam doll is a perfect representation of my Soviet childhood. They were very popular in the eighties, but disappeared almost immediately after Estonia gained its independence.

Kai Lobjakas: A coffee pot

This coffee pot is an example of a good and dense variety of pieces available to be found here produced by local glass and ceramic factories where many people specifically from this area used to work.

Tauri Tuvikene: An expired pack of juice

This is a normal pack of juice, although of a sort that would not be available from mainstream shops. However, what is even more significant than the uniqueness of the pack is that it is sold after the 'best before' date has passed by an outlet that specializes in selling such products. This shopping outlet with its queue of buyers really struck me as significant when I visited Jaama Turg. It also made me think about what will probably be lost with the inevitable redevelopment of the area: cheap goods for those who need them.

Marika Agu: Candies

My mother doesn't eat Russian candies.

Merly Mändla: A towel with tropical motifs

Tropical motifs have been 'in' at Jaama Turg for some time – not a fad, not a trend – a classic.

One of the objectives that was initially in my mind was to bring people to the market and make them approach its normal functioning. Another of the aims of this exercise of rescuing things was to turn the exhibition space of the gallery into a social laboratory to study the reactions and feedback from the public. The objects rescued in this project may themselves be considered as an enactment of border-crossing, as they establish an affective relation to the context in which they were extracted and serve as a condenser of complex meanings (Buchli 2002). Objects might function as cultural nodes mediating social agency, capable of generating complex responses and making things happen – *qua* artefacts (Gell 1998). Likewise, the exhibiting of objects impels the audience to connect the present of the thing to its previous temporalities, establishing also a relationship between them which might lead to new cultural configurations and meanings (Bal 1996).

The exhibition provided me with the chance to release control over the values and meanings attributed to the Jaama Turg. As artists do, I was able to make visible social and cultural connections that were silenced or ignored. Indeed, the space of the exhibition became an open field site, and the displayed items mediated between the everyday functioning of the market and society at large. This strategy helped me to confront a great number of locals with my observations, engaging with a wide public *during*, not merely after, fieldwork (Murawski 2013a), enhancing the sociocultural meanings of the site (Jarillo de la Torre 2013) and popularising the discussion by playing with distance, intimacy and representation. Such a *conceptual fieldwork* helped me to relate to the people and the site I was studying differently (Ringel 2013), and also offered new ways of seeing and experimentation, as well as the chance to learn from open-ended or incomplete procedures (Schneider and Wright 2010). This combination of anthropology and contemporary art made it possible to not only represent reality, but also to do so in such a way that the representation itself became part of the research, producing situations that gave the chance to study meaningful reactions through public engagement (Ssorin-Chaikov 2013).

Otherwise, the shape and location of the EKA gallery – a lobby at the entrance of a central building of the Estonian Academy of Arts – helped to bring to the exhibition people who would probably not visit it otherwise. For instance, I overheard a conversation between two middle-aged women who crossed the lobby and stopped to see the exhibition: 'I don't quite understand it' / 'Probably it is just about nostalgia' / 'Look at the *tšeburek*, this is nowadays fashionable' / 'the lock is a good one!' / 'And the garlic, this garlic is authentic' (figures 3.7 and 3.8).[6]

The case of *Ringvaade* also deserves mention. The team that made this programme broadcast by Estonian National TV was first interested in the bizarre situation of a 'Spaniard' exploring the 'strange' market and bringing 'trash' to a gallery. The triple picturesque charge made an attractive story for TV. However, journalist Keiu Virro was sufficiently savvy to see that the issue contained deeper layers than oddity or nostalgia. From the initial questions of 'Is this art?' and 'Why is the market important for you?', she became involved to the point of being willing to participate in the project. In addition to what Keiu saw with her own eyes

Fig. 3.7 Garlic displayed in the exhibition, EKA Gallery. Source: Author, 2014.

Tänavaturukunst.
Balti jaama turg kolib galeriisse

Street-market-art. The Jaama turg goes gallery

EKA G Gallery (Estonia pst 7 / Teatri väljak 1)

7.5 – 23.5.2014

Käesoleva näituse tarvis palume 23 inimesel päästa Balti jaama turult üks ese. Need esemed lunastatakse galeriis unustusest. Kas me eeldame, et jaama väli-turule tormab nüüd hordide viisi aardeotsijaid, kes kõik tahavad päästa oma pärli? Kas me peaksime palkama lisavalvuri, kes hoiaks silma peal väärtuslikel esemetel, mis galeriise välja pannakse?

In this exhibition we invite 23 people to rescue an item from the Jaama turg. These objects will be redeemed in the gallery from oblivion. Shall we expect that a horde of treasure seekers will go now to the open-air market to rescue their own gem? Should we hire another guard to look after the precious items displayed at the gallery?

Kuraator/
Curator:
Francisco Martínez

Osalejad/
Participants:
Anna-Liisa Unt,
Andres Kurg,
Annika Toots,
Eva Dino,
Eva Sepping,
Flo Kasearu,
Gustav Kalm,
Jaanus Samma,
Jürgen Rendl,
Kai Lobjakas,
Liisa Kaljula,
Madli Maruste,
Marika Agu,
Maros Krivy,
Märt Miljan,
Merlin Mandla,
Kristina Norman,
Ott Kagovere,
Patrick Laviolette,
Siobhan Kattago,
Taimar Peterkopt,
Tarmo Jüristo,
Tauri Tuvikene.

Fig. 3.8 Poster of the exhibition at the EKA Gallery, May 2014, by Ott Kagovere.

(people offering bread for free to babushkas and marginals), it helped that both Flo Kasearu (a local artist) and I commented on the social value and normal character of the Balta during our interviews.

Another case that deserves attention is the 'act of vandalism' done by Galina. The day after the opening, gallerist Merilin Talumaa called to inform me that an object was missing (the Kazakhstan chocolate) and that she had found a handicraft bag replacing it. I went to the gallery and asked the janitors if they had seen the person who had taken the chocolate. Finally, the item appeared and we were informed that the bag was put there by a 50-year-old Russian-speaking lady who worked nearby. The next day, I came to the gallery to add an extra table for spontaneous donations. Unexpectedly, Galina returned with more objects to display and a poem about the spiritual importance of stuff. I explained to her that we accepted just one item per person and asked why she had wanted to change the exhibition. Galina answered that some of the objects looked boring standing alone and impelled me to look at her stuff: 'This is beauty'.

Since March 2014, the Jaama Turg has had a new owner: Astri Kinnisvara (Astri real estate, which already controls several shopping malls in Estonia). For the *finissage* of the exhibition, we organized a roundtable in which Kairi Kivi (agent of the company) explained that the new owners aimed to reduce the current functioning of the market by half, intending, nonetheless, to maintain the character and variety of vendors. Initially, they planned to improve the overall appearance of the site and reorganise the activity to reach the new neighbours of the gentrified district of Kalamaja. According to Kairi, the limestone façades from the 1870s would be saved and the interior market would be located on two floors. Meanwhile, the exterior market would be partly covered and complemented with cafés and restaurants. In addition to Kairi Kivi, Teele Pehk (an activist from Linnalabor / Tallinn Urban Lab NGO), Jaanus Juss (founder and board member of Telliskivi Loomelinnak),[7] Lena Grishaeva (vendor at the market), and Jaak-Adam Looveer (an official in charge of urban planning in the city) participated in the public discussion about the future of the market organised at the gallery. With respect to concerns about the social impact of these changes, both landowners (Kairi and Jaanus) argued that 'developers should not bear this responsibility on their shoulders' and that the changes in the social composition of both the market and the neighbourhood were 'natural', 'logical' and 'inevitable'.

During the discussion, Kairi Kivi stated several times that 'shopping mall' was not the right term to describe the plan of the new developers, proposing instead the *hipster*-friendly term 'urban square'. Kairi also expressed her wish that, in five years' time, it would be possible to buy the same items that were displayed at the gallery. Furthermore, we agreed to bring the exhibition to the Jaama Turg, where it will stay permanently, depicting the identity of the site. At the debate, the new landowners finally disclosed their plans publicly and questions were raised about the way neighbours and vendors would participate in the decision making of the project. Kairi acknowledged that the owners had not thought of it, adding later by mail that they intended to involve different 'interest groups'. After the public discussions, the owners asked the Koko studio of architects to improve the project by preserving the character of the current marketplace without undermining the main objective of attracting the new middle-class neighbours of Kalamaja.

In recent years, some other open-air markets have emerged in Tallinn, enjoying a different degree of institutional support.[8] The combination of a street market focused on organic and handicraft products with the traditional one, more price competitive and accessible, could have helped to stop the process of economic and material depauperation in which the Jaama Turg fell, without necessarily stimulating a dynamic of gentrification. This process – which forces traditional neighbours to move further to the periphery, privileging the moving in of expats and middle classes – has been active for several years in Kalamaja and Telliskivi, the neighbourhoods whereby the Jaama Turg is located.[9]

Several dwellers of the neighbourhood contacted me asking for information about the plans of the real estate, worried about the possibility that the market would disappear and about the intensification of the gentrification process. Overall, I received positive feedback during the two weeks that the exhibition was open and also for a few weeks afterwards. For instance, a class of the Tallinna Mustjõe Gümnaasium visited the gallery as a surprise excursion after finishing their exams (the teachers had read about the exhibition in the daily newspaper *Postimees*). Articles in the media were written, as were comments on these articles and messages in the guest book of the gallery. However, the discussion mostly triggered concerns that the market was a remnant from the past, rather than a debate on the future development of the city.

The promised land of shopping malls

Estonia has two square metres of shopping floor space per inhabitant, ranking third in Europe.[10] In the city centre, the first shopping mall (Kristiine) appeared in 1999, replacing trading arrangements that had emerged a decade before, such as street markets, ground floor shops, kiosks and a variety of informal retail practices. Initially, these temporary retail activities were allowed by the municipality to complement official services of distribution of goods and to promote individuals earning a living through self-initiative. At the time, the expansion of these informal retail activities also meant significant revenue through fees for the municipality. These supposedly interim forms began to dominate the cityscape, becoming one of the material symbols of the so-called transition.

Indeed, the appearance of malls and hypermarkets was celebrated as a sort of material confirmation of years of political and economic promises and reforms (Garb and Dybicz 2006). The transformation of the retailing infrastructure and services mirrored ongoing social changes and the aspirations of consumption at large, testing not only a new economic order (Färber and Gdaniec 2004) but also the very construction of the new Estonia. For instance, Sigrid Rausing (2004) has shown the pivotal role played by consumer products in a process envisioned as 'returning to normality'. As she points out, negative contrasts with Soviet Russians and positive identifications with Scandinavia have been central to informing consumption patterns and identity construction in the country, since after the socialist break-up, consumption was particularly related to collective identity and national aspirations, evolving later into a matter of the satisfaction of individual desires (see also Keller 2005). As writer Tõnu Õnnepalu ironically described: 'Europe or not, this is not important anymore. The main thing is to have a shopping centre, a hypermarket. A shopping centre is the paradise on earth that the Soviet power promised, but never delivered' (Õnnepalu 2002, 9).

After the Soviet break-up, shopping malls appeared as something more than a site of exchange, as something like an ideological model, fostering a 'right' to consumption. Shopping malls have been associated with social aspirations and individual imaginaries of exclusivity, emerging hand in hand with the crystallisation of new lifestyles and mirroring society to a great extent. And yet, the development of 'civilised formats' and the restructuring of urban retail space (transferring control into the hands of big businesses) have been the outcomes of concrete legislative measures and tax support, rather than a natural course of evolution. For decades, Tallinn has been organised around new delineations between public and private, of which the proliferation of shopping malls is a prime example, offering commercial and depoliticised solutions to social problems (Bodnár 2005).[11]

Plants placed in shopping malls intensify the perception of a tree, with leaves that are greener and more perfectly formed than those of normal trees. The hyperreal spectacular shape of the elements that comprise malls relies on ersatz traditions, staged through weightless pastiches that cancel authorship and constrain imagination. This generation of 'atmospheres' and 'ambiences' (Miller 1998) is, however, far from neutral, extracting life from the flux of reality. In the shopping mall we also breathe recycled air, the lights are artificial and rarely mix with atmospheric luminosity. The sounds of the exterior, thanks to architectural precision, do not penetrate the fortified walls of the enclosure and the frequent absence of windows denies any communication with the exterior.[12]

And yet shopping malls comprise a multifunctional dimension besides providing goods and services. They manage the leisure of individuals, functioning as places where socialisation rituals are practised, organising collective rhythms and consumption, as well as imposing de facto authority and order (Voyce 2006). Malls create their own temporality and pedestrian routes, separating people from the outdoors through a threshold that makes clients believe they are safe (Freitas 1996). As a self-regulated system, the shopping mall is designed to anticipate whatever its visitors need: neither cold nor heat exist, there is no random assembly of mechanical and natural sounds, just as there is no conflict of styles. Shopping malls unify the cityscape with their massive typography and repeated mix of styles and decors. Nonetheless, the supposed public character of shopping malls is rather 'illusory' (Manzo 2005), since these spaces are organised according to the social control strategies of the owner, informally created instead of being explicitly manifested. Malls appear to be everything that they are not: they contrive to be public, even though they are private; they seem to offer a common place for recreation, even though they seek profit; they are 'representations of space masquerading as representational spaces' (Goss 1993, 40).

As sociologist Anna Zhelnina shows (2011), order in a mall is internalised through social facts. They are constructed through personal interactions as well as in the assembled elements of a place. Contrary to street markers, shopping malls are places where inequality is produced and affective interactions are obliterated. Shopping malls are locations for social differentiation through consumption, semipublic spaces where those aiming to belong to an ideal middle class have to demonstrate 'taste' and financial means. In Eastern Europe, terms such as 'civilised' (*kulturno* or *tsivilizovannyi*) and 'modern' (*sovremennyi*) were applied to shopping malls by both common people and city officials. By emptying the content of terms such as 'civilised', 'European city', 'prosperity' and 'modernisation', entrepreneurs and officials brought new types of space to Tallinn that had not existed before, such as shopping malls and entertainment complexes. Zhelnina (2009) has explained how in St Petersburg, the discourse of 'transition to civilized retailing' was used by the city administration to explain and legitimise legislative measures and budget support to one kind of economic actor at the expense of others. As she shows, this process has altered not only the format of the trade outlet and the goods sold but also the interrelations between customers and vendors, removing 'nonstandard' relations whether illegal or displaced to the periphery. Also, in St Petersburg, Pachenkov studied the emergence in the 1990s of dozens of flea markets and how they were eliminated by city authorities for the celebration of the 300th anniversary of the city, so as 'not to disgrace and shame the city in the eyes of the respectable foreign guests' (Pachenkov 2011, 198). A market still stands on the outskirts of the city, Udelnyi, which indicates that postsocialism is not over there. Where it has disappeared, the process is complete; while wherever street markets still exist, the concept is still needed (Schlögel 2012).

Concluding considerations

In this chapter, I investigated how differently positioned social actors negotiate changes and produce their own material culture in a street market of Tallinn. More than resisting or contesting capitalism, the Jaama Turg demonstrated an unusual quality to fill the gaps and failures of the neoliberal economy and the excesses of postsocialist transformations. The Railway market functioned as a suture and hot location – an inclusive site of cohabitation and exchange, reminding us of the slippage between value and values in a capitalist economy. As the research demonstrates, the Jaama Turg provided a social glue and cultural air in Tallinn, enhancing public interactions and feelings of empathy and difference.

Contrary to shopping malls, this postsocialist bazaar functioned as a mechanism of the daily production of reciprocity. As shown in the last part of the chapter, the disappearance of certain trade arrangements in postsocialist cities and the emergence of new more 'civilised' ones was not a spontaneous and natural process as usually presented, but the direct outcome of changes in consumption, official policies and municipal actions and inactions (following a 'mallification' and 'touristification' of Tallinn). Once the market disappeared, the access to public space for some groups and participation in social life has become more difficult, thereby decreasing urban diversity and integration.

To be clear, I do not wish to romanticise marginality or informality. Illegal activities and the need to cope with risk in a precarious position often result in dread and human intimidation. Yet, I aimed to show how this particular market had a positive affecting presence in the everyday life of the Estonian capital and was not simply residual or dangerous, as had been depicted most often in public opinion. In this sense, the best option would have been to upgrade the market's material and social conditions, maintaining and recognising it, instead of actively neglecting it for decades and finally transforming it into a shopping mall for hipsters.

~

A few days after the opening of the new Jaama Turg (May 2017), I was invited by Keiu Virro (former journalist of *Ringvaade*, now working for the newspaper *Eesti Päevaleht*) to visit the market together, talk to the vendors and comment on the new setting. As I said in the newspaper interview, there has been improvement in the material conditions; the site is cleaner, lighter . . . yet I suggested avoiding the dichotomies good and bad, or nice and ugly, in order to understand the transformation of the site without simplification, paying attention instead to what is lost in the process of change, and what would be the contribution of the new place to the city at large.

The few vendors who stayed seem to be satisfied with the new setting, orientating their business activity to a younger and richer target audience, as they explain. However, those who lost their jobs, not being able to pay the almost threefold increase in the price of a stand, those who used to come to sell their home-made stuff, and those who came to buy cheap products have lost in this transformation, remaining more isolated and invisible in the suburbs. In this sense, the public space, conviviality and the configuration of diversity in the city has been affected, segregating even more who comes to the centre and for what, and enhancing ongoing gentrification processes. In short, Tallinn has gained a new space for retailing services in the form of a shopping mall for hipsters, adding more supermarkets, gyms, global cafés and bakeries, yet it has lost a place (another one to the list) that was distinct and, therefore, contributed to the identity of the city.

4
Spending time with buildings

For somehow we know by instinct that outsize buildings cast the shadow of their own destruction before them, and are designed from the first with an eye to their later existence as ruins.

Sebald (2001, 23–4)

The birth, death and maturing of Linnahall

Linnahall is a massive half-empty structure in a prominent space of the Estonian capital. Despite being semiruined, almost from its inauguration, the building has thoroughly reached the magnetic function for which it was designed: connecting the city with the seaside. Yet this site has also acquired meanings not envisioned by its designers. Linnahall comes to have a unique history, standing simultaneously as a relic of a bygone era and as a sign of the beginning of a new one (Kurg 2006a). More than its biography, this chapter studies the building's existence in time and its preservation against all odds, pointing at different forms of temporal agency. The consideration of this building as 'Soviet' poses the problem of how to present the biography of the site, which shows plural life stages instead of a linear process of change. In this sense, I propose the term 'maturing' to understand the ageing of the building along with its society, maintenance workers and the young generations who seasonally reappropriate it.

Buildings stand in a process of constant unfolding, being subject to renovation, extension, neglect; processes correlated with individual subjectivities and societal transformations. In this light, Neil Harris (1999) argued for studying buildings as entities with stories that can be as revealing as individual biographies, and in many cases that follow life stages such as birth/initiation, childhood/coming of age and finally death/burial/sainthood. And yet, these cycles would be – as life rituals – constructed forms, since buildings are not born but made, and not dead but abandoned. Further on, there are many issues other than natural disaster in the life stages of buildings, as for instance the land they occupy and market forces, or how architecture is used to reflect or legitimate power. But I agree with Harris that both the physical collapse and the surgeries performed on the buildings through reworking (plumbing, electricity, heating, and so on), are important occasions for collective thought and action, creating new opportunities and temporalities, and helping us to understand the terms of physical as well as social life.

Mature buildings possess a particular transgressive energy, deconstructing normative spacings and condensing fragmented situated stories. They are containers of meaning (Bevan 2006), keeping invisible memories alive, reflecting multiple contested histories and plural narratives. For instance, Linnahall transcended its own death and remains as an adversary of temporal sequencing. The building is caught somewhere between disposal, history and landscape, reminding us of entropic disintegrating orders (Smithson 1972).[1] Paradoxically, ruination and the end of its functional use did not mean the end of Linnahall, but merely a new availability of the venue, being the disposal never finished. In this sense, the building fits Thompson's formulation of rubbish, as something in which a form of value dies, while another may be born.

Linnahall might have failed to promote socialism as a political view and as a way of envisioning the future, yet its impact in Tallinn's urbanity has been wider than its functioning life, probably because of its openness to critical and imaginative reinscription. Nonetheless, the affecting energy of the building is not unintentional, since it was part of the original aim of its architects. Linnahall has served as a catalyst for the redefinition and transformation of urban space in the Estonian capital, turning traditional port areas into a site valued for its scenic waterfronts. Likewise, Linnahall could be understood as a social condenser, with a magical-electrifying capacity of generating estrangement, enabling a world that is 'otherwise', and defamiliarising the actual understanding of the public space (Murawski 2017a).

In his study of Warsaw's Palace of Culture and Science, Michał Murawski points out how that Stalinist building still condenses much of the city's complexity in one place, crystallising material forms of the new society and culture despite enduring as a still-socialist zone. According to

Murawski, its nodal location within the city, enormous size and symmetrical shape, and its capacity to trigger extraordinary affective responses fulfil the modernist ambition to suffuse architecture with socially consequential energy and power (Murawski 2013b). Something similar could be said for Linnahall, which changed the city's centre of gravity. Even if its materiality is decaying, the building encompasses recollective features, capable of binding multiple temporalities and voices still. And it does so partly because of its palatial monumentality, symmetry and centrality, lending it the quality of the colossal, visible from afar, erected in an area that is open and accessible to view, keeping the worshipper at a distance and creating a mystical protective zone (Yampolsky 1995). This ambivalence is one of the reasons to preserve Linnahall in its current condition. Indeed, one of the reasons that make Linnahall achieve its ambiguous plenitude is the entropic decay of the building. We can say that Linnahall has had a larger and more interesting afterlife than its period of usefulness. Precisely because of its current opacity and resistance to fixity, the building racks up values that are at once fragile and incontestable, lingering on, transgressing cultural categorisations and generating affectual responses.

Palace of the great utopia

Linnahall was replete with anticipation and expectations. Ironically, the town planners of Tallinn were correct (back in the seventies) when claiming that the building would function as a time-bomb, slowly cleaning up the surroundings and attracting life towards the water (Bruns 2006). Linnahall was planned to function as both a building and a public outdoor space, being the first modern attempt in Tallinn to connect the city with the sea. Built in 1980 and originally called V. I. Lenin Palace of Culture and Sport, Linnahall stands as a fairly recent but nonetheless controversial Soviet building in the Estonian capital. The site has a 4,600-seat concert hall, an ice rink, an exhibition and dance hall, cafeterias, and hundreds of square metres of walkable roofs, terraces and squares. Otherwise, during the 1990s, the location of Linnahall attracted some new facilities: a heliport, a nightclub, a bar and even an outdoor children's pool that had earlier been used to collect cooling water for the ice rink; also the concert hall began to host Jehovah's Witnesses meetings, Miss Estonia contests, trade fairs, bingo games. Rave parties were organised there, Boney M gave a concert in 1992, and Russian superstars frequently staged their retro-glamorous shows at the venue (Alla Pugachova performed there at least four times – always sold out).

Fig. 4.1 Events in Tallinn for the 1980 Olympic Games. Source: Urve Rukki, Rahvusarhiivi filmiarhiiv.

The starting point for establishing the building was a directive from Moscow, saying that there must be a sports arena with large capacity in each union republic capital. At that time, Tallinn was one of the many candidates for holding the Olympic sailing regatta, the other choices being Leningrad, Riga, Klaipeda, Sochi and Odessa. The decision was made in 1974 and 200 million rubles were allocated to build several of the landmark buildings of the city (figure 4.1). Twenty thousand construction workers and thousands of volunteers were hired to erect fifty new buildings in Tallinn, including the Olympic Yachting Centre at Pirita, the TV tower, the Central Post Office, Tallinn Airport, Hotel Olümpia and Linnahall. It was precisely to host these workers that the 'dormitory suburb' of Lasnamäe started to be erected, later presented within the Estonian imaginary as 'Russification pumps' (Kalm 2001, 349). Of the numerous constructions, Linnahall was the largest and most prominently sited, being spread out over a large area between the old city centre and the coast, on previous industrial harbour sites. Built with concrete bricks covered with limestone[2] as a multipurpose cultural centre, it earned several architectural awards[3] and received much attention from the press.

The first public building opening up to the seafront, Linnahall was situated on the coast between an industrial area and a factory site owned by the military, standing over the railway lines that separated the site from

Fig. 4.2 Construction of Linnahall, 1979. Source: Harald Leppikson, Rahvusarhiivi filmiarhiiv.

the access route. Its location determined the low height of the building, in order to preserve the views to the medieval old town from the sea. Because of its insistently symmetrical shape, the building resembles a Mesopotamian ziggurat. The original idea was to contextualise the building in the seventeenth-century bastions of Tallinn. The main architect, Raine Karp, has also recognised his fascination for the architecture of medieval fortifications. Significantly, his two later major structures[4] in Tallinn demonstrate a bulkiness similar to Linnahall, using similar typologies and building materials (figure 4.2).

The building has no façades and the roof is a public promenade functioning as a bridge over the industrial railway tracks that had blocked public access to the seaside. Once one enters, and climbs the entrance stairs, the stage appears down below as a symmetrical amphitheatre (figure 4.3). For architect Andri Ksenofontov, the building is simultaneously closed and open: 'Linnahall is heavy and powerful on the outside, yet strangely buoyant on the inside' (2006, 18). Architect Triin Ojari has called it 'a concrete fossil' (2012, 151), while Kurg describes Linnahall as a 'windowless concrete and grey limestone construction typical of a bunker or depot; it is easy to miss it at street level, and its considerable size can only really be appreciated from an aerial photograph or map' (2006, 47). The immediate associations of grey are not optimistic, but dull, deprived, of bleakness, as a shade of sickness, yet as Þora Pétursdóttir foregrounds

Fig. 4.3 Construction of Linnahall, 26 February 1980. Source: Valdur-Peeter Vahi, Rahvusarhiivi filmiarhiiv.

(2017), grey is also a liminal shade, tinted by tranquillity, allowing elements to rest, toning down our definitions and preconceptions.

However, in local artistic and architectural circles, the building was seen as too 'rational' and too 'grand', besides lacking the 'irrational substance' of the playful postmodernist design of the period. As Kurg points out, 'it was considered an alien monument, official, formal, Soviet. Even if in the 1980s it was packed with members of the public enjoying the first Western rock bands to play in Estonia, or attending flower parades, it was generally still regarded with contempt rather than pride' (Kurg 2006, 48). Nonetheless, it is also important to note that relevant events connected with the regaining of Estonian independence took place in Linnahall, such as, for instance, a nonofficial declaration of the sovereignty of Estonia adopted on 26 November 1989. And on 20 August 1991, the new government of Estonia went to Linnahall to read the declaration of independence from the USSR (figure 4.4).

Linnahall was built in a rush, as if it were also part of the effort to construct the communist future in the present (Ssorin-Chaikov 2003). The building has been astonishingly short-lived too, despite the privileged location and resources that were devoted to it. Tallinn municipality is still the owner of the ground on which Linnahall is situated. Indeed, the ruination of Linnahall is not simply a symbol of the abnormality of socialist materialities

Fig. 4.4 Declaration of Sovereignty on Linnahall, 26 November 1989.
Source: Viktor Rudko, Rahvusarhiivi filmiarhiiv.

and their supposed denial of the effects of time (Fehérváry 2013), but a
signifier of official indifference, negligence and abandonment. In 2000 the
leadership of the concert hall held negotiations with potential investors
from Sweden, aiming to convert Linnahall into a conference centre and also
planning a business activity for the surroundings. A year later, the municipal government unexpectedly announced that the Swedish plan was not
beneficial for the city, and supported the construction of the Saku Suurhall
arena with capacity for 10,000 spectators. The mayor of Tallinn announced
that Linnahall would be closed down upon completion of the new arena. In
2002, the municipal government issued a proposal for removing Linnahall
from the list of protected monuments, depicting the building as an
unwanted presence to be eradicated. However, the Docomomo expert
analysis did not allow this, confirming Linnahall as an outstanding representative of Estonia's twentieth-century architecture (figure 4.5).

Wrong way of decaying

Linnahall stands as an architectural remain, jilted upon its birth. Once the
building was consigned to obsolescence, entropy and scatology took hold
organically. Architecture, graffiti, debris, nature, signs of decay and the

Fig. 4.5 View of Linnahall from the energy plant, 1980. Source: Harald Leppikson, Rahvusarhiivi filmiarhiiv.

territory manifest themselves as indistinctive, as a whole space of ruination, floating in an atmosphere of spatial melancholia (Navaro-Yashin 2012). My interest in Linnahall already emerged during my first visit to the site. As anyone, I was fascinated by its monumentality, its particular capacity to affect the visitor and its actual state of 'unfinished disposal' (Hetherington 2004). One of the problems of Linnahall was its wrong way of decaying, too quickly for some, too slow for others, not passing away and therefore coming to animate something else (Frederiksen 2016).

Besides a wasted legacy, Linnahall is part of a wider 'ecology of remains' in which the effects of the past are activated (Stoler 2013), yet too new and built with too cheap materials to reach the noble status of a ruin (Yablon 2010). The building stands still and seems to speak through inert silences, through a static history, as if it had become a ruin along with the failure of the ideology and regime from which it emerged (Buck-Morss 2000). In a recent article (2018), Murawski examines how scholars working on postsocialist societies have extensively produced accounts exaggerating collapse, failure and calamity, and eliding instances of success and endurance of the built environment. For instance, Murawski notes that postsocialist assessments of failure have been most often presented as a consequence of a too rigid planning, of being incapable of making room for the complexities of social life and the contingencies of the passage of time. Further on, we can also correlate the active negligence of particular buildings and certain types of architecture with a strategy for the erasure of the memories, history, ideas and identity attached to them, as an enforced or induced forgetting (see also Bevan 2006).

During recent years, I have visited Linnahall with relative frequency. The building stands in a constant flux, at the mercy of arbitrary forces, in a constant change and unfolding. Linnahall shows thus that architecture does not finish when it dies, but can adopt new forms of use, experience and significance. Despite its size, poor construction materials, terrible maintenance record and running costs, the building has learned to adapt over time, being constantly refined and reshaped by its roof occupants. Was Linnahall designed for that? And how long should a building live? Stewart Brand ([1994] 2014) argues that buildings are meant to evolve, yet some structures resist adaptation, and others lend themselves to change. As he points out, buildings have transformations rather than endings, changing organically and being altered at different times; hence the importance of maintenance and repair, as an evolutionary and sustained shaping.

I have had also the pleasure of sharing several conversations with Peeter and Rein, guards who watch the building in 24-hour shifts. Armed with their own patchwork weapons and being the 'first face' janitors to the public, they perform all kind of functions, for instance placing cubed buckets when it rains to avoid the corrosive damage from water. For Peeter (52 years old; figure 4.6), to guard Linnahall is 'a cool way to earn a living', and he confesses that his love for the building grows every day. Peeter laments, however, that the building is neglected, and concludes: 'It is my experience that if a building is left soulless it gets destroyed, just like people'.[5] For Rein (74 years old; figure 4.7), 'it is not only the place which falls apart, also a part of me is affected every time I see something new broken in the building. After that many years working here, I feel it as a part of my body'. Rein first worked as an engineer in the building, in charge of its maintenance. Once Linnahall was closed, Rein was offered one of these positions as a guard to complement his meagre early pension. Back then, 540 people were employed; today just four guards and a manager look after it.

Both Peeter and Rein have told me the story of a 'narkoman' (in their description, a person who is high after consuming drugs) running into the building at night and hiding himself inside. Peeter called the police to help him arrest the 'narkoman'. Soon they found the man, who said as an apology that he did not want to break anything, but just to stay there for a

Fig. 4.6   Author with Peeter. Source: Liina Luhats, 2012.

Fig. 4.7   Rein. Source: Photograph by Kristiina, 2016.

while 'because it feels good and safe'. There is a feeling of peace and companionship inside, noticed by the guards and by many people with whom I have been in. For instance, Rein underscores that despite working alone at night in such a big building, he rarely gets scared and never looks over his shoulder when walking around. Peeter plays, however, with the idea of ghosts, saying that the walls echo all the performances held there.

After spending several hours in Linnahall, I also felt the entropic presence and haunted company of the building. However, it strikes me still the mutuality in which Peeter and Rein approach it, as if it were a 'conjoint being' with an 'interdependent existence' (Sahlins 2013). The way in which they talk about the building produces the feeling that the weight of Linnahall is held on their shoulders, giving meaning to their lives outdoors – not only refusing to accept the building's death but making latent some sense of shared fate. Attachments to such places incite identifications, responsibilities and interconnectedness, a sense of mutuality (or even love) with the building associated with feelings of responsibility (Pétursdóttir 2016; Errázuriz forthcoming). This raises the question of how to study the correlated maturing of people and buildings. As Rein concludes, 'the building is not only part of my identity, but of the identity of the city, if not of the whole country'.

Roadside picnic

Despite the *Lonely Planet* guide deigning to confer no more than ten words on Linnahall (and that in the section on live music), tourists and locals are constantly dropping onto the Soviet ziggurat. By looking at them, I was intrigued to unveil what Linnahall evokes to people with different backgrounds, and if they also share the phantom pain felt by Peeter, Rein and myself. Hence I carried out 25 informal interviews in 2012.[6] According to my informants, Linnahall has become not only a ruin but also an uncanny remnant of the past stages of their lives, expressing a distinct testimonial quality. Among the interviewees, only three were favourable to the idea of tearing down Linnahall and one of the informants changed her opinion a few weeks after the interview, contacting me to make sure that I had changed the record. Also, I found a generational issue within the answers, as various generations had reappropriated the site differently, informing alternative histories along the way. Younger interviewees presented Linnahall as a site of alterity, an edgy landscape to be tamed (e.g., by graffiti); while older informants mostly referred to the building as a source of sorrow and pain. 'It is a shame because of the lost

Fig. 4.8 Author with Kristina and Anette on the roof of Linnahall.
Source: Kristiina, 2016.

Fig. 4.9 People walking on the roof. Source: Author, 2014.

chance. It should be possible to do something better with it', argued
Harri (Estonian speaker, 55 years old). Also Lille (Estonian, 71) commented: 'It is a beautiful building. Nowadays, I feel shame, because I
attended very nice concerts there. The current shape of the building is a
shame. It is really a shame'.

People walk on the roof of Linnahall in a loose way, constructing
their own pace and path (figures 4.8 and 4.9). The most populated

moment of the day is sunset, which gathers a great number of people (the number varies depending on the season). The muteness of Linnahall transfixes into a transcendental phenomenon, attributing to the building an aura that goes far beyond political concerns. For instance, I observed several people praying around the building, as if it had a cosmological significance.[7] Maritta (Estonian, 30 years old) is one of these people who comes 'to read the bible' on the roof when St Olav's Church (Oleviste kirik) is closed. The liminal character of Linnahall – producing a threshold experience – was noted by Tamara (Russian, 17), who gets from the building 'a very good feeling. It is a pleasure to sit here with friends, and talk, and walk and look at the sea. In case I am in a bad mood and the weather is good, I come to Linnahall and think'. In a similar vein, Indrek (Estonian, 40 years old) remarks:

> It is cool to go there. . . . It is different, and it has a nice emplacement, in front of the sea and the wind. Also, I get totalitarian feelings, because of the architecture; and the image comes to my mind of the Soviet congresses that were held there, when old people with yellow moustaches were congregated in the building. But this place has links with the punk subculture too, since it was a gathering point and many concerts were organised in the venue. People still go there on New Year's Eve and also to drink a beer; clearly, it's a plus that the roofs are walkable.

The neglected stands as an invitation to disorder and playfulness. Linnahall is an area of transgression which throws you into the fringes. Victor Turner relates conscious experience with the notion of 'I pass through', distinguishing between 'mere experience' and 'an experience', the latter referring to a development through varied stages (Turner 1969). Overall, liminal experiences form a realm where questions instead of answers emerge, instilling an inquisitive attitude from one's own surroundings. The crowd that gathers on the roof is varied. In a way, everybody is welcome and finds their place on Linnahall. As Vitalija (Lithuanian, 28 years old), for instance (figure 4.10) says:

> We had picnics there. True, it was a bit weird, but it worked very well. For me, this place is related to friendship and a kind of escape from everything else. The wind is strong, the sound unusual . . . it's something brutal, unexpected and relaxing. At first, when you see the building from the old town, it looks very monumental, as something that has not been finished. First, you see the old factory and the

Fig. 4.10   Vitalija on Linnahall. Source: Vitalija Jadvyga, 2012.

gas station next to it . . . when you start going up the stairs you experience something unusual . . . especially the first time you go there . . . more and more stairs are appearing, so the architecture plays with you, and, on the top, you see the sea. There is a mixture of wildness, an order that has not worked out, and at the same time you feel the possibility of change, so you feel the power of the moment. There is history, also the sea, and you are a kind of in between. Also, it produces a relaxed feeling because the place seems to be frozen in time, as if it doesn't care what's happening around. Different people are meeting there, and somehow I believe that everyone finds their own place on Linnahall.

Linnahall is a liminal building in many ways. There, I feel part time-traveller and part voyeur. With subsequent visits, I discovered a transcendental place in which one could disconnect from the everyday routine. The building in itself can be taken as a rehearsal stage, as if the walkable roof would exude the inner function of Linnahall and host new performances through which the meaning of the place is continuously reshaped and actualised. Otherwise, there is a large group of local people that still have not set foot on the dockside territory many years after the grounds opened for public access (Feldman 2000). The seaside areas near the city had been closed for military and industrial reasons for centuries. Not surprisingly, three informants confessed that they had been somehow avoiding this site for many years. For instance, Kadi (Estonian, 43) says:

> Linnahall did not exist on my personal city map for a long time. It was kind of transitional space for me. Somehow it seemed a foreign territory due to the concerts taking place there attracting a predominantly Russian-speaking audience. There are these invisible lines between Estonian and Russian communities. There are events where you see hardly any Russians and vice versa. And Linnahall was somehow a Russian place. Just recently I started to realise what a great place is. Concretely it was the last year, due to some sound artists who showed me the sound potential of the space outside there and also inside. Seeing the place through foreign eyes helped me to suddenly see it on its own terms. And now it has happened that I have walked again there – on the stairs, roof, by the seaside . . . and the place has returned to my map of Tallinn.

At the back of Linnahall, there has been a nightclub for many years called Lucky Luke's (figure 4.11), which is now called Poseidon. As the press tells it, its owner Erik Kruusimägi has criminal records for cocaine trafficking and shows a swastika tattooed in his arm. In November 2015, a British client was thrown out of the bar because of her skin colour. Right behind, the Estonian police organises trainings of arrest and drugs detection with dogs in the Linnahall, shooting with fake bullets. Also, the artists of the Estonia theatre rehearse from time to time on the old stage, preparing for musicals such as *Shrek* and *Billy Elliot*.

Nowadays, the surroundings are available for new housing. The seaside promenade activated during the European Cultural Programme was destroyed three years later to build a highway. Likewise, the nearby district of Kalamaja has witnessed an intense gentrification process. This raises questions about the suitable balance between private and public ownership and shows, once again, the benefit that the accessibility and public use of the shoreline brings to the whole city. The municipal authorities have attempted to rent out Linnahall to private investors several times, but such efforts have been fruitless.[8] At the beginning of 2012, local authorities reported that the city was still close to signing an agreement with Ronald S. Lauder (Estée Lauder's son), who would eventually invest €63 million in Linnahall.[9] A few months later, we learned that the

Fig. 4.11 Old Lucky Luke's bar at the back of Linnahall, 1992. Source: Erik Prozes, Rahvusarhiivi filmiarhiiv.

negotiations with the entrepreneur to transform the Soviet concert hall into a mega-casino had broken down, despite important concessions offered by the local government. Entrepreneurs representing a famous rock café chain also came to see Linnahall and negotiate terms for renting the ice rink. The point of disagreement was, however, the need for renovation, or more precisely the limitations for it; since the potential renters wanted to refurbish the space with minimum concerns possible about protecting the heritage. Finally, in September 2016, the board members Tõnu Prööm and Väino Sarnet confirmed that Linnahall's concert hall would be repaired, the work to start in 2018. The budget will come from privatising 11.5 hectares of the public land surrounding the building, a detachment that might signify memory amputation. Meelis Pai, chairman of the Linnahall supervisory board, explained that the reconstructive and demolition works would be orientated towards transforming the building into the centre of conference tourism in the Nordic and Eastern European regions.[10]

In September 2017, a few weeks before the municipal elections, Märt Sults, member of the parliament and candidate for Tallinn, organised the painting of a mural on one of the sides of Linnahall as part of his campaign, even arranging public funding for it. 'Linnahall is a memorial, no matter what', reacted Siim Raie, director of the National Heritage Board, which ruled that the mural was illegal and had to be cleaned. Asked about it, Peeter responds diplomatically that it is disrespectful but understandable, as the building is being reduced to stones and waste. For those who calculate everything in terms of financial profit, for property developers, Linnahall is 'just a waste of developable land, too low and with too much indefinite space, but most importantly it could not be marketed piece by piece. Its logic lay in the Soviet period where, within the context of state ownership, its designers had not had to worry about the cost of the land' (Kurg 2006a, 51); and yet for most of my informants the building was a fringy space where the public and private, memory and history, dissolve their boundaries.

Buildings mature

Buildings generate affects not just in their preservation and persistence, but in their negligence and disposal too (DeSilvey 2006; Hetherington 2004). We can talk of Linnahall as standing in excess and holding affective power. The study of affect refers to the felt atmospheres and the sensorial aspects of space (Brennan 2004), which prime subjects to act in particular ways and lend meaning to places (Wanner 2016). This building is a good example of how architecture stirs a spectre of affects, coming to hold memories of relationships and attachments, rendering this building exceedingly difficult to dispose of. Years after its construction and abandonment, Linnahall stands as an inclusive site of alterity, turned into an involuntary memorial which disturbs the current order of things in Tallinn.

Although social time dictated the end of its use as a building, natural time has not yet terminated its existence. Nowadays, the building takes the form of a multitemporal field in which the past accumulates itself (Olivier 2011), and history physically merges into the setting (Benjamin 1998). We project ideas in material forms, and through them we construct memories and imaginaries; Linnahall is a place in which large- and small-scale histories entwine, standing as something that reminds and as something to remember – a 'material mirror' (Miller 2005) of the historical world created by those who lived before us. The building enfolds time, as much as it is enfolded within it. Through its multiple durations and improper standing (parasitic on history and people's biographies), Linnahall provides an *eventscape* where a long-timescale process produces an effect in a much shorter timescale, enabling the experience of several temporalities in a single *durée* among those who encounter it, conveying vanished worlds and futures that did not come to pass, inspiring diverse memories as a prism, which gathers meanings and scatters them again, yet not randomly, since a prism has a given number of faces and scatters the light in particular directions (Humphrey 2005).

Comparisons can therefore be drawn between the biographies of persons and the biographies of buildings, highlighting the eventful discontinuation and change of states they might go through. An example of this is the repeated effort of Peeter to capture seasonal changes through the building as well as the social relations around Linnahall. Peeter generously shared a folder with the hundreds of pictures of Linnahall he has accumulated over a decade. In them, we can recognise several tropes: family relationships (visits of his mother and grandson; figure 4.12); the recollective power of Linnahall (marking the passing of time); multiple reappropriations of the building (people, animals and vegetation). Yet as I see it, what this case also shows is that the boundary between personal imaginaries and material forms, between our maturing and the ageing of the built environment, is often not that clear. In this sense, buildings might be considered as an extension of our intimate subjectivity (Pallasmaa 2005), and the relation between a building, its dwelling and maintenance, and our personal biography can be understood as reciprocal, characterised by mutuality (figures 4.13–4.15).

Fig. 4.12 Visit of Peeter's grandson. Source: Peeter Mägi.

Fig. 4.13   Steps on the snow. Source: Peeter Mägi.

Fig. 4.14   'Look what a beautiful light here'. Source: Peeter Mägi.

Fig. 4.15 Graffiti on the wall. Source: Peeter Mägi.

For Grete (Estonian, 26),

Linnahall brings all sorts of memories, starting from childhood and how I tried to drink Fanta from a glass bottle and the straw was always too short for it. I often went ice-skating on the rink . . . and then came the period when I hung around with my friends there, on the right slope, because it was more hidden. Ha, I remember our famous, cheap, crappy wine called Kosmos, which went together with Coca-Cola in those gatherings. At that time, we didn't go to the performances anymore; I think that they showed only commercial musicals. Nowadays we still go there to watch sunrise during summer mornings . . . I've been always fascinated by the greatness and monumentality of the building, iconic but forgotten!

Ruination paradoxically undercuts claims of temporal continuity, breaking the linear sequence of events and offering a 'counter-narrative in which testimony becomes guided by voids rather than points of presence' (Trigg 2009, 89). In every new encounter with Linnahall, we experience a sense of time collapsing, which generates an evocative relationship between materiality, nature and history, awakening a transcendental repositioning of the self. Likewise, the building bears a burden of signification for the observer, witnessing and reflecting social changes simultaneously. Linnahall uniquely expresses something of the threshold character of Tallinn, whereby unfinished modernisations and socialist sites of disrepair coexist with the neoliberal brave new city.

As other elements of the socialist legacy, Linnahall has been presented as residual and in need of recycling, unworthy of restoration or protection, close to zero value. And yet, when or what was the turning point that made this building obsolete? Decisions to abandon or rehabilitate are always informed by value judgements, not simply by the cost of time, money or effort required. Paradoxically, we have been taught to recognise Soviet remnants as ruins even before they crumbled. The ironic part of it is that the melancholic plenitude of the building arrived only after its neglect. In that scheme, Linnahall is a social transgression of the (postsocialist) natural order, a marginalised structure that continues to inform social affects but that ceases to function in ways it once did.

The building resists final definitions and an easy placement in the timeline. Linnahall might be read as vestige, remnant and relic, but the consideration of this building as 'Soviet' brings to the fore the difficulty of presenting its biography and poses broader questions concerning the conservation and maintenance of the building. The situation of abandonment adds a new layer of meaning to Linnahall, a new availability repeatedly taken by younger generations. As a spatial structure, Linnahall fulfils the same functions as a monument: paralysing the flow of time, creating the experience of temporal metamorphosis (Yampolsky 1995). Yet this affectual energy is combined with age value in the building left to decay, expressing a victory of nature over history, unmasking the human pretension of fixity. Linnahall appears as a memorial despite being in movement; we should even substitute 'because' for 'despite', since one of the reasons this site has become a generator of landscapes and entails cultural value for the different generations is the way the building embraces entropy in ruination, in a state of passing through.

The threat posed by things that have been categorised as waste is that they still have some identity, since they can disturb the order of things. It is this stage of 'half-identity' (Douglas 1966, 160) that makes them powerful in their dissonance. We tend to have concern for ruins, as heritage, yet we are intolerant of ruination, as a process (Pétursdóttir and Olsen 2014). Things of the past seem to be of value if they serve for something – attract tourists, form identity – yet there is also the option of letting things be, falling into decay or being appropriated outside of official discourses of heritage; in other words, accepting how things are, also in their messy state (ibid.).

Ruins appear as relics that not only speak about loss, but also about contingency and nonlinear processes of change. They emerge as a landmark of redemption and variability, partly due to their fragmentary composition. Certain sites and things enable alternative memories, an assumption which collides with the idea of memory as a humanly initiated phenomenon. The upgrading and degrading of materials, the invention of new uses and the loss produced in decline show that decay might also be a necessary step in the upgrading process. Decay has the merit of inscribing time in things, hence the curation of certain sites is argued as a generative process in itself. In addition to practices of preservation and reconstruction, the strategy of a curated decay has emerged, proposing to put time to work in the shaping of the legacy (DeSilvey 2017; Moshenska 2015; Pétursdóttir 2013). For instance, Caitlin DeSilvey explains it as a 'procreative power of decay' which generates contemplation through the embodied responses of 'repugnance and attraction' (2006, 320). Hence, she proposes the notion of 'entropic heritage': a 'maintenance policy applied to buildings to uphold their structural integrity yet preserve their ruined appearance' (326).

In postsocialist contexts, we have often been impelled to choose between abandonment and speculative redevelopment. Yet there is an alternative beyond this dichotomy, which is maintenance and curation. Through a careful conservation and stabilisation, Linnahall could be turned into a curated ruin too. Kevin Lynch (1990) has also argued for the value of decay as a necessary part of life, yet foregrounding that waste always implies negligence. As he recognised, the wasting of places stems from human actions and inactions, as well as from choices made during the period of production.[11] In the case of Linnahall, its size and the poor materials used prevent any possible restoration of the building, making hard any possible use and maintenance without subsidies. And yet, Linnahall produces new meanings in its persistence and obduracy, as a time-bomb that it is still ticking after the explosion.

Decay teaches us that life is composed of ends and new beginnings, and that something is always lost and something is gained in the life cycle of upgrading and laying down. In his writings on ruins, Simmel presented material decay as a human and nonhuman process, since in remains, nature begins to have a brute, downward-dragging, corroding power, producing something new that is 'entirely meaningful, comprehensible, differentiated' (Simmel 1965, 259). Akin to this theory of ruination, Benjamin (1999) approaches ruins as sites open to interpretation, able to catch historical paradoxes and to teach us about the transience of modern projects. The encounter with material decay produces a sort of mimesis

Fig. 4.16   Lobby of the concert hall, Linnahall. Source: Kristiina, 2016.

favouring the work of imagination. For instance, Linnahall triggers affective responses and encompasses a threshold quality, creating a sense of dislocation and disclosing nonteleological possibilities of evolution.

Even those who have not visited Linnahall in many years, or those who are in favour of tearing down the building, do not reject the affective value of Linnahall. Meelis (Estonian, 39) is an example of that. I met him on the roof, looking at the sea and drinking a beer. He went to the harbour to walk a friend to the ferry and stayed there for a while, just relaxing. Meelis believes that Linnahall is hopeless: 'I would prefer the building to be demolished. Look at the building; what do we need it for? It's too expensive to repair it'. And even so, Meelis usually stays on the roof after walking friends to the harbour.

Very few of the interviewees saw the building in a direct relationship to political categories. Their narratives rather approach Linnahall as a 'storehouse of personal memories' (Meier 2013, 471; figures 4.16, 4.17 and 4.18). Memories of the past are thus recalled in a highly selective way and the exercise of reconstruction appears to be influenced by subsequent biographic and political events, by the indexing process of intermingling present experience with past temporalities and personal trajectories. Reflexive nostalgia, as a negotiation of collective belonging, has been a very recurrent answer among the informants. In the view of Kärt (Estonian, 23), Linnahall evokes:

Fig. 4.17 Concert hall, Linnahall. Source: Liina Siib, 2016.

Fig. 4.18 Walkers on Linnahall, 1980. Source: Harald Leppikson, Rahvusarhiivi filmiarhiiv.

nostalgia, nostalgia, nostalgia. It was the place where school-markets were held when I was little. You got all the pencils and books and stuff like that. Also, I went to some concerts, plays and music festivals when I was a bit older. And there was an ice rink where we used to go skating with my family or school mates. A lot of funny memories! But I think the most important usage Linnahall has had since I was a teenager is as a place to drink and hang out. Actually, the milieu was always quite dirty and obscene, but that's what made it so cool and rebellious for youngsters. Well, the views are great too. The architecture in its roughness and measurements is also remarkable.

This nostalgia is not just of youth but also of alternative orders and temporalities. For Ott (Estonian, 28), Linnahall generates:

good feelings, nostalgia, relaxation . . . I have a special relationship with this place. When I met my girlfriend then we used to hang out there a lot, watch the sunset, or the sea, etc. But we have been hanging out there with other friends as well, so in general, I associate it with leisure and with my friends. Also nostalgic, because it reminds me of my childhood in the Soviet Union.

And for Maren (Estonian, 22):

I feel a kind of sad and romantic nostalgia, thinking about these Soviet superstars performing there, like Alla Pugachova, everybody adoring her. . . . And now the building is kind of decaying and this fantasy of excess, camp, kitsch and weird sincerity with it. I imagine it was a really magical place in its glory days.

The 'democratic' character of Linnahall has been praised in the Estonian pavilion at the Venice Biennale of architecture (2012). Eero Epner, one of the contributors to that project, remarks that the gigantic complex is free of consumerism and ambiguous enough to be appropriated in diverse ways by different people. An inspiring volume, entitled *How Long Is the Life of a Building?* and edited by Tüüne-Kristin Vaikla, reflects on an array of questions such as: why do we value certain buildings over others? What should be done with the buildings from the 1960s and 1970s that currently stand unused? Which of them could be used for today, and who might need these buildings tomorrow? Also, what kinds of values do modernist buildings represent and how could they be preserved for the future? And why is socialist architecture being abandoned – do their materials and technologies depreciate or is it an escape instead? After noticing that 750 objects from the postwar era have been selected as architectural heritage yet more than 60 per cent of them are marked as abandoned,[12] and also after considering that perhaps there are still too many Soviet-era buildings, several of the contributors to the book ask what to do if the circumstances and conditions in which those buildings were built do not exist anymore: Does a function have to be found for them? Are they not old enough to be recognised as heritage?

Otherwise, the case of Linnahall demonstrates that ruination is preceded by neither a period of absolute usefulness nor the end of a building. As shown, the ruined quality might even happen prior to its use, due to size, location or political contingencies. Further, the level of degradation of Linnahall is not neutral; it points at failures in social life, depending upon political decisions, local regulations and economic disinvestment. Otherwise, the disposal of things inherently entails an ambiguity, as it means almost opposite things simultaneously: to get rid of something and to have something available – at our disposal (Hetherington 2004) (figure 4.19). As a wasted legacy, Linnahall exemplifies this ambiguity. The building continued its existence after reaching zero

Fig. 4.19 Tokens of the changing room, as material remains of occupation. Source: Kristiina et al., 2016.

value and zero expected life-span, and did so in a timeless limbo, where, at some later date, it had the chance of being discovered (Thompson 1979).

Concluding considerations

Affectual responses are based on the monumentality, centrality and multifunctionality of buildings (Murawski 2013b), but they are also related to their longevity and endurance. As a remain, Linnahall is charged with its own retractability. The building stands as a problematic legacy; not just because of its lack of functionality and the small economic surplus produced on site, but also because of its hetero-memento character. The presence of Linnahall disturbs and interrupts the hegemonic discourse of transition as a linear journey: from bad to good, from tyranny to democracy, from oppression to freedom, from abandonment to design. Linnahall is in this sense auratic, having the capacity to look back at us and generate a feeling of loss.

The work of memory often needs a material mediation which triggers lived experiences, evokes different temporalities or carries mirroring qualities. The building remains crafted by both time and by new generational reappropriations, standing stubbornly in spite of being left to decay. Its modern status as unintentional memorial signals the loss of its practical usefulness, yet also the need for caretakers to guard this landmark and help with its maintenance. What has to be preserved and in which way are still relevant questions in postsocialist contexts, not just because of architectural protection, but also because of the social logic, ideas and personal memories that they encapsulate. As a relic of another time, Linnahall encapsulates diverse modes of being, enhancing feelings of empathy and difference, recalling memory: not how it was, but rather how it has been forgotten.

Linnahall is better understood if compared with: (1) Machu Picchu – a temple affected by time; (2) the Berlin Wall – an archaeological site in constant progress; or (3) a playground, as a cultural space continually reappropriated by the young and where we take risks, break norms and disconnect from the normal flow of everyday life. If we think of Machu Picchu, of the Acropolis, of the Alhambra, it seems obvious that we are talking about heritage. However, all these fantastic sites were neglected and abandoned for centuries and gained their status through their maintenance as curated ruins, rather than through their reconstruction. Here I propose two alternatives for Linnahall: either a multifunctional reactivation through small uses operating in an accessible way and oriented to the occupation and maintenance of the building – what Alari Allik (2012) calls a 'transfusion of fresh blood to the altar-temple'; or for an arrested decay through a set of measures that does not obliterate the offences of time and keeps the building accessible as a landscape (an alternative supported, for instance, by architect Karli Luik).

5
Tallinn 2017 chronotope

Thinking the contemporary city through amalgamations

In this chapter, I elaborate on a survey of the contemporary cityscape of Tallinn, with an account of existing urban assemblages. The observations take as a departure urban fragments (zones, buildings, façades and so on), yet strive to embrace the city as a sociocultural whole, as a coherent object of study which remains always unfinished, in the making. Short-term adaptations and long-term patterns are considered by showing the coevolution of the social, the spatial and the temporal in urban changes, bringing to light diverse spatiotemporal horizons. Relying on empirical examples, literature, architecture, visual signs and traces and gaps in the cityscape, I outline both how the built environment is reflecting the ongoing sociality and the accumulation of changeless elements and unfinished projects in the cityscape, exploring then the way it might condition new processes of adaptation and reshape the spatial identity of the Estonian capital.

Radical social transformations become apparent in the external aestheticised form of material culture, creating a fragmented as well as an aesthetically and historically diverse urban landscape. In this light, the research draws on the assumption that ruptures and obduracies can be comprehended through material expressions of the past that remain in the cityscape in the form of gaps and interruptions. From previously existing practices and forms, new ones are generated in a way similar to the process of rewriting – adding and eroding. This process can be partly described as a hybrid, since transformations are mediated through local infrastructures and configurations of legacy, institution and power. But in some cases, the degree of contradiction between the elements forming the cityscape is that high, or the process of reception-translation so parallel (instead of mixed), that we have to talk about Frankenstein formations rather than hybrid ones.

The notion of amalgamations is proposed to conceptualise the particular heterogeneity found in the cityscape of Tallinn, which is redundant and mismatching in its entanglement of space and time. We can even talk of aesthetics of amalgamation, illustrating the tension between history, memory and decay, and of how the affective charge of the urban aesthetic forms contributes to shaping a sense of place. This notion is related to the concept of chronotope (Bakhtin 1981), which refers to how temporal and spatial relationships are intrinsically connected, constituting a narrative unity.[1] Here, chronotopes and amalgamations are not understood as an ontologically autonomous something, but rather as a field of spatiotemporal relations. We can see amalgamations as a form of constellation (Benjamin 1968; 1999), a 'thought image' that evokes a noncausal connectivity defined by multiplicity, rupture and fragmentation, which happen in relation to other places, processes and historical elements. These constellations or chronotopes have no clear boundaries and are superimposed on each other, forming outward-looking nodes (Gordillo 2014; Massey 2005) and showing how 'space becomes charged and responsive to the movements of time, plot and history' (Bakhtin 1981, 84).

The study of material compositions is a privileged point from which to access vanished worlds and cultural meanings, acknowledging their mounting quality. Different kinds of elements and cascading effects create a particular texture and entanglement that reaches a point of expressivity, as an unforeseen precarious composition, made of what is left behind by change, repairs and interruptions. Materialities persist, acquiring new meanings through lived experiences, being part of the metabolism of the city. In contrast to the fleetingness of our remembered impressions, the materiality of forms is a reality that endures. As fragments, different patterns enter into the existent constellations of the present and are manifested in everyday life through an uneven sedimentation of practices and materialities. Yet the fragmentation of the cityscape does not imply simply some joyous coexistence between sameness and difference, nor that the material environment is a mere leftover from past actions, but rather points at a relational placement and a synthesis effect (Löw 2008).

Particular arrangements in our quotidian space generate specific meanings, make certain experiences and narratives more viable, draw symbolic boundaries, and carry with them a set of values, codes of behaviour and affective drives (Cresswell 1996; De Boeck 2015; Löw 2008). But how is the accumulated experience of a society materialised in the urban space? Social life, with its practices and representations, actively produces an own temporality and historical now. Tallinn appears as a city where disparate temporalities coexist and juxtapose radically, containing within a multiplicity of spatiotemporal relations. New transformations come on top of old ones (often unfinished) and are applied in a very short time, complicating the process of adaptation and integration. Walking along the harbour, one can trace, for example, the shadow play of evolution and metamorphosis in the city that makes visible the act of change and its nonlinear outlines. One comes across construction sites, metal tunnels for boarding ferries, a museum of contemporary art, car parks, alcohol shops, casinos with glossy neon lights, forgotten warehouses, factory skeletons, abandoned buildings with graffiti on their walls and a former prison turned into a tourist attraction with a terrace café exhibiting the painting of a naked woman holding the flag of the former Estonian Soviet Republic (figures 5.1 and 5.2).

In a way, the shoreline landscape is a disparate constellation of diverse times and projects of modernisation – conditioned by factors such as a long military occupation, intense industrialisation and rapid privatisation. Like archives, cityscapes maintain a representation of the past, as a topography of commemorative signs and markers, but also through the amalgamations formed in the ongoing process of dwelling, building,

Fig. 5.1 Café at the prison. Source: Author, 2014.

Fig. 5.2 Terrace at the former Patarei prison. Source: Alex Bieth, 2014.

investing . . . traces are not simply scattered throughout a city, they form assemblages and material systems entropically brought together. Different temporal topographies collide and become partially interwoven as indexing recombinations, making multiple temporalities coexist within particular spaces, uncovering the lingering presence of various legacies in an altered form.

And what does one temporality do to the other, or how is this multiplicity assembled? The meaning of various periods and the experience of time change along with the material form of the city and the uses of the space (Laszczkowski 2016; Tilley 2017). The cityscape appears thus as a collage characterised by becoming and obduracy, by changes and continuities, by juxtaposition and coexistence, always operating at multiple temporal and spatial scales. The cityscape is therefore taken as a relational entity, where multiple sociomaterial assemblages converge, each of them with its self-contained processes of heterogeneous associations (Farías 2011) and particular interactions with the beyond (Massey 2005). For instance, Tallinn does not merely mirror transition and postsocialism: we can recognise other materialisations of change, related to obduracies, scales, temporal horizons, material rhythms, social orientations and idiosyncratic ways of building an urban system. Further, the adoption of neoliberal initiatives and rationalities across the region has intersected with local politics, histories and legacies to the point that even if the 'socialist'

Tallinn has undergone intense erosion, many of the dwellings, utilities and public spaces built by these regimes continue to be cherished by their inhabitants and users (Bodnár 2000; Collier 2011; Murawski 2018).

In this account of the Estonian capital, I put the focus on the study of long-term mutations of the cityscape, giving an account of how globalisation, neoliberalism and Soviet legacies are intensively negotiated and crystallised in urban spaces. Yet material forms demonstrate obduracy or, in other words, a tendency to resist change; these responses to fragmentation and change are also part of the inventory of a city's material culture, as enduring archetypes and inertias based on mental models, social embeddedness and traditions (Hommels 2005). The concept of amalgamation draws attention to the contingency of social forms, epitomising the arts of transience and emergence, foregrounding how different materialities, scales and temporal frames come to cohabit a given setting, becoming codependent and culturally charged as an entanglement (Laszczkowski 2016).

Places in the making

As a plural time-space, there is a myriad of ways in which Tallinn can be described and embodied. Last time that my friend Alex came to Tallinn, he complained that his visit was about to end and he had seen just the 'Disneyland old town', a few bars and Kanala, the open-air recreation area where we had been playing ping-pong every day. The next morning, we rented a couple of bikes and went out for a thorough exploration of the Estonian capital. Amazed by the wide unexpected differences within the cityscape, Alex took dozens of photos during the exploratory journey. That day, we acted as *vélo-flâneurs*, engendering our own action system, embodying the form and sociality of the city in a ludic and kinaesthetic way. We can call it an ethnographic go-along, riding along sand paths, motorways and stone-paved streets, sweating when stopping at the edge of a zebra crossing, falling into trappings and dead ends, zigzagging to avoid the wounds of the city or discovering temporary uses. A bicycle journey might help to sense the intensities of everyday affective cityscapes; it is a haptic experience of the body coming together with the urban environment, which largely exists outside the linguistic realm, activating many strings that pull memories, imagination and consciousness into awareness (Jones 2012; Laviolette 2011; Martínez and Laviolette 2016). While cycling around, centres of gravity, sensory hotspots and amalgamated trails of history were revealed. The *Geist* of Tallinn came to us as an organic spatiality; we were riding through the intersection of time and materiality, since the city manifested itself as an enduring human experience. In our two-wheeled exploration, material forms and urban compositions etched into our personal memory, sailing over the crossroads, hitting the gaps, interpreting bodily the urban knots, enacting the heterogeneity and polycentricity of the Estonian capital.

Instead of reducing urban encounters to 'points of collision', we can choose an interrogative approach that pays attention to emergent forms in the conduct of life, whereby elements come to hang together as an assemblage that has its own sensory aesthetics and lines of force (Farías 2011; Stewart 2014). Further, the materiality of the cityscape produces distinctive public feelings and resonates with various affects, influencing the capacities to act and be acted upon by intensities, entanglements and obduracies. Local affective history and spatial identity are constituted as tangible and perceptible too, affected by the past through material and immaterial networks and obduracies, as a lived spatiality, layering different images of space that do not simply overlap but mutate (Navaro-Yashin 2012). Memory sits in places; events of history shrivel up and become absorbed in settings, turning the past into an aesthetic category in its own right (Benjamin 1998). Piles of history accumulate and coexist along in the cityscape telling about empires, modernity, and excess; carrying a temporal index; producing particular forms such as amalgamations – a conglomerate of mismatching elements that show how the process of laying down occurred through erosion, rupture and assemblage instead of a clean sedimentation.

Urban materialities do not simply mean 'matter', since the physical stuff of the city has a rich symbolic value and condenses power relations, affects and temporalities (Buchli 2007; Văetişi 2011). In Tallinn, the acceleration of landscape is perceived as a lack of contextual fit, symbolic saturation, yet also by a need for (material and social) sutures. For instance, we may take as paradigmatic the Rottermann island in the centre of Tallinn: the location of a bread factory in the nineteenth century, of an intense industrial activity in Soviet time, and now transformed into a business and entertainment area after a new architectural visage juxtaposing past traces and industrial structures with modern glass configurations. The temporalities experienced in the encounter with Tallinn's cityscape appear often out of sync, looking like disjunctions and making time be experienced as heterogeneous and 'uncontemporaneous' (Kracauer 1969; Pinney 2005). These out-of-sync temporalities can be recognised in scraps, ornaments and other elements disjointed from their original networks (Laszczkowski 2015).

Tallinn appears to be composed of spatial and temporal elements and perspectives that relate but do not add up, generating a sense of multiplicity that reminds us of Gisa Weszkalnys's description of Alexanderplatz in postunification Berlin (2010). Also, Karl Schlögel (2003) has tried to explain the hybridity of processes of change by distinguishing between 'hot' and 'cold' locations in urban spaces. Hot places are those in the making, while cold ones appear as already consolidated. Hot locations appear at different scales of analysis: intersubjective, neighbourhoods, cities, societies, global . . . conditioning patterns of interaction, being part of a changing common sense (*sensus communis*), acting thus as a suture: they connect, alleviate and bridge, providing terrain for inclusiveness and communication. In medical terms, a suture is an element that stitches wounds. In anatomy, a suture is a joint between rigid pieces.

Andres Kurg (2009b) notes how the interconnections between the pieces forming the city were often designed retrospectively, after surprises such as realising that shopping facilities were inaccessible to pedestrians or far from public transport nodes. Whether in the form of gap or suture, interruptions make us aware of other experiences and regimes, of what has been forgotten or erased, yet not quite. In the case of Tallinn, we can see it through the unbalance between constructiveness and destructiveness, making this city appear as richly unfinished. It is not difficult in Tallinn to encounter a succession of abandoned properties, areas of high-speculation and consumption, forgotten ghettos of socially disadvantaged populations, calm residential areas with big gardens, quarters with wooden houses, and even a so-called creative city, where different expats, local hipsters and tourists find each other.

Even if the cityscape is rapidly changing, when I traverse the city still I get the sense of crossing many spatio-temporal borders. An example of this is the Šnelli area, next to the former Railway street market, and whereby a football pitch, medieval walls, ruinous factories, a hotel with Nordic design, vague post-industrial spaces and forgotten railway roads coexist. Not much further, we could find another area that is under a gentrification process (Kalamaja) but which used to include an Azerbaijanian bistro, an intriguing nightclub called Kolm Lõvi (Three lions), the 24/7 Tseburek canteen and a *piroshkis* kiosk for late-night partygoers hoping to escape a hangover, as well as an Eastern European–style casino, a Peetri pizza bistro, a grill kiosk and a bus depot.

In Tallinn, built legacies show an ambiguous ending. Series of past durations are recognisable in vestiges, spiralling trajectories and built forms that are contemporary yet unsynchronised, rather coexisting alongside, overlapping and amalgamating themselves. A suture-based theory is proposed as a means to study urban gaps (De Boeck and Baloji 2016). In postsocialist cities, the need for sutures has been the consequence of the accumulation of unfinished projects of modernisation and successive ruptures at community and landscape levels as much as the neoliberal acceleration of the contemporary city. Sutures and amalgamations cause the vibration of the past to resonate in the present, demonstrating a particular sensibility to changes, in the form of patterns of entanglement and transmission.

Such constellation reinforces the sense that the old is not that old, nor is entirely past. The old rather appears in the present deposited on and accumulated with other past temporalities. Throughout amalgamations, we can learn how the past radiates into the emergent material culture, illuminating the porous and eventful layering of social transformations. This quality, related to material duration, contributes to the thickening and indexing of urban phenomena, appearing as a form of memory (Olivier 2011). Amalgamations portray this double reality of change and continuity (becoming and obduracy) through intended and unintended compositions and morphologies, as an entropic condensation and saturation of power relations and temporalities.

There is thus a link between social changes, urban memories and collective moods, conditioning our affective investments and creating a sense of place that is also informed by the unbuilt, the erased and the wasted. This correlation has been beautifully shown by Ingrid Ruudi's exhibition on the unrealised architectural projects planned in Tallinn in the liminal period 1986–94, yet never built due to the radical openness of an era described as 'a fluid and hazy process' and 'a phenomenon in itself', where Estonian society appeared 'in the stage when it is hard to define whether it is being constructed or demolished' (Ruudi 2015).

The exhibition *Unbuilt: Visions for a New Society, 1986–1994* manages to symbolise urban incompletion, reminding its audience that architectural projects are the product of socially constituted relations. As Ruudi concludes, 'Just a few years later, by the mid-1990s, belief in the possibility of having a say in social processes seemed to have reached its very lowest low' (2015, 32).[2] This case could also be approached through Vladimir Paperny's (2002) dichotomy Culture One and Culture Two. As described by the Russian architectural historian, characteristics of Culture One are porosity, improvisation, horizontal quality and centrifugal dynamics that favour diversity. In the middle of radical changes, authorities are minimally concerned with architecture, so architects are left to themselves, and tend to generate ideal projects – as a fired act of creativity – that are almost never realised. However, Culture Two emerges

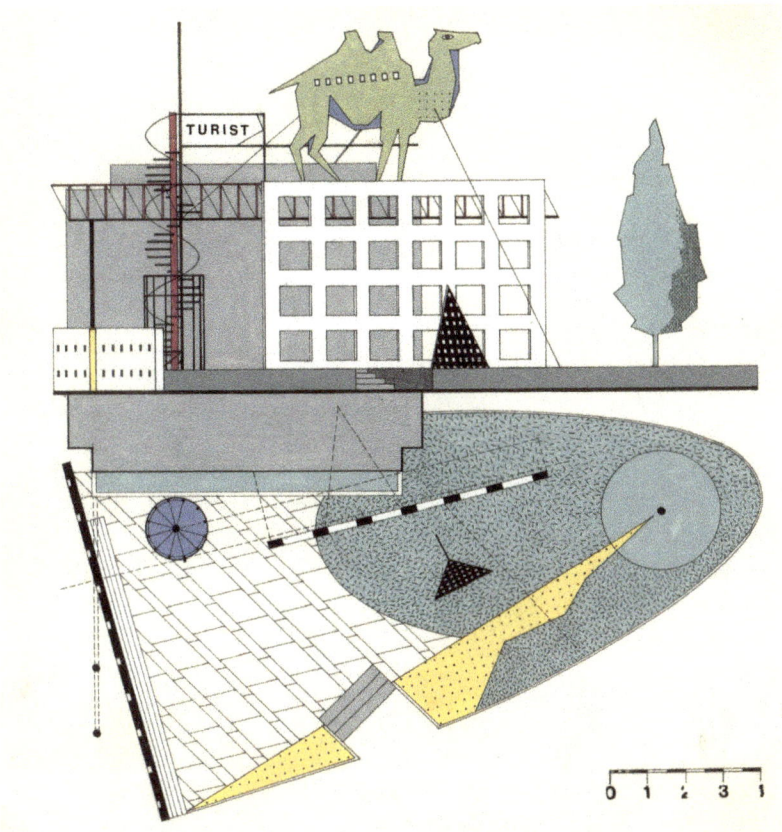

Fig. 5.3 Designs for Camel Park, Vilen Künnapu and Andres Siim.
Source: Andres Siim, 1987.

in periods of settlement and is characterised by vertical architecture, reinvigorating centripetal forces and appearing more hierarchical. Society ossifies and architecture is rediscovered as a vehicle of values and spatial expression of the system. Culture One aims at the emancipation of space and is oriented to the future, breaking ties to the past and denying any legacies, declaring itself to be the beginning of history. By contrast, Culture Two turns its gaze towards the past and strives for eternity, for ending history.

The unbuilt projects were turned by the curator into storytelling devices, since the objects that formed the exhibition acquired an autobiographical patina, lingering stories about ourselves. In postsocialist countries, the 1990s were the decade when the seeds of business and entertainment centres, banks and religious buildings, suburbanisation

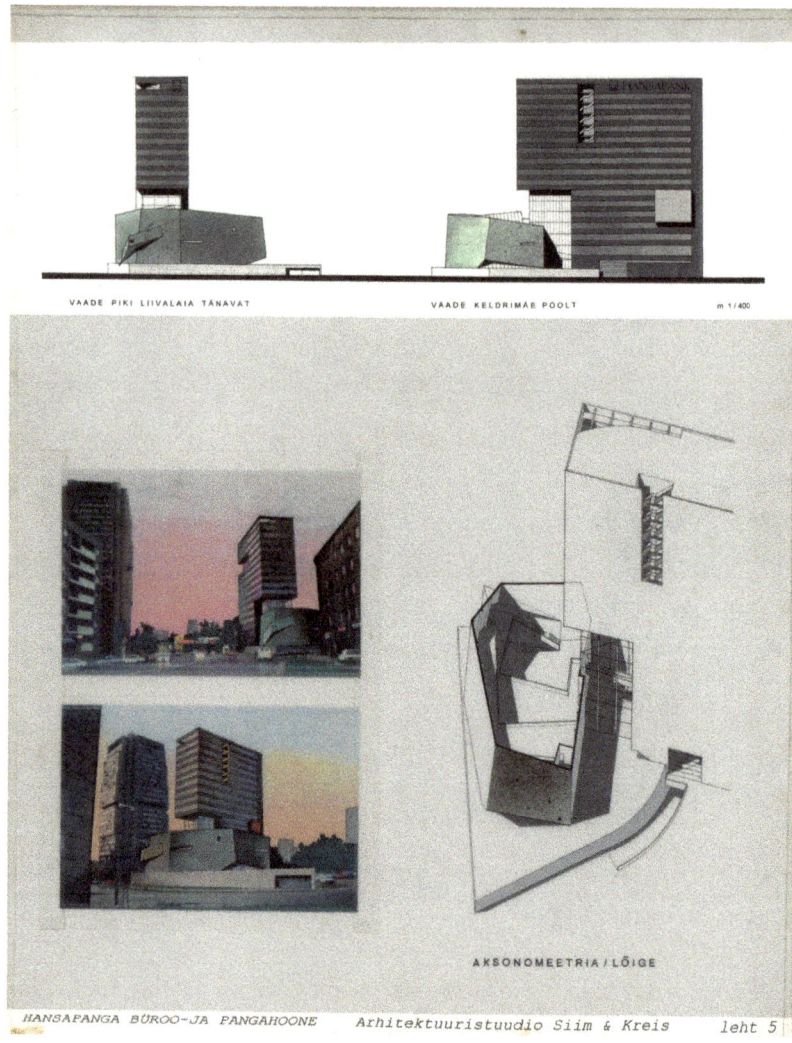

Fig. 5.4 Designs for new business district of Tallinn, Siim & Kreis.
Source: Andres Siim, 1994.

and enclosures were planted. Yet as Ruudi emphasises, there were alternative imageries to transform the city, starting with a symbolic rejection of the actual urban environment (figure 5.3 and 5.4). Despite being unaccomplished, these 'unbuilt' projects were intended to conceive a new society, as well as to discern what the changes were about. They managed to reconfigure the planning conditions of Tallinn by making 'excess' available for other projects.

Within a few years many things were decided in an irreversible way; new themes, designs and typologies (business and entertainment centres, banks and religious buildings, and semipublic spaces), yet the liminality of the time produced a distinctive cityscape and a particular way of pushing together unrelated actors and events. The study of urban amalgamations talks about how social transformation takes form materially and about the realisation and failure of projects. Interruptions within material forms turn out to be expressions of the past which make us aware of other experiences and varieties of urbanism.

Urban archipelago

In 2002, Mari Laanemets and Andres Kurg edited *A User's Guide to Tallinn*, a compilation of insights describing how Tallinn was ten years after Estonia regained independence, and the way local people related to citiness:

> The meaning of the places and objects of the city is constantly changing, and precisely due to different practices – the churches turned into garages; the industrial buildings turned into museums. . . . There are no permanent architectural objects – one day, any of them could undergo a reversal or a transgression. There is no place that couldn't be used by different interest groups, marking the familiar and fully-developed cityscapes with completely new codes and messages. Indeed, city life means not so much living in the buildings as living in these changes and events. This also means the changing of the identities of districts in the course of time, or to be more exact, lots of identities through lots of different consumers. . . . Every object or place has its own virtuality which is coexisting with it and can actualise in the course of time. The actualisation, however, needn't always happen in the same way, but differently each and every time. Actualisation is a repetition, but it's the repetition of the different.[3]

Inspired by *A User's Guide to Tallinn*, I tried to approach the city by relating microscale situational ethnographies with comparative historical processes. The research underscores how Tallinn is characterised by the interplay between what has not been demolished and the emergent. Not surprisingly, urban planning in Tallinn took place without a master plan for a whole decade after the country regained its independence, since the city's Soviet master plan was declared obsolete without there being a new one right away (Feldman 2000). The result was that 'the city grew one piece after another . . . following an island logic, being composed of different unrelated chunks which in some cases had already been separated from each other historically' (Kurg 2009b, 38).

The transformation of Tallinn into a modern city began in the 1890s, after the construction of the railway and along with the construction of industries in the suburbs. The railway brought the modern world to Tallinn in the form of factories, schools, theatres, stores, workers' strikes and barracks. The first city plan dates from a competition organised in 1913 and won by Finnish architect Eliel Saarinen. Delays, war and regime changes kept Saarinen's plan from being implemented. In the 1930s, there was a new plan to develop the city centre, once again interrupted by regime changes and war. By 1944, 52 per cent of the residential space of Tallinn had been destroyed, so in the subsequent years, a new Stalinist quarter was built and working-class neighbourhoods expanded. Yet Soviet projects showed preferences for the suburbs of the city, where they could develop their planning ideas from scratch. From the 1960s, prefabricated apartment blocks (designed to last 50 years) were developed in Tallinn, first in Mustamäe, then Õismäe and finally in Lasnamäe, which remained uncompleted as their financing and political will to complete them disappeared with the end of state socialism.

A dark side of the modernisation of Tallinn might be the demolition of wooden houses, accentuated in the late 1970s by the construction of infrastructure and buildings for the Moscow Olympic sailing events. Current landmarks of the city date from that period, such as the Pirita road, Linnahall, Postimaja, the TV tower and the Olümpia hotel. The 1990s brought a financial district to the city, and in the 2000s, half a dozen shopping malls. The result is a conglomerate of small historical areas, as the city has never been completed in any period (Jagodin 2012).[4] During the last decades, the city has evolved as a capital, keeping cosiness yet losing a certain naïveté. Despite sustained efforts at erasure, Tallinn conserves many socialist features, in the form of ornaments, buildings and even entire Soviet modernist projects such as Mustamäe, Lasnamäe and Õismäe. However, it was not only housing but a new urban order and system of values that were also brought to Tallinn through Soviet planning and architecture, with their own notion of normality and cleanliness, as well as with delusions, repression, dirt and deviation (Kurg 2007).

The associations given to each of the three projects (Mustamäe, Lasnamäe and Õismäe) were, however, different, depending on the period in which they were built. Perhaps the best example to see this evolution or divergence is to compare the book and the film of *Autumn Ball*. The novel was published by Mati Unt in 1979, with the story taking place in Mustamäe, the first block-building project in the Estonian capital, starting in the 1960s and seen at the time as an attractive location since it offered many conveniences, such as warm water and central heating. Unt dedicates part of his novel to reflect on this location, a copy without an original behind. In this respect, Epp Annus (2015) describes *Autumn Ball* as the first manifestation of postmodernism in Estonian literature. Annus notes, for instance, that there is a lot of looking and watching in the novel, but little walking, and that the existence of lit windows can be taken as a lens through which to observe life.[5]

The film *Autumn Ball* was directed by Veiko Õunpuu in 2007. The action takes place, however, in Lasnamäe (figure 5.5), a similar residential satellite district, yet initiated in the late 1970s and stopped in 1991; initially, it was built with the aim of providing housing to the builders and factory workers involved in the construction of infrastructure for the 1980 Olympic Games and mostly inhabited by Russian speakers. But if Mustamäe was characterised by an optimistic and positive attitude from the beginning (being the place where couples just married moved), the construction of Lasnamäe appeared as a negative project in the eyes of locals, considered as 'placeless', grimy, oppressive, 'a tumor' and 'a huge centre of immigrants' (Viires 2003). For many Estonians, Lasnamäe is considered an uncomfortable reminder of the Soviet occupation, a sort of 'imperial debris' (Stoler 2013). Not surprisingly, Lasnamäe is shown in

Fig. 5.5 Lasnamäe. Source: Anne Vatén, 2013.

Õunpuu's film as an alienating urban space, where people happen to live with little interaction with the surroundings.

In her work about how people enact national identities in diaspora spaces, sociologist Maarja Saar has noted that to live in Lasnamäe implies an open negotiation of how to be Estonian. One of her examples is this interview with a 22-year-old ethnic Estonian woman who had recently moved to Lasnamäe:

> When you see youth in the city, I am quite sure I can tell which people are from Lasnamäe. This slutty attitude, and especially the girls dressed like Russian chicks, cheapness, this comes from Lasnamäe. Arrogant attitude, dirty words. For Russians, it is normal to wear a lot of makeup and shoes with leopard skin. I think youth in Lasnamäe are so Russianised, being in gangs, hip-hop culture, acting rowdy. (Saar 2010, 70)

In this way Saar concludes that not only identity but also places thought of as not-Estonia must be reimagined if integration is to occur.

A copy without an original behind

The built environment is one of the main legacies of socialism and its ideology of dwelling (Buchli 1999; Fehérváry 2013; Murawski 2018). For the Soviet regime, architecture and urban planning were considered to be important instruments of social engineering. To that end, socialist states adopted many modernist design and planning principles, so that the socialist city is characterised by visual monotony, compactness, grand scale of public projects, infrastructural thinking, oversupply of industrial and undersupply of commercial functions, and special typologies such as *mikrorayons*, boulevards, memorials, metros, high buildings and social condensers (Czepczynski 2008; Hirt 2013; Murawski 2018). The beautification of these cities was then a lower priority than public health and social equality, and central planning was monocentric, functional, strictly zoned, with mass housing favouring residential mixing and meant to provide equal access to transport, recreation and public services (Szelenyi 1996).

Socialist ideology emphasised industrialisation and mass housing as vehicles for progress and modernisation. Urban areas were particularly seen as key spaces of socialism, where the design of the cityscape was intended to forge new forms of social relations (Stenning 2005). Many of the objectives expected of the Soviet housing project were fulfilled, such as reshaping of the way of living (*byt'*) and forging a citizenship connected to the state. Later, the restitution of policies and elimination of price subsidies, reprivatisation and enhancement of trade resulted in deplanning, diversification of housing supply and a growing income differentiation within Estonian society, turning the Soviet planning into 'a brilliant failure' (Varga-Harris 2015, 1).

Ideology does not exist in just linguistic form; it also appears in material structures. Architecture acts like a prism: ideas shape and are deflected from architecture and infrastructure, motivating inferences and interpretations, serving as practical models out of space (Humphrey 2005). The reinforced discontinuity within the cityscape has not been the result of random architectural choices, but of particular decisions and factors such as neoliberal policies and the embrace of new values, which followed a sort of anticontinuity strategy. The withdrawal of state control and regulations, postmodern ideas and eclecticism, the global opening, the search for 'shocking' differences and exclusiveness, and the entry of private investors – with their individual likes – into urban life led to a bizarre hybridity of postsocialist spaces and polarising consequences, contributing to the redundant coexistence and semantic contradictions within the cityscape (Hirt 2012).

In Estonia, housing was privatised primarily to the prewar owners; centralised state planning shifted towards neoliberal economy, and a different power balance between private ownership and municipal policies was established. This produced changes in the cityscape with new dispersions and concentrations, new uses and occupations, giving rise also to questions about how to defend public interest in this new context. Postsocialist transformations multiplied a series of polarisations, while housing dynamics expose shapes that are at once mixed and fragmented, as the residential mobility of privileged groups forcefully confronts the relative immobility of the lower social strata (Marcińczak, Gentile and Stępniak 2013). Mostly, people with low income were the ones who suburbanised because of the oversupply of flats in the periphery created by the Russian-speaking residents leaving Estonia. But people with high incomes also moved to suburbs, in their case, to newly constructed buildings – following the pursuit of a dream of a single-family house with a private garden. Different classes then moved into different areas, being integrated differently into urban life (Leetma and Tammaru 2007).

Postsocialist transformations have accentuated the sense of an urban archipelago, which is deeper than the logic of 'winners' and 'losers', or urban segregation and economic inequalities. The appropriation of public spaces for private uses, the extension of spatial enclosures and suburbanisation also involves a reconfiguration of private and public responsibilities. Abrupt changes in postsocialist cities reveal the imperatives of liberalisation and the effects of globalisation in an intensified form, denoting diversity instead of uniformity (Bodnár 2000). Once Estonia regained independence, the subsequent processes of privatisation and changes in ownership had a strong impact on Tallinn's urban space. The most important part of this process of political legitimisation was legal continuity with the first Republic of Estonia (1918–40); thus the properties nationalised in 1940 were returned to their prewar owners. Likewise, and on a symbolic level, there was 'historical' pressure to erase from the city any physical representations of the Soviet era. The economic changes of the mid-nineties also gave rise to a building boom in Tallinn, which led to the construction of a number of 'business towers' and expansive shopping malls. As Kurg explains:

> The changes were also easily accomplished and readily accepted due to the sharp conscious break with the demonised past. Deregulation, which coincided with ongoing land reform, left the municipality of Tallinn with less property than ever before. (Kurg 2006a, 48)

What time is this place?

When I meet people abroad who have been to Tallinn, they often tell me that they loved the city. I usually respond with two questions: When did you go to Tallinn? Did you manage to get out from the old town? It requires an effort to step aside from the tourist hordes, particularly during the summer season. The influx of international visitors to the old town brought both positively and negatively perceived changes, such as the renovation of old buildings, development of retail and recreation services, a cosmopolitan atmosphere, street congestion, banalisation and commercialisation of historic areas, segregation and so on. The social isolation of the old town has also been intensified, as it has become an open-air shopping mall and a theme park for tourism.

In Tallinn, there has been an acceleration of landscape development in the last decades, facilitated by deindustrialising processes, a neglect of modernist architecture and the extension of spaces of intensive leisure and consumption. Accordingly, many modernist landscapes and architecture have vanished, or are about to disappear, producing an epistemological disruption and a sense of mismatch between societal and personal time. If one asks the question of what time is this place in Tallinn, we might find a wide diversity of answers, depending on the positioning of the person towards urban memory and his or her projections towards the future.

As other Eastern European cities, Tallinn has been conditioned by perennial new beginnings, which resulted in gaps and a pattern of discontinuity in the cityscape (rather than through layers of sedimentation and linear change). Historical breaks are still characterising social patterns and the material culture in Tallinn, a city which has even received different names depending on the power ruling the territory at the time.[6] Past elements and material traces condition any forthcoming transformation within the city, creating a particular sensibility and facilitating small variations to produce great changes in the totality. In Tallinn, these inconsistencies and casualties also belong to a dense unitary fractal, in which certain patterns (regular and irregular) tend to repeat. To follow Johann Arnason's line of thought (2005), there are regions and societies where the sequence of patterns of transformation can be reconstructed in terms of an internal logic, whereas in other cases, like Eastern Europe, the sequence depends to a great extent on historical and geopolitical contexts. This exposure to externalities manifests itself in the cityscape as a response to the constant need for foreign investment, central plans of industrialisation, military occupations, dependence of tourism (in 2014, 34 per cent of the alcohol sold in Estonia was bought by Finnish tourists), and the succession of political ruptures that made the city become a capital, then a province, then a capital, and finally both a capital and a province.

We can see this localisation of foreign patterns in the accumulation of projects that would have been completed differently in other international contexts, or more precisely in the sedimentation of their remnants, as they are often unfinished or neglected, yet linger on, pointing at conflicting temporalities. For instance, there is a building behind the house of Tatari 21b, a construction stopped at the end of World War II and never completed. Also, of the half-dozen street signs that still remain from the Soviet time, such as the one in Koidu Street, where it is possible to see not only the Russian past through the Cyrillic letters, but also its later erasure or whitewashing (figure 5.6).

Another example would be the Maarjamäe memorial complex, a cemetery and a monumental landscape design in which around 3,000 bodies are buried (mostly Germans, but also Russians, Finns and Estonians). First, Soviet soldiers were buried there. Then, in 1941, the Nazis dug the bodies out and buried their own soldiers on the site. Two decades later, an

Fig. 5.6 Koidu Street with the erased Cyrillic letters. Source: Author, 2013.

obelisk was erected there to commemorate the Soviet troops killed in 1918; in 1975 a series of sculptures and architectonic elements (carved hands, a flock of birds, aircraft landing runway, ten symbolic graves, and so on) were added to remember the Soviet defenders of Tallinn against the advancing Nazis in 1941. In 1998, another symbolic layer was added, with sets of triple granite crosses in the style common to German World War II military cemeteries. The final layer to the memorial has been entropically given by nature itself, since decades of official neglect of the site are visible in the crumbling structures and grass covering the mound. As a result, the Maarjamäe memorial is nowadays visited as a site of alterity and as an engaging landscape, instead of being taken as a space for mourning and remembrance.

In Tallinn, these past elements remain as a matter of an unfinished world in a space in motion, combining highly transitional places with microhistorical remnants that oscillate between monumentality and rubble. The last example is the Alexander Nevsky Orthodox Cathedral, which stands on a prominent site of the old town with a magnetic presence. Nevsky Cathedral is another remnant of a bygone era, yet not a plaque or a statue, but a landmark of contested memories performed every day and upon which ghosts, fears and hopes are continuously projected. For the Orthodox population the cathedral continues to serve as a place of worship, and for Estonian nationalists it has been the target of *ressentiment* for a century. 'Estonians do not like it. And yet there it stands, restored in all its provocative beauty and grandeur' (Della Dora and Sooväli 2009,

Fig. 5.7 A wedding at Nevsky Cathedral. Source: Author, 2013.

217). And yet, Nevsky Cathedral also constitutes one of the most visited tourist heritage attractions in the city (figure 5.7).

The design, maintenance and materiality of legacies can speed up or slow down the process of wasting. The phenomenon of spatial degradation and upgrading was encapsulated by Lynch with the aphorism 'What time is this place?' (Lynch 1976). Past formations persist over social changes in their materiality, reminding us that processes of transformation are not totally independent from former traces and regimes of knowledge, hence the need for this study to grasp a longer time frame. Further, if we ignore the way the actual saturation, redundancy and amalgamation were produced, the elements that occupy Tallinn seem to merely coexist without order, harmony or design.

Concluding considerations

By paying attention to the perception of historical accumulation in urban spaces and how how these temporalities are interrelated in a multiplicity, the chapter has given an account of the way the meaning of various periods and the experience of time change along with the material form of the city and the uses of the space, as well as the relationship between its parts and the whole. The research co-related the evolution of legacies and visual signs with the transformations in the use of space, of the 'users' themselves, and of the urban memories of the city. Through multiple examples, I argue that history, sociality, materiality and urban memories had to be thought of as entangled entities. Different pasts and an array of scale effects intrude on the present and in the urban space, producing particular urban assemblages and specific forms of material culture such as amalgamations and sutures. In short, cityscapes are perceived in the moment and in the process, made up of multiple beginnings and endings, contested and volatile. Historical breaks and past transformations are still of importance today, conditioning social patterns, the material culture of this city and the urban memories formed.

6
Narva, a centre out there

The political periphery?

> Beeline, Tele2, Beeline, Tele2 . . . once I arrived at Narva, these two
> phone operators from Russia and from Estonia – started to alter-
> nate without asking. They impelled me to turn off the automatic net
> detection of the mobile phone and make a strategic choice, which
> was not based on any logic of belonging but simply in order to save
> money. In practical terms, it meant acknowledging border-effects
> and activate the manual mode of the phone, and of my mind too.

This anecdote from my field notes reveals how close Russia is, and illustrates
what it means, in practice, to be in a borderland. Narvians cross civilisations
by walking; they decide to stick to one culture or another, or to both, to use
one language or another, or both, depending on practical, contextual and
seemingly banal reasons. Overall, borderlands are places of contradiction,
interstitial zones of displacement and disembedding; there we are immersed
in a process of constant translation of models of behaviour, cultural codes
and lifestyles, without totally converging on any of them. Borderlanders
appear thus as agents of hybridity, challenging homogenising foundations and arrangements, melting fixed definitions, calling for new categories. It is in this sense that historian Oscar Martínez (1994) presents those
who inhabit the border as mixers, as mediators. For borderlanders, the cer-
tainties and norms of the social order are shown as contingent and performative; they answer identitary questions based on tactical decisions, rather
than simply following established classifications and forms of cohesion.

Narva is a good example of a juncture that both separates and unites.
This city marks the border between the Russian Federation, NATO and the

European Union, and stands as a contested place of continuous negotiation and translation of bigger forms and wider processes. As much as borders divide and discriminate, they also enable stable relationships. Indeed, borders can be considered as an intricate part of the European identity; they do not necessarily entail the distantiation of a community from its neighbour, but also a formal connection that may provide opportunities for engagement across boundaries.

Borderlands bring to the fore heterogeneous narratives and imaginaries, introducing liminal elements to the process of identity construction. Indeed, identity in the borderlands appears often as both incomplete and continuously differentiating. It also entails a strong performative character, as the hilarious exhibition of St George ribbons by Narvians shows (figure 6.1).[1] A walk in Narva makes evident the polycentricity of Estonian society. There we can notice how five distinctive scale effects were constructed in a relatively brief period of time: Soviet, Estonian, European, Russian and 'local'. As noted by Kaiser and Nikiforova, 'each of these scale effects has been naturalised and sedimented through everyday citational practices in Narva, and each set of discursive practices, in turn, intersects with the others, constructing, contesting and reconfiguring the scalar hierarchies produced' (2008, 559).

Fig. 6.1   St George Ribbon exhibited in Narva. Source: Author, 2015.

Globalisation, tourism, technologies of information, transnational-ism, financial flows . . . in spite of all that, people in Narva recount how the world became smaller for them in 1991, rather than a space of fluid-ity and diversity (de Montesquiou 2010). Anthropologist Daphne Berdahl described borderlands as a 'place of intense and inflexible lucidity', whereby existing social and power relations are deeply enmeshed. In her ethnography carried out at the borderland that divided Germany for half a century, Berdahl noted (1999) that the disappearance of social bound-aries was not followed by the disappearance of the symbolic ones, but by an intensification of them. In the case of Narva, the opposite process occurred – people had to learn how to live separately. They were forced to deal with a border that was not there in their childhood or when they moved into the city; so since 1991, Narva has been undergoing an exam-ination of its heritage, as a form of resilience of local identification.

The political intensity of the border is also demonstrated in the capacity of its dwellers to reinforce, resist or undermine state power almost simultaneously in their everyday actions; also in the redundancy of ele-ments semantically contradictory, which creates a curious cosmological pastiche. For instance, in tourist shops we can encounter souvenirs depict-ing Nicholas II, Estonian folkloric apparel, Orthodox icons and Lenin next to each other (Brednikova 2007, 53). We can also visit a Swedish lion commemorating the Scandinavian period of the city, a Tsarist-era monu-ment to those who fell during the Great Northern War, a restored World War II German military cemetery, a White Russian military cemetery and a Soviet memorial, all of them on the same road (Kattago 2008). Eventually, this array of different narrations of memory and society coexisting along-side one another exposes the limits of the 'nationalising' state (Smith and Burch 2011). Whilst the sovereignty of the Estonian Republic is enacted in Narva through the display of flags on public buildings and the use of the Estonian language in official documents, we find ourselves surrounded by Soviet-era traces (e.g., the statue of Lenin in the courtyard of the cas-tle) or symbols of Russianness (in a bust of Pushkin erected in 1999 on a street dedicated to the poet).

Walking on Tuleviku Street (figure 6.2), not far from the centre of Narva, I asked six locals about the meaning of this Estonian street name. The first five openly recognised that they had no clue about it and are ignorant of the Estonian language. The sixth, a middle-aged woman, demanded half a minute to think and unconvincingly answered: 'I believe it means "Street of our past"'. *Tuleviku* in Estonian simply means 'of the future'. This example shows the sense of being separated, in a distinct milieu. Drawing on descriptions, formal and informal interviews, two

Fig. 6.2   Tuleviku Street. Source: Author, 2013.

round tables and a review of literature on Narva, I examine cultural constructions that give meanings to the boundaries between nations, as well
as bordering affects and material, and symbolic specificities associated
with 'living in-between'. By focusing on day-to-day narratives, experiences
and imaginaries in Narva, I aimed to study how people living in this city
make sense of the place in which they live, deal with the proximity of the
border and negotiate post-Soviet identity construction.[2]

As I found, in Narva, 'Estonians' are often referred to as neighbours,
rather than as belonging to one and the same family. Narvians rather
appear as a separated community – they were divorced from a previous
family without finding a new one. As a result, an autonomous space-time
has been consolidated in Narva, which functions as a mediation between
bigger cultural worlds and political powers, and which affects relations
and representations within Estonian society as a whole.

'Rare people are those who do not have borders'[3]

One of the things that surprised me the most in Narva was the striking
normality in which the inhabitants of the city described the proximity of
the border; also that the residents praise the status quo and are afraid of

changes in a city crossed by the EU–Russia border and which is affected by unemployment and decay. For instance, students Vika and Natasha (both 18 years old) showed a certain astonishment at my questions about how the border is felt, and presented their answers as self-evident. During our conversation, Vika and Natasha agreed with each other's statements, nodding their heads. For them, the frontier does not condition their everyday life, they even claim not to notice it: 'We don't feel it. We live a normal life', said Natasha. 'I don't know what people think there in Tallinn or in Tartu. I don't go often to any of these places. I spent all my life in Narva and I like it', added Vika with a challenging smile.

A few hours later, I visited a club called Geneva; roughly 200 people were there but seemingly nobody spoke Estonian. Instead, I heard English, Spanish, German, Portuguese and predominantly Russian. Most of them were not tourists, but 'expats', working for a hydroelectric plant managed by Alstom. Vladimir is a Russian citizen. He also works in Alstom and in his free time goes fishing on the Narva River between the castles. 'There's a border. That's all' ('граница есть, но все'), then he takes ten seconds and adds: 'Of course it makes a difference. We all are Russians, but it seems like someone needs a border'.

Vitaly is a Russian citizen who likes fishing and has no interest in seeing what is there on the other side: 'I already know it: alcoholism and unemployment. If I want to know about Russia I watch the TV and see what's going on in Moscow and St Petersburg', he says provocatively. Vitaly chats endlessly, probably motivated by seeing me writing down what he says. Then he stops and comments in a mannered way: 'Look at both castles; there one sees where civilisation begins and where it ends'. Volodia also likes fishing, yet he has a different view on the topic from Vitaly. While changing his clothes in a sort of metal booth in front of the castles, he remarks that 'on the other side there are much more berries, mushrooms and fishes. The forest is much richer in resources, so the border is just uncomfortable. If there were no border, it would be possible to create employment there too, and not just here, how it currently happens. Do you know? It takes an hour to cross it'.

I also conversed with a few people in front of the border administration.[4] For instance, Viktor comments: 'There's a border, that's all. Life here is normal. Why should it influence our lives? I go there from time to time. I still have relatives on the other side'. Tamara was coming out from the border control. She lives in Ivangorod and finds it 'very positive that the border exists because people should be controlled. This is not Africa'. Also Valentina, a woman over 70 years old, accepts the existence of the border as something inevitable: 'What should we do? We've got used to it. Before we were together; now separated. The destiny is thought up by high intelligent minds'.

Roughly 100,000 Estonian Russians carry a grey passport that reads 'undetermined citizenship' and labels them as 'alien'. The Estonian government uses the category 'undetermined citizenship', instead of 'non-citizens' or 'stateless people', which implies that citizenship is not absent, but yet to be determined, and that this person will have the right to make claims on a state. Nonetheless, this status complicates getting a job and does not allow people in this category to vote in national elections. Most of the grey passport holders are elderly people born in the USSR (hence they did not cross any border). Furthermore, Estonia's language policy, citizen laws and economic measures (deindustrialisation, privatisation, retreat of state support) have ensured that members of the Russian-speaking community find themselves with lower incomes, higher HIV, criminal and unemployment rates and lower life expectancy than the Estonian-speaking ones (Kasearu and Trumm 2008; Kus 2011; Leping and Toomet 2008).[5]

The disappearance of personal and economic stability in Narva, accompanied by a continuous emphasis on ancestry and language in Estonian political discussions, left the majority of Russian speakers outside the public space. For instance, the implementation of the requirement to have ancestors in Estonia before 1940 or to pass language exams turns the integration of the Russian speaking minority into 'a challenge' (Hallik 2002). Arkadi sits on a bench on the hill and ironically presents himself as an 'alien': 'I speak Russian and my passport is grey. So language is my identity'. Tatyana sits at the upper platform on the hill and looks to the horizon, thus to Russia: 'I don't go there because I have nothing to do there anymore. I don't care; I'm too old for that. And for me it's easy to go to Russia (she has a grey passport), but I cannot travel in Europe'. 'Nobody needs us', laments Galina, a retired teacher who sits on the viewpoint on the hill. *But is Narva not Europe?* 'Narva is neither Europe, nor Russia; Narva is the border', Tatyana concludes. Walking around the frontier with two friends, Patrick and Dan, I keep thinking about these words. Tatyana is probably right. Narva and Ivangorod are neither Europe nor Russia; they belong to the border and create a distinct milieu with its own normality and way of constructing identity. These two cities are monuments in themselves, but also a kind of laboratory in which categories such as 'Europe', 'West' and 'East' are appropriated and reshaped by ordinary citizens in their everyday lives (Pfoser 2017).

In my first visit to Narva, I stayed at the Centre Hotel, where Darya worked as a receptionist. I also asked her about how the proximity of the border is felt and how it conditions the everyday life of Narvians. 'We've got used to the border. And borders are also a business', she replied without any hesitation. *Hmmm . . . won't you get more tourists by opening the border?* 'Then we'll get not only tourists, but also immigrants. The best for Narva would be to open a corridor and let tourists enjoy both castles at once', Darya suggested. To me, it is paradoxical to hear this in a city that has been entirely repopulated by immigrants. Quite probably, and as the Estonian historian Kaarel Vanamölder commented after reading an early draft of this chapter, Narvians have a distinct discourse indoors and outdoors, to which I would ask, is this an expression of the Soviet *habitus* or a common safety practice in borderlands?

Languages are a vehicle of revealing but also of concealing, allowing people to live in different historical dimensions and memory regimes. In the case of Estonia, the Russian language gives access to other cultural worlds, in which the media plays an important role in reinforcing certain values and alternative visions of the past and present. In recent years, there has been a step back with regard to the politicisation of the Russian language; not in the sense of claiming equality and better integration, but of making use of language as a geopolitical tool. For instance, when I asked locals to comment on the Russian annexation of Crimea and the war in the Donbass, they all reproduced the version of the facts promoted from Moscow, nonetheless introducing certain nuances. 'You all in Europe are ignoring the suffering of the Ukrainian people. Not only you are not conveniently informed, but you are not interested in knowing the truth', Vladimir said to me, and became passionate on the topic while smoking a cigarette at the entrance of his house. *But could something similar happen in Narva?* 'No, here it is too late to claim for independence', he concluded. 'In this city there is no separatism', commented Anatoly, 'Nationalism is just limited to a few morons. There won't be any problem, meanwhile Tallinn treats us well'. Anatoly believed that 'Kiev is to be blamed for what is going on in Ukraine. We can see that there is separatism in other countries, like in Scotland and Catalonia, yet they are not bombed for that'.

In their precarious ethereal existence of migration, we can see lots of birds crossing the sky of Narva, crossing political frontiers before the dark tunnel of winter comes, as well as Russian citizens crossing the border to buy products such as milk, cheese or salami, which have been forbidden in their country as a political response to the sanctions introduced by Western countries for the military annexation of Crimea. Those waiting in the queue hold closed bags (to avoid border guards checking the products) and are reticent to give any explanations or statements. Economic activity in the borderlands tests the power of authority structures, the boundaries of law and the limits of global processes: 'Borders are economic resources to be consumed like other resources in a variety of ways . . . shopping at the border is part of the process of shopping the border itself' (Donnan and Wilson 1999, 122).

Standing next to the bridge, Vladimir was smiling while looking at the people passing through the border. He is a Russian speaker with Estonian citizenship, and ironically said: 'They never complain. I think that the political agitation promoted by the TV has convinced them all'. A year later, when I came back to Narva, the fishermen were not as talkative as in my previous visit. When I went to the peninsula between the castles to talk about Ukraine they replied with disdain: 'Another journalist' or 'We are good in Europe. Nothing more to say'. Next to the former site of the administration of the border there is a tiny kiosk which used to be crowded but has lost some clients with the redesign of the infrastructure. Inside the booth, talking through a small window, a sympathetic lady sells a bit of everything, from hamburgers to cigarettes and newspapers. She became tense, however, when I asked about Ukraine: 'My husband cannot stand Putin. But in my case, I do not believe any of them. What I want is all to remain the same'. This statement might sound paradoxical in a region that has lost thousands of inhabitants in the last decades, and counts the lowest salaries and birth rates and the highest unemployment in Estonia; yet it has its logic: as the seller says, 'all the time, politics forces us to change. We are tired of that'.

Brokenness can be contagious

Narva used to be a prestigious industrial city, but experienced hardships while entering into the twenty-first century. Nowadays, Narva is presented as the third city of Estonia, whilst in Russia Ivangorod is just a peripheral village. In Narva's recent history, we could point out three particularities: its frontier location, migrant processes and its industrial activity. The Kreenholm factory has been part of the city since 1857 (figure 6.3), located on the western bank of the Narva River (an area formerly called Juhkentali). Founded by Baron Ludwig Knoop, Kreenholm soon became the largest textile factory in the Russian Empire. By the end of the nineteenth century, the population of Narva was 30,000 inhabitants, of whom 5,400 were employed at the textile factory (*Eesti Entsüklopeedia* 1994).[6] In the late 1980s, Kreenholm employed over 10,000 workers and was able to

Fig. 6.3 Kreenholm, 1958. Source: V. Samussenko, Rahvusarhiivi filmiarhiiv.

export its goods, not having to rely on approvals from the corresponding ministry in Moscow.

In 1992, following the break-up the USSR, the company was renamed AS Kreenholm Manufaktuur and impelled to find new export markets beyond the former Soviet Republics. Finally, in 1995 the Swedish Borås Wäfveri (BW) acquired the factory, hoping to achieve cost synergies in its production. Yet decisions such as dividing the structure of production into eight separated entities and unpopular replacements of the head of the factory led to the decline of Kreenholm. Other factors did not help growth in global markets, such as the financial problems of the Swedish matrix, a poor reputation for buying cotton produced with Uzbekistan's child labour (Marimekko cancelled a contract because of this) and the Bronze Night events related to the relocation of a war monument in Tallinn (damaging its presence in the Russian market). But the main reason argued by the owners was the difficulty of competing with Asian producers.

Kreenholm's bankruptcy is an example of late modern practices of production, in the form of financial speculation, technocratic management, real estate interests and industrial delocalisation to Asia. In 2007, the firm sold all its real estate (32 ha) to Narva Gate (a company connected to BW) for €22.37 million.[7] The production was gradually reduced and, despite having worked on a profit margin for many years and receiving financial support from the World Bank, the activities of Kreenholm ended

Fig. 6.4   Ruins of the Kreenholm factory. Source: Author, 2015.

in 2011 (Vissak 2014). The deindustrialisation of Narva, a problem whose cause is postsocialist, made the city even more vulnerable to global economic crises and hardened the negative image and prejudices against its population. Accordingly, in Narva we can find that the 'anti' is not directed towards the Soviet past but rather towards the global present.

Nowadays, the old brick buildings of Kreenholm stand alone, naked, haunted, as physical markers underlining decline (figure 6.4). All the machinery, furniture and documents have been taken away and those buildings not considered 'historical' were demolished. The ruins of Kreenholm appear both political and affective; they not only embody the absence of industrial activity but also negligence and disinvestment in Narva. In a way, this city can be considered the Estonian Detroit; its empty apartments and crumbling buildings are reminders of what has occurred to the social and material heritage during the last decades, they transmit disaffection and generate feelings of marginality. These are the working effects of disrepair, operating through aesthetics, the spread of affects, and modes of state engagement (Chu 2014). Brokenness can be also considered a form of peripherality and dispossession, a situation of being excluded from collectives that previously provided social and economic frames (Humphrey 2002b).

The way central governments treat border cities vacillates between care and abandonment, without any middle term. Both castles appear as relics enacting power; the Estonian one is repaired, the Russian semi-ruined. Both together look like a postcard, standing on a dramatic landscape. While walking on the promenade at night, we can hear voices and the sound of the TV and radio coming from the other side of the river. In the newly created promenade (around the bastions of the city), there is also a strong symbol of power and multiple and competing narratives of belonging. The project of repair and regeneration was funded by the EU and on the pavement along the promenade there are written the names of all the EU members and the years of accession. Two political messages seem to be clearly articulated through this: first, here is where the EU starts – this is in, there is out; second, look how the material standards are on this side of the border and compare. The restoration of administration buildings, infrastructures, parks and various tourist attractions in Narva seems to convey the sense that belonging to Europe is superior to belonging to Russia, demonstrating how the category of Europe has an enormous discursive force still (Dzenovska 2014).

Here, repair appears as a form of communication that connects people to the state. Both the negligence of Narva for decades and the current effort to repair it show that the city has been at the centre of Estonian politics since 1991. Tanel teaches history in Narva and jokes that the EU is the new empire interested in the city. He argues, however, that Brussels would have to invest more than money to make a difference here.[8] A recent symbolic case of repair in Narva has been Alexander's Cathedral.[9] Built in 1884 and named in honour of the then Russian emperor, the church bell tower was destroyed in WWII and reconstructed only in 2008. Over €2.5 million of public funds (40 per cent coming from the EU) were spent to help restore the Lutheran church, which also acquired the status of cathedral. Part of the renovation cost was paid with a loan, however the congregation was unable to pay it back, and in 2015 Alexander's Cathedral went bankrupt and the repair work was left unfinished. After different rumours about the fate of the cathedral, in June 2016, the Estonian state and the Estonian Evangelical Lutheran Church (EELK) bought it for €375,000, half of which was paid by the state and half by EELK.

The exterior of the cathedral has been beautifully renovated and conditioned with lighting to illuminate it at night. Also, the bell tower is fully furnished, hosting a modest exhibition about the history of the building. The chapel, however, remains in a state of repair, held with construction beams and exposing the auratic patina of a difficult past. Religious services have not stopped in the meanwhile, yet the Narva City Hall and Estonian Ministry of Culture are exploring different possibilities for adding new uses to the building. In this light, the department of interior architecture of the Estonian Academy of Arts has organised a workshop to study how to make use of the cathedral as a concert hall. In the public presentation of the results, organised on 9 March 2018 in both Russian and Estonian languages, the chairman of the city council, Aleksandr Jefimov, stated that 'this building is a presentation card of Narva, representing its culture and history'. I also had the opportunity to talk to the EELK pastor Vladimir Batuhtin, who commented that 'the repair shows a normal relationship to the things that are own, and a will to maintain legacies over centuries. . . . For us the visit of these students is interesting, they are like a mirror where we see ourselves'. After noticing my accent, Pastor Batuhtin asked about my opinion about Catalunya. Not convinced with my diplomatic reply, he made explicit his support for the Catalan separatism, and argued that Europe should be organised as a confederation of regions, and not of nations, adding that such confederation might include current Russia too.

Another example of how the present is strongly intertwined with sensitivities generated in the past is the resonance acquired by the maquette of pre-1940 old town of Narva. Fjodor Šantsõn has created over twenty years a 1:100 scale model, a sort of miniature park exhibited in the former town hall (figures 6.5 and 6.6). The maquette shows a nonexisting city, a place without a place, a retro-utopia that serves nonetheless as a catalyst of affective place making (Mikula 2017). 'It is sad to work with something that it is lost', acknowledged Fjodor in one of our multiple encounters in the town hall. He started to prepare the layout in 1992, at home, rebuilding the town through the available photos, comparing locations in different seasons. In 2008, he was invited to bring the model to the town hall, and then, in 2015, he was given the highest Estonian award, the Order of the White Star, by President Ilves. 'Homeland is where your roots and dead people are. Mine are in Belarus, despite having lived all my life in Narva', shares Fjodor.

Šantsõn started to work as an electrician in a school of Narva, where he built his first model, a palace for children to play during the winter. However, the first thought of building models emerged in the early eighties, while he was visiting the Museum of Architecture in Leningrad and seeing reproductions of the Nevsky Prospekt.

For some people, the maquette has meanings that I did not plan to generate. For instance, every year there are visitors from Sweden

Fig. 6.5 Fjodor Šantsõn and the model of Narva. Source: Marika Agu, October 2017.

Fig. 6.6 Fjodor Šantsõn in his workshop. Source: Marika Agu, October 2017.

who come as if this were a site of pilgrimage. Some of them are originally from Narva, bring photos with them, comment about how the city was when they were born. . . . Some of them even say that in 1939 when they left, that street or that façade wasn't exactly like in the maquette. I always reply that my maquette reproduces Narva as it was at the beginning of the twentieth century, not in a specific year, but there are also other kinds of comment. For example, a couple of years ago one of the original Narvians told me that 'now a Russian is doing more for the Estonian identity than most of Estonians'. . . . Also a woman who lives in Pärnu came to visit the maquette with her granddaughter and told her, 'look, that was the window of my room eighty years ago'. . . . For me [the visitors] are important because of their archives too; some of them emigrated even to Australia, and private collectors do not always facilitate access to old documents, they want money, so the people of the diaspora who visit the model are an important source of information.

An alien city

Already in the early thirteenth century, the Danish kingdom established a military defence on the site of Narva to protect the commercial routes that flowed into Russian lands. This wall was turned into a castle and over the centuries different Western powers dominated, such as the Teutonic order, Livonian knights and the Swedish monarchy. The name, Narva, comes from the river that crosses these borderlands and means 'agitated waters'. In 1492, the Tsar Ivan III (Prince of Moscow) ordered the construction of a stronghold on the eastern side of the river. Near the walls, a settlement was created, which received the prosaic name of Ivangorod (City of Ivan). These borderlands have witnessed continuous conquerors and great battles, such as the one involving King Karl XII of Sweden and Peter I of Russia. The first railway constructed in Estonia (completed in 1870) connected Narva to St Petersburg and Tallinn. Then, in August 1890, Narva was the site of a meeting between German Kaiser Wilhelm II and Russian Tsar Alexander III.[10]

In the aftermath of the empire's collapse, the newly independent Republic of Estonia gained control over the whole town of Narva, including Ivangorod. The line of that frontier was mutually recognised by Soviet Russia and Estonia in the Tartu Peace Treaty of 1920. During World War II, Estonia was occupied by both Nazi Germany and Soviet Russia. Indeed, Narva was one of the front lines to the point that artillery (mostly Soviet) devastated 98.2 per cent of the buildings (Weiss-Wendt 1997). After the war, the Soviet government did not allow the former inhabitants of Narva to return home, and decided not to reconstruct the baroque old town of Narva, but to rebuild it as a modern socialist city (Brüggemann 2004). As Narva's fate epitomises, the twentieth century has been a period of intense construction and destruction. We can see it for instance in the latent absence of the old Narva and in the variation of the number of inhabitants in the town:

1939: 22,400 inhabitants
1945: 6,600
1990: 82,200
2017: 57,130[11]

In the postwar period, Narva underwent a rapid industrialisation process and saw immigration of Russian-speaking workers from far away as well as neighbouring regions of the USSR. As pointed out by sociologist Elena Nikiforova (2004), the first wave of migration came for economic and political reasons. But gradually, Narva started to attract people also because of the relatively high living standard and easy access to new apartments. Later on, migration came as a chain, often pulled through relatives already living there, and, to a great extent, the city was regarded as an actually existing utopia of work and peace. Moreover, cities in the Soviet Union did more than merely accommodate residents' daily needs; they also planned to transform people's understanding of place and self, and link them to the Soviet project (Qualls 2009).

In the aftermath of the Soviet disintegration, the border came back to Narva and the population decreased to 65,000 inhabitants. Among the current Narvians, 96 per cent are Russian speakers, and half of them hold a Russian passport.[12] In the early 1990s, Narva, and the region of Ida-Virumaa overall, were identified as potential sources of secessionist politics. In July 1993, then mayor of Narva Vladimir Chuikin organised a referendum in order to make the district independent from Estonia. Of the residents, 54 per cent participated and 97 per cent opted to support secession. However, the Estonian Constitutional Court did not recognise the results.

During the Soviet era, to live in Narva was considered to be the 'near abroad', somehow mentally inhabiting Europe (de Montesquiou 2010, 47). The river functions as a mental border too, but the bordering effect goes beyond the line. As Peeter Tambu, former chief architect of Narva, acknowledges: 'Whenever I'm leaving Narva it seems to me that the border is somewhere near Jõhvi or Kohtla-Järve . . . it is another world'.[13] Also, Marika Alver, former director of the Narva art residency, has put it in a diasporic sense: 'Estonians in Narva are like Estonians in Toronto'.[14] Likewise, for many Narvians, 'Estonia' seems to be far away and they do not see the point of studying that language. This tells us something about the disparity between official representations and localised practices.

For many, the choice of citizenship was connected with future plans and life strategies, rather than by a definitive political position (Brednikova and Voronkov 1999). This is also noted by Nikiforova (2004), who argues that in Narva, identity seems to be not only based on abstract belonging but also related to practical questions and social networks, according to which future plans and daily life are organised. Some of my informants acknowledged that they have never been to Tallinn, demonstrating a border effect that goes beyond the frontier line. Likewise, people from other parts of Estonia have referred to Narva as an alien city. Asked about it, Narva-born art historian Elnara Taidre observes that: 'Many Estonians – especially the younger generation that have never been to the place – formed a view of Narva based only on information from the media and the collective repertoire of anecdotes . . . later I came to understand that such prejudices are shared not only by Estonians, but by Russians too'.[15] Elnara adds that she used to celebrate with a glass of champagne both the Russian and the Estonian new year, yet the family stood up for only the Estonian anthem. In this line, Estonian artist Eva Sepping, who is interested in public performances of nationalism, carried out an experiment on the last night of 2014. Sepping went to Narva on 31 December in order to video record the midnight fireworks of Narva and Ivangorod. As Sepping recounts, she had two basic questions in mind: would Narvians follow Moscow or Tallinn time for the fireworks? And which fireworks were bigger? On the first night of 2015, and surprisingly, there were almost no fireworks in Ivangorod, and those organised in Narva followed Tallinn time.

Borderlands have their own system of integration and exclusion which often functions parallel to or even apart from the general hegemonic order. Architect Kaja Pae finds that Narva is characterised by 'a super-abundance of character . . . and connections' (2011, 133–4). In spite of being three hours by car from both Tallinn and St Petersburg, the mental distance to these cities has changed in the last decades. If during the Soviet era Leningrad was considered a closer city, seen by many as one of the advantages of Narva, in recent years, the perspective of inhabitants turns towards Tallinn, while for Leningraders, Narva has become a gateway to the European Union (Nikiforova 2004, 154). Indeed, the new real estate project planned for the former Kreenholm factory is named 'Narva Gate' and marks Russians living in the Leningrad region as their target group. As Jaanus Mikk, chief executive of the firm acknowledges, 'the local people are the best because they are able to serve our potential clients in their own mother tongue' (cf. de Montesquiou 2010, 203).

In a workshop organised in Narva by the Estonian Centre of Architecture, participants asserted: 'Narva residents live in the city as if they were living in the countryside. They are not open, temperamental Russians but rather Russian-speaking Estonians' . . . 'For residents of Narva the capital is Tallinn but the president is Putin' . . . 'I'm bored in Narva. What could I do that wouldn't be boring here?' I took part in a roundtable to discuss these matters, and organised a second take of the discussion (both in 2017).[16] Ivan Sergejev, chief architect of the city, insists that emptiness entails also an opportunity. Instinctively, one would think that having all this space empty does not help local people to move on, yet the very emptiness might offer the chance to envision a new future and form of participation in the regeneration of the city (see also Pelkmans 2003). Narva itself has been conceived as a town under construction for almost a century, going through several traumatic ruptures. However, as Sergejev points out, local people are not simply afraid of changes but also afraid of the future, and tired of discourses about having potential. To this, Kristina Kallas, director of Narva College, adds that 'Estonians want to see potential in Narva, but they don't want to see the reality of Narva. . . . Because the reality, they don't like it, so that is why they are trying to draw the curtains on it and pretend that it doesn't exist'.

Professor Kallas also reflected on the limits of the vocabulary we use for analysing nation-states, giving the example of the terms 'national majority' and 'national minority': 'this vocabulary is not contemporary, and I think it confuses a lot . . . if someone asked me if I was a member of a minority or not, it's difficult to answer because sometimes I am and sometimes I'm not. In one way I am, because I was born in this region here, as an Estonian – so I was sort of a minority here, because everyone around was Russian. And then I moved to study in Tartu, and I felt like a minority there, because everyone was so Estonian there, and I felt Russian there, and now I'm back here in Narva, and I feel like a minority again. So it's like constantly floating in and out of this minority status'. Kallas concluded that the current complexity with regard to national identity and sense of belonging requires a redefinition of what it means to be an Estonian, a thought provocatively caught by Sergejev to reflect on how the Estonian government is more and more choosey about whom to take in and how this is correlated with a decreasing institutional responsibility towards citizens:

'I think it's really perverse though how we're entering into this era of e-residency. The real reason is that I think Estonia wants to choose its citizens, and that's essentially what's going on with the e-residency programme'.

Border cities or cities on the border?

Until 1991, Narva and Ivangorod lived one life despite being located in different republics. In Soviet times, the cities had common systems of transportation, power supply, telephone communication, sewerage and water purification. As pointed out in Jauhiainen and Pikner's (2009) study, changes within the water system in Narva and Ivangorod revealed the complexity of the transition process, in which diverse logics and manners coexisted and very different agents had to cooperate in order to supply key services. The economic activity of Narva has been affected by the setting of the border in many ways. As in other border cities, there are those who try to take advantage of the situation, for instance by smuggling tobacco, petrol or vodka. In 2008, a 2 km pipeline was discovered under the Narva River that pumped 6,200 litres of vodka across before being discovered.

Borders function in oxymoronic terms: they are temporarily forever. All boundaries are drawn relationally to create order out of chaos, entailing their own exceptions and violations (Douglas 1966). They are embedded in societies and encompass an arranging quality, generating specific meanings and affects, and making certain experiences and narratives more viable. For instance, the proximity of the border urges one to imagine how things are on the other side, how is the life of my neighbours elsewhere (figure 6.7). As in a Lefebvrian triad, borders are cartographically represented, abstractly conceptualised and practised in personal ways. Infrastructurally and symbolically, they confine and configure the choices made in our everyday lives, urging a different search for meaning. Even if these social infrastructures are contingent and dependent upon temporarily produced entanglements, they influence the way we produce other orders, interconnections, as well as personal perceptions and interpretations. But if it is the bordering process that affects societies, rather than the physical border per se, should we talk about border cities or cities on the border?

Narvians have a particular sense of connection and disconnection with other spaces; here, daily life involves a density of scales and separations, as well as dynamics of relative positioning. Even if marginality seems to be increasingly detached from conceptions of geopolitics and culture, being narrated more and more in terms of globalisation, and making

Fig. 6.7   Narva. Source: Tõnu Tunnel, 2017.

notions of culture, identity and space lose their traditional meaning
(Browning and Lehti 2007; Gupta and Ferguson 1997), the world is still
full of borders locating people in particular ways. For instance, Estonia's
entry into the EU and the Schengen area meant abolishing the simplified
border-crossing regime established after Estonia regained its independence.
On the edge of the European Union, this zone has a severe visa policy, yet it
is also a bridge between two towns that were not that long ago united. In
that sense, the edge of the territory, marking the point where the EU ends,
is 'transported into the middle of political space' (Balibar 2004, 109).

Nowadays, silent individuals cross a heavily surveyed bridge that
functions as a passage connecting a longer road – from Russia to Europe
and vice versa. Accidental border crossings still occur, as for the fishermen
Mikhail Sukhoshin and Alexander Ladur, who crossed the dividing line of
the Narva River in November 2014, and were sentenced to two months
and nine days in prison.[17] Borders are crucial sites of political and spatial
enclosure – simultaneously constituted and contested. A border determines the limits of the possible, generating both mobility and immobility,
shaping the potentialities and constraints of human agency and imagination. Yet any boundary entails of necessity the potential to be trans-
gressed, continually at risk of being surpassed or seen across. Borders
may produce order . . . and disorder. They function as Simmel's (1997)
doorways and bridges – uniting and separating simultaneously. They
put into contact diverse historical narratives and political scales. Simmel

Fig. 6.8　Narva. Source: Tõnu Tunnel, 2017.

explains that the concept of separation has meaning because connecting paths were built. He distinguishes between the two forms of connections: bridges, connecting what is separated, and doors, separating what is connected. The particularity of doors, however, is that they can also be opened. So a border can also be considered a threshold rather than simply a barrier (figure 6.8).

We usually associate borders with the migration of people, but in fact, borders themselves often 'migrate' and move over the populations.[18] This 'migration of borders' destroys old communities and shapes new ones, causes resettlements, creates new minorities or homogenises populations inside the new borders (Bös and Zimmer 2006). Borders are neither objective entities nor eternal: they are artificial constructions in both their physical materiality and their sociocultural meanings, emerging from an amalgam of social and institutional practices (Paasi 1995). The liminal situation found in Narva is not due to only physical or geographical reasons, but also discursive ones. Narva exists not only as an area apart within Estonia but also as a quintessentially European and global periphery. This town is laid in a zone of tension between antagonistic forms of logic, so it has a suturing quality. In medical terms, a suture is an element that stitches wounds. In anatomy, a suture is a joint between rigid pieces. Both notions fit this case, demonstrating material and discursive repairing might have implications in narrative politics of belonging.

Frontiers are not just lines drawn on maps, or territorial demarcations; they activate distinct processes and entail an affectual quality, wherein rules, interactions and embodied imagination are intensively played out. The border produces social situations that are negotiated through repetition; as a corporeal experience, the border is embodied and cognitively internalised, as if it were an affectual extension of the self. Concrete affects are formed through encounters and accumulation, influencing feelings of belonging, attunement and the temporality of communities. Borders are more than a state's periphery, they are lived as a distinct milieu, a unique human environment with an active role in the way society is articulated and the government exerts power. Any border is a *limen*, a physical and psychological threshold; as such, it produces a borderline effect that varies within and across cultures.

In Narva, we find particular modes of reality, symbolic world and material culture, which are context-bound and require localised strategies for meaning-making. We can talk of a borderland knowhow, which involves strong reflexive and performative dimensions. Yet borderlands do not have the same meaning for everybody, being differently interpreted not just by both sides but even within each side, looking different depending on who you are and where you come from (Delaplace 2012). It is interesting to see how many Estonian speakers adapt to local circumstances and try to learn and speak Russian. This illustrates the local yet collective dimension of Narva, as a centre out there (Turner 1973), a cultural site with heightened symbolic, industrial, military, historical and spiritual value.

Borderlands situate us in a different position towards patterns of normality, producing a sense of passage, as if we were in a liminal phase. As noted by Victor Turner (1974), the liminal already connotes a space: a boundary, a frontier, a transitional area. Turner describes liminality as 'cunicular' – like being in a tunnel between the entrance and the exit. Liminal spaces are sites of creativity, but also of danger and frailty. Homi Bhabha, too, posits hybridity as such a form of liminal or in-between space, where translation and negotiation occur. These are 'third spaces' between contending and contradictory positions – hence not zones of resolution, but of continuous collaboration and contestation that raise feelings of ambivalence, disruption and displacement. For Bhabha (1994), the reflective capacity of such a space starts at the boundaries, and enables the negotiation of collective experiences and values, initiating new signs of identity and a spatial politics of inclusion.[19]

In a chapter entitled 'Liminality and Communitas', Victor Turner defines liminal individuals as 'neither here nor there; they are betwixt and between the positions assigned and arrayed by law, custom, convention and ceremony' (1969, 95). They are threshold people, necessarily ambiguous, since this condition and these persons elude the classifications that normally locate states and positions in cultural space. Narva appears to me as a zone of vulnerability and translation, whereby 'plurality and alternative models of living' are generated, 'capable of influencing the behaviour of those in the mainstream' (Turner 1974, 65). There is in this town a different understanding of the individual and the collective from other Estonian cities, as well as an inversion of the prevailing norms, and a distinct form of mutuality (in the sense that locals feel for each other and understand themselves as a community – 'мы нарвитяне / we are Narvians').

Life at the edge produces a particular regime of knowledge and sense of belonging, generating distinct affects and cultural practices too. As Yuri Lotman (2005) noted, the Baltic countries may function as an 'interpretative filter' for 'translating' Russia to Western Europe. Within this European borderland (neither fully Western, nor Russian), Narva is the very place where the translation process happens in quotidian terms. On the eastern side of the Narva River, Russia stands as a poly-peripheral country constituted by broad regions and a plethora of disparate communities and cultures (Medvedev 1999). On the western side, the Baltic region (and Eastern Europe in general) embodies a 'betwixt and between' self-image that creates cases of 'nested liminalities' (Mälksoo 2009, 65).

Narva appears thus as 'a discursive battlefield that reflects the difficult relations between Russia and Estonia after the restoration of Estonia's independence' (Pfoser 2014, 269). Still the boundary treaty between the Russian Federation and the Republic of Estonia has not been ratified. This matter is becoming a soap opera, since when Tallinn agrees, Moscow doesn't and vice versa. In the last years, the main problem was a preamble referring to the Treaty of Tartu of 1920 introduced by the Estonian parliament in the final reading. That note potentially opens the way to claims for compensation from the Estonian side, since the border back then included also Ivangorod. The conflict in Ukraine has activated the will to demarcate the border on the Estonian side, while Moscow keeps playing a rhetorical tennis match. Hence, the Estonian government ordered a fence to be built along the eastern border with Russia.

Loss speaks in Russian, success in Estonian

The castles of Narva and Ivangorod are printed on the old Estonian 5 krooni notes (figure 6.9) and represent a curious meteorological forecast. From

Fig. 6.9 5 krooni note, 1992–2011.

the Russian side, an ominous and heavy dark storm advances. This example fits into what Michael Billig defines as 'banal nationalism' (1995) – a way of flagging the nation through the ordinary engaging activities. As he puts it, the nation is not simply reminded in the weather map graphically, but also with the 'here' and 'there', the 'we' and the 'other; discursive constructions which often go unnoticed. Symbolic material aspects equally permeate daily life, making nationhood a familiar space. Tim Edensor (2002) talks, for instance, of the smell and soundscapes of public places and ordinary habits such as timetables or ways of sitting, washing and playing, which make nations sensually present and shape the way people experience it, adding a cognitive and affective dimension to national identity.

Estonia itself has been traditionally depicted as a borderland, a somewhat messy place existing on the edge of Europe and between the great powers. As in the case of Finns (Browning and Lehti 2007), Estonia is conceptualised as a nation emerging from the periphery, historically subordinate and lacking power, in search of self-esteem, not simply describing the current position but also prescribing how things ought to be (ibid.). Yet in current day Estonia, the places and populations at the margins are precisely those questioning the postsocialist success story, absorbing the negative effects of the changes, and highlighting multiple inequalities and exclusions (Pfoser 2017). Overall, post-Soviet border-lands entail pejorative connotations and are often represented as adjacent territories, and their inhabitants as not comfortable elements of a more general group – the imagined community. Narva is no exception, and for decades, locals have been depicted by media as 'out of place' and symbolically toxic (Douglas 1966), participating in the construction of identity by enhancing sociocultural boundaries and highlighting differences with the rest of Estonia.

Fig. 6.10   Fishing between the castles of Narva and Ivangorod. Source: Author, 2013.

The break-up of state socialism produced very different reactions from the varied communities present in Estonia (figure 6.10). For most Estonians, it was perceived as an opportunity to restore and secure their cultural identity and independent state, while for most Russian speakers it instead had the effect of producing an identity crisis, thus increasing the difficulties for adaptation and integration (Kirch 1997). Accordingly, the Soviet period is still acknowledged by many Narvians as a personally meaningful time, linked with progress and industrialisation (Pfoser 2014). Also, Russian-speaking workers in the Narva region feel part of a global subaltern class, depicting themselves as 'Afro-Russians' or 'Estonian white-skinned Negroes', as exposed in Eeva Kesküla's research on Estonian miners (2012).

In this light, social scientist Alena Pfoser argues (2014) that the label of 'occupant' does not help to integrate local populations in the rest of Estonia, since it questions the actual belonging of the Russian speakers, directly associating them with a regime which is already past. Estonian society is still characterised 'by divisions on ethnic lines and historic memory' (Brüggemann and Kasekamp 2008, 427), in which many Estonians recurrently present themselves as superior to Russians, who are considered 'uncivilised' and 'Oriental' (Annus 2012). This is partly based on the need to assert the nation's self-esteem (Hroch 1985), relying on the argument that for centuries a nondominant ethnic group (Swedish, German, Russian) has held the political, economic and cultural power over the majority population (Estonian).[20] As a result, since independence has been regained, Estonian identity has been constructed as being continually under threat, as an endangered entity that must be protected from non-Estonian (Kuus 2012).

The paradox, however, is that the securitisation of 'memory' and identity (making certain historical remembrances secure by delegitimising others) leads to new dilemmas and a reduced sense of security (Mälksoo 2015). Also, the interpretation of the past and the framing of the inherited becomes a geopolitical battleground. More important than the coexistence of one of several languages, and a frequent source of misunderstandings and tensions, is thus the different approach towards the recent past. This has led to a huge separation between the two main cultural worlds – namely the Russian-speaking and the Estonian-speaking ones, demonstrating once again that 'geopolitics has its ideological foundations in chronopolitics' (Fabian 1983, 144).

Narva appears, however, as a location of ongoing hybrid processes, asserting a constant cultural clash that dismantles any definitive classification. This town is not only a political regional node, but also a cultural site with heightened symbolic value. There, identity appears as unfinished, as being in a constant making – as a quotidian negotiation and translation of vectors that come from elsewhere. Hence, the integration of Narva and its inhabitants into the ongoing cultural, economic and political processes would have positive effects, such as redrawing the contours of the nation-building project in Estonia and shifting towards a more multicultural and multiethnic understanding of the social composition (Smith and Burch 2011). Estonian identity has been often portrayed in security terms, as well as fused with the state; however, identities are not only constructed through interactions with other states, but also in interaction with their own societies and the multiple identities and discourses that constitute these groups (Mälksoo 2009). Therefore, Maria Mälksoo (2014) proposes a mnemonic pluralism informed by different readings of the commonly experienced past. Also, Maarja Saar (2010) has claimed that Estonianness needs to be reframed in order to deal with its integration problems, making the society more inclusive and more considerate of differences, meeting the Other in the same ground and in the same time (Fabian 1983). Hence, to regenerate Narva in its peculiar mixture of the centrality and marginality means to make the Estonian society more inclusive and to acknowledge its plural composition (figures 6.11 and 6.12).

Fig. 6.11   Railway Station of Narva. Source: Tõnu Tunnel, 2017.

Fig. 6.12   Narva. Source: Tõnu Tunnel, 2017.

Concluding considerations

Borderlands are spaces where large differences are compelled to meet often. Despite being clearly drawn on maps, borders rarely correspond to the ambivalent and fluid way in which people experience them in daily life. They are erected to banish uncertainty about the difference between here and somewhere else, yet they might become the opposite and contribute to establishing greyness (Green 2015). The discussion demonstrates that Narva can be taken as a space of translation and negotiation, and also that the repair and rebuilding of the city reinforces communal ties and favours a plural constitution of Estonian identity, showing both the limits and potentials of nation-building projects as sources of cohesive spaces of interaction. Further, and agreeing with Dace Dzenovska's research on Latvian border guards (2014), the study of the affective dimension of the bordering encounter and how the idea of Europe is distributed in political spaces requires analysis of Eastern European societies not only in relation to the socialist past but also the global present.

This city is the borderland of a borderland, hence a centre out there producing distinct affects and identifications, as well as bringing questions to the construction of identity. The study of local narratives makes evident how discourses of sameness and otherness are dynamised in Narva, and shows a wide range of levels of adhesion and deviation. This city appears as a mixer to help overcome disconnections at both a collective and an intersubjective level, playing a suturing role within Estonia and also between Russia and the EU. In Narva, we can experience sociocultural hybridity and an intense translation of varied temporalities and scales. Everyday life there shows a distinct mode of normality that contests narrow understandings of border, nation and territory. Identity in the borderland appears thus as incomplete and plural, invoking different degrees of belonging, and helping us to rethink notions such as borders, national identity and territory, as well as the scale effects that are generated by different connections and separations.

7
A memory-constructing space in Tartu

The condenser of Estonian culture

The twentieth century has been one of unprecedented extremes, paradoxes and clashes of historical projects, and Estonia is a vivid example.
This chapter studies dynamics of memory transmission and foregrounds
how the existence of 'spatial scars' defies single narratives about memory
and politics. The research contributes to the debates about mediated forms
of remembrance and the intersection between sites of history and collective memory, by showing the changing 'how' and 'where' of Estonian
national identity. The focus is put on Raadi, a former airbase on the outskirts of Tartu, which was chosen in 2003 as the site of the new building
for the Estonian National Museum (ENM). This is a site where contradictory projects of modernisation are entangled; hence it is a relevant case
study to approach processes of commemoration, the politics of memory
and the discursive construction of national identity. In Raadi we discover
that in short periods of time things have been with very different ambitions and in different languages, as if the site were in a foreign country.
Historical breaks and unfinished projects of modernisation appear in gaps
and absences, in a form of patchwork landscape and spatial scars, rather
than through layers of sedimentation and linear change. Indeed, the amalgamation of memories and happenings in the area has played an important role in the conceptualisation of the new ENM as a 'Memory Field'.[1]

The construction in Raadi of the new building of the ENM gives an
opportunity to reconsider the way that Soviet legacies are culturally represented in Estonia. The new ENM is a modern concrete and glass building designed to resemble the runway of a former Soviet airfield. This
building is meant to be a multifunctional condenser of Estonianness, conducting and defining what Estonia is supposed to be, crystallising the

culture and material forms of the new society (Murawski 2017a). Significantly, many of those who believe the role of this institution is to guard folkloric heritage, mark historical events and define identity in the country were disappointed with the open character of the memoryland. For them, the building-symbol should have been a modern expression of Estonianness, since the ENM has the mandate to establish how the past is conceptualised and represented, as well as to articulate historic narratives. This task is done through publications, public displays and events, yet also through the very building of the museum and the place where it stands. By all these means, it delineates the memorable and projects a sense of belonging, marking who is included and excluded through discourses of legacy to be preserved and pasts to be remembered – by the double task of any memory work: remembering and forgetting.

Ethnological exhibitions do not simply bring the past to the present, but they also create the present as such (Bjerregaard 2015). In this light, any representation of the past tends to reduce the traces of historical heterogeneity, prioritising instead the articulation of a coherent and epic narrative of social development, which always begins in the past and leads to the present as if the development were irreversible. Furthermore, there is a remarkable range of ways of addressing the past, depending on factors such as whether longer or shorter time periods are activated and how personal and collective memories are brought together. In this logic, museums act as historical agents; they don't simply embody ideological discussions, they also function as 'visualising technologies' cultivating these ideas (Macdonald 1996).

Nonetheless, memory does not simply take narrative form; the past is also placed through monuments and buildings, as well as materialised through items, which contribute to the forming of values, forging a sense of belonging and organisation of lives, and avoiding any recreation of the old beyond the hegemonic narrative. The so-called spatial turn emphasised the awareness of the constructedness of places as meaningful locations (Cresswell 1996). In this process, memories play a crucial role, since it is through historical stories that places acquire symbolic meaning and are linked to cultural and political communities (Halbwachs 1980). The term *lieu de mémoire* was coined by Pierre Nora in an attempt to describe how places acquire referential meaning, becoming an allegory of history, 'where memory crystallises and secretes itself' (Nora 1989, 7). Memorials serve to express a collective version of history and cast legitimacy upon it as well, since they give the past a 'tangibility' and a 'familiarity' (Dwyer and Alderman 2008), produce a 'geography of belonging' (Hodgkin and Radstone 2003) and offer to each member of society an image of membership and 'effecting consensus' (Lefebvre [1974] 1991).

The representation of the past appears therefore not just as a factor of struggle but also as an important political resource that facilitates the managing of people's memories, and through them the regulation of people's position in society (Foucault 1975). Modern architecture of memory is built through museums, monuments, and archives, as well as commemorative practices, all of which serve to materialise history and narrate what to forget, what to remember, establishing also the canon of how to do it. However, museum engagements with 'the past' do not always entail 'remembering', but might rather follow strategies of commemoration, marketing and romanticisation of traditions, privileging continuity and homogeneity in history as well as reducing the past to something controllable and useful for the present (Pétursdóttir and Olsen 2014). And yet, what all these strategies of past presencing eventually manifest is a preoccupation with the incorporation of memory, heritage and identity into a project of collective representation (Macdonald 2013).

In Estonia, the ENM governs memory and commands the public attention to the past. This institution articulates a dominant idea of tradition based on the assumption that Estonian culture and identity have been under threat for centuries. Yet through representations of the past not only is a sense of belonging constituted, but a hierarchy of generations is established as a parallel process. I agree with Raili Nugin (2015) that the attitude to history has been crucial in determining the line separating generations. She calls it 'generational habitus' and remarks how the remembering of the Soviet period and the Singing Revolution appear as key representations in defining generational boundaries.[2] The term 'winners generation' (Titma 1999) has also been coined to refer to those who gained influential positions in the economy and politics after the change, which corresponds to the cohort born around 1965. Yet we can go even further to argue that these representations and narratives of the past are used as a cultural resource and symbolic capital in Estonia and that by cultivating these memories, the Estonian government harvested a hierarchy of generations and temporal belonging. This has produced the condition where any effective inclusion within the social system and public debates can happen only in the winners' terms, which in turn reinforces the hierarchical integration.

Bygone futures

Raadi appears as a good site from which to approach the recent history of the Baltic region. As said above, continuities and discontinuities are thick in this region, which has suffered a succession of ruptures with new effects at each modernising project and historical turn. There is in Raadi a particular amalgamation of historical strata – allowing us to parachute into different spatiotemporal experiences of modernity. The Raadi area can be also understood as a 'carrier of history' and a 'chronotope of modernity'; what is shown within the layers and historical elements present at Raadi is not simply change, but also its tempo and the models and ideals leading the transformation. Hence, the study of this place brings to light diverse temporalities and uncovers multiple projects of modernisation, showing how they have contributed to what is nowadays Estonian society.

There is, however, a gap between the abundance of traces of the Soviet period on the site and their eventual destruction and designation as having zero value for the construction of Estonian collective memory, as the very survival of historic evidence is the first intervention in the process of making the past available (Schofield, Johnson and Beck 2002). When I first visited Raadi, the construction works of the new building of the ENM were about to start (figure 7.1). It was November 2013, and the old air traffic control centre was still there (abandoned and with graffiti on the walls). Since then, however, the demolition of buildings has been extensive. In each new visit to the site, I noticed the progressive disappearance of old traces. Indeed, it is ironic that in order to construct memory fields, many of the remaining elements have to be erased. Yet modernity itself is characterised by a deliberate erasure of the past to facilitate a new start – which is always based on other memories of the past (Connerton 2009). The landscape of modernity appears as an amalgamated

Fig. 7.1 Former hangar of the military airport. Source: Author, 2015.

patchwork, made of rarely stable components and narratives. As noted by Zygmunt Bauman (1991), any modern project seeks order and stability, but ends up creating a social world that is unstable, restless and unresolved.

I visited Raadi several times more. We can find still a few remaining ruins of the airbase, partly occupied by mechanical businesses and dealers in construction materials. Besides the main runway, on which plants were growing freely and water puddles multiplied, there are a few constructions still standing associated with the first hangars and the storehouse of the airfield. These buildings were kept as carcasses, and all the elements within their interiors have been taken away. Around the main storehouse there are half a dozen small hangars, hundreds of used tires and piles of construction materials and rusted metal. On the other side of the airfield, behind the museum, we find the curated ruins of the old manor.

'Traces signal the limits of representation; they are the materials of knots of histories at the margins', observes the anthropologist Valentina Napolitano (2015, 47). Through the analysis of traces and regimes of temporality we can learn many modalities of imagining and experiencing the past. They enable dialectical engagements with 'gone' histories, which show how the past concurrently passes and endures, and helps to make us understand how cultural constructions of time play out. In the case of Raadi, we can see how the evaluation of this place as dirty and disordered carries social and political weight, naturalising orders of worth through 'trash talk' (McKee 2015). Indeed, by its very depiction of rubble and nothing being there (Gordillo 2014), many elements in this place were denied being a part of the geographies of the present.

In his Moscow diary of 1926, Benjamin (1986) wrote that the result of the Bolshevik revolution was not just a civil war, but also electrification, canal construction and the creation of factories. In Raadi we find the existence of some of those modern projects. The study of these remains demonstrates the evocative relationship between materiality and history, as well as the lost futures that communism had offered. The legacies of the twentieth century have frequently been remembered within national narratives, leading people to ignore the remains from uncomfortable pasts, as if neglect were part of a strategy of coming to terms with the past, instead choosing to apply repair practices to deal with them. Hence I claim that Soviet remains can be taken as a legacy too, as something given by ancestors that has an effect in the present.

Despite socialism's claim to being more progressive and modern than capitalism, after the Soviet breakdown, a narrative was extended equating socialism with obsolescence. In this vein, Susanne Brandtstädter notes how 'postsocialism not only replaced one type of modernity with another, but it also replaced a socialist modernity, which used to define the capitalist project as backward and flawed, with a capitalist modernity, which *now* defines everything socialist as unmodern' (2007, 134). These battlegrounds of redefining and reappropriating the meaning of modernity speak of its character: being constantly in the making, constituted by discontinuous modes of temporalisation and repeated attempts to order space. Some authors, such as Koselleck (2004) and Hartog (2003), point out how modernity brought a temporalisation of history, affecting all aspects of human experience and establishing regimes of historicity, which sewed together different temporalities and ordered social experiences by giving meaning to the relationship between past, present and future. In Raadi, different perspectives of the future intersect and overlap, along with the tensions with which they are invested. This place encompasses a testimonial quality, informing a more complex configuration of memory in Estonia.

The cultural excavation of Raadi discloses traces of multiple events that occurred there and the scars of modernisation processes, as well as different worlds and visions of the future. I propose therefore to take the Raadi area as a chronotope of modernity, where it is possible to investigate changes in the experience and configuration of space and of time in Estonia. Places like Raadi condense historical narratives and modern transformations in a process of amalgamation (constantly piling up and eroding), showing in turn the limits of 'past presencing' strategies – as a way of drawing the past into the present (Macdonald 2013).

Historical background

The Raadi area is located two kilometres northeast of Tartu. Originally, it gained relevance because of a manor house (Raadi Mõis), a socioeconomic structure present since the sixteenth century. The last private owners of the manor were the Liphart family, German aristocrats who became prominent in the region by distilling and selling spirits. At the dawn of the twentieth century, an airfield was created in Raadi, and a nephew of the owner, Sergey Utochkin, took to the air in Raadi for the first time in 1912 in a biplane Farman IV. He gained the permission of his uncle to use what was then a cavalry field for an intermediate aircraft landing following the route Gatchina–Tallinn–Haapsalu–Riga–Tartu–Narva–Gatchina (figure 7.2). By this period, the manor had already suffered several renovations.[3] In 1918, after Estonia gained its independence, the 2nd Estonian squadron of flight was allocated the site, and in 1919, two hangars were built. The airfield was expanded in 1925 and again in 1930. Also in the 1920s, the

Fig. 7.2   Flight of Sergey Utochkin in a biplane Farman IV over Raadi, 14 May 1912. Source: E. Köhler, Rahvusarhiivi filmiarhiiv.

manor was given over to the University of Tartu, which placed the Faculty of Agriculture there and shared part of the main building with the Estonian National Museum. The manor served as an exhibition hall where an ethnographic exhibition focusing on peasant culture opened. The library counted over 30,000 volumes (figure 7.3).[4]

Fig. 7.3 In front of the Raadi manor house, 1933. Source: Photographer unknown, Rahvusarhiivi filmiarhiiv.

Following the Molotov–Ribbentrop pact, the site witnessed the evacuation of the collections and the loss of two Estonian-made PTO-4 aircraft and three recently bought Czech-made S-328 bombers. Once the Soviets took control of Raadi, they extended the airport area. During the war, Nazi troops established headquarters there and began to upgrade the airfield with a concrete runway. Raadi was repeatedly bombed by Soviet aircraft, which destroyed the manor house. Another relevant episode for Estonian art took place at the site. Many of Pallas's Academy art students were arrested overnight and later exiled to Soviet hard labour camps for supposedly circulating flyers with cartoons of Stalin and for blowing up a Red Army monument at Raadi.

After the war, the Soviets rebuilt the airport (the runway was extended to 2500 m in 1956, and an additional 500 metres were added in 1975). Raadi became a major bomber base for 50 years, menacing NATO with the famed Tu-22m 'Backfire' bombers with nuclear strike capability. Over 100 bombers were based here, making it the largest military airfield in the Baltic. The secrecy of the airfield turned Tartu into a closed town (foreigners were not allowed to visit it), bringing the Cold War to the civilian population and keeping the city from expanding to the northeast. In a way, the site and the noise of the jet engines turned into a metaphor for the overall situation of Estonia under Soviet occupation. Ironically, it became a tradition among university students to infiltrate the area at night for celebrations. In the last years of the Soviet Union, and related to the public movement against the occupation, several demonstrations were held calling for the ENM to be returned to Raadi (Runnel, Tarand and Tamm 2014). In 1989, the Soviet army made a partial withdrawal from the area, and the land was appropriated for the 'Estonian National Museum at Raadi'.

On 15 January 1991, a Soviet Air Force Tupolev Tu-16K Badger crashed on landing at Raadi when the wheels locked. The pilot and copilot ejected, but four other crew members were killed.[5] In 1992, the Soviets left Raadi and the airfield was listed as available only for emergency landings. In 1994, Polish President Lech Wałęsa used Raadi to land in Estonia. The last plane took to the air in 1996. By then, several small companies had already set up their business in the hangars; they were mostly dealing with the importation of cars, metal trade and mechanical repairs (symbols of the early *transition* period). Additionally, car races were organised, and people practised for driving tests. As documented, several fuel spills took place at the airfield, resulting in heavy soil and groundwater pollution.[6] Between 2008 and 2009, the EU funded a project to clean the grounds of Raadi (particularly dangerous due to water infiltration at the nearby lake). Nonetheless, the site remains in the local imaginary as a symbolically polluted area.[7] This is also partially due to the Raadi area being used as a place for executions in medieval times (Malve et al. 2012).

A scar left from a century of modernisations

The 1990s were a decade conditioned by the revaluation of the past, nationalist exaltation, attempts to imitate Western 'normalities' and rapid economic and cultural changes. In Tallinn, for instance, there was a project for the ENM which tried to use an architectural form to reference the contour of the map of Estonia (Ruudi 2015). In 1994, an exhibition on Estonian culture was shown in a temporary building at the centre of Tartu, mainly focused on the display of nineteenth-century peasant life and other folkloric motifs. Yet the Raadi area was not entirely forgotten and a competition for future development of the manor was arranged. The resulting ideas were diverse and ranged from a centre for the study of Baltic German culture to a museum of Estonian folklore or a multifunctional cultural building. Five supposed descendants of the family refused what they considered to be below market-value compensation and sought the land's return. Finally, in 1998, the central manor area was returned to the ENM by order of the Tartu city government.[8]

Runnel, Tatsi and Pruulmann-Vengerfeldt (2014) have published a study on the media discussion preceding the erection of the building of the new ENM in Raadi. As they show, newspaper articles published between 2001 and 2004 awakened a nostalgic reflection among an older generation of Estonians, to whom the remembering of Raadi 'brought a sparkle in the eye' (Mikelsaar 2003). In the media, the new museum was presented as a collective dream, *becoming* a symbolic object of national importance, whose completion had come to appear as necessary and self-evident (Latour 1996; Weszkalnys 2010). The decision in 2003 to rebuild the museum in this area was even compared to a 'divine act'.[9] Many intellectuals contributed to the public discussion about the appropriate role and location of the ENM. For instance, Marek Tamm (2005) acknowledged the historical role of the museum 'in the creation of the Estonian nation', yet emphasised that the museum's identity was bound to change, since 'the golden age of nationalism is now behind us'.

Surprisingly, the jury of the architectural competition nominated a project that positioned the museum building as an extension to the runaway on the airfield. The concept, developed by three young architects established in Paris, Dan Dorell, Lina Ghotmeth and Tsyoshi Tane, ignored the nationalist understanding of the museum as the repository of the country's romantic peasant past. Indeed, Dorell, director of the studio behind the winning project, said that their inspiration came from the way in which the Berlin Wall has been integrated into the urban space, acknowledging its historical value yet turning the negative associations into positive meanings.[10]

In a conversation held at the construction site, Dorell explained to me some details of the building, such as the low consumption of energy and the original will of the architects to make the top part of the museum accessible as a walkable roof (figure 7.4). 'We wished to have a small area where people could take advantage of the view as part of the experience in the museum with an incredible panoramic view'. However, this idea was discarded by the officials for security reasons, and the hope is still to gain access to some parts of the roof. According to Dorell, the building could act as a catalyst in Tartu for a new way of living, yet for that reason 'it would be important to preserve the green character of Raadi, improve the connections with the city centre and plan carefully what is gonna be built in the surroundings'. In this sense, he defined as negative the project to build a resort with a golf course at the end of the runway of the former airfield (this land is owned by the county of Tartu, not by the city hall, unlike the building's territory).

Traces bear witness to the different factors leading up to the present, hence they refer to something that entails both a past and a future.

Fig. 7.4 Architect Dan Dorell explaining the project for the museum. Source: Author, 2015.

The architectural engagement with the airfield reflects the plurality of traces found in Raadi, instead of promoting a single narrative of the past and ignoring other historical traces beyond the hegemonic account. The project takes the area as a legacy, as something received from predecessors which talks about other lives – manifested in different uses of the space, varied temporalities and alternative social ideas. This model of a memory field developed in Raadi invites us to narrate intervals and durations in an open-ended way, taking unfinished projects as meaningful and constitutive.

Identity-forming spaces are characterised by an accumulation of narratives, but their reconstruction and representation are concerned with silencing as much as with remembrance. Through this project, however, a memory that was meant to be forgotten was acknowledged and became present again. Over the last decades, memory politics have dominated public debate in Estonia, making the national past endure into the future yet ignoring that there is far less consensus about historical representations than is officially depicted (Kirss 2017). Hence, these discussions of national identity should emphasise fluidity and complexity in contrast to essentialist categories rooted in models of the past, acknowledging that divergent views of the past lay at the core of the difficulties of integrating the Russian-speaking community (Burch and Smith 2007; Della Dora and Sooväli 2009; Kattago 2009b).

In its description of the project, prosaically entitled 'New Building. Estonian National Museum. What Is This? Where Is This?', the website of the ENM shows a meaningful contradiction. On the one hand, the text remarks, 'the architects wish to change the area surrounding the new building as little as possible and preserve the locality's characteristics and forms of nature'; and on the other, the institution presents the Raadi area as an 'empty space' in need of 'a more powerful voice'.[11] There were those who felt that such a decision was humiliating, undermining Estonian identity and somewhat perpetuating the occupation (Hallas-Murula 2006). Several people claimed that the museum's representations of the past should be a string of 'beautiful events and secure symbols' and that the 'memory field' project only served to glorify the occupation and open up old wounds (Runnel, Tarand and Tamm 2014, 330). Even the judging committee of the competition acknowledged that:

> the ideological premise behind this entry is somewhat unexpected and surprising, given Estonia's dramatic recent history – the devastating Soviet occupation lasting more than half a century. This history cannot and must not be banished from the nation's memory by denying the traces still present; rather, these traces should be given a new meaning that inspires hope. This is a design that opens up discussions. (ENM 2006)

More rationally, Andres Kurg (2006b) contributed to the debate by presenting the airfield as a scar left from a century of modernisation. He argued that collecting this history together and explaining it was a task to be done by the future ENM. In Kurg's view, the tension between 'appropriate' and 'inappropriate' elements reflected within the 'memory field' project is like the dialectical tension present in any configuration of cultural memory. 'The architects understood the airfield as a signifier of the polarity of the Cold War', notes Kurg, while 'for locals it also signifies pollution, confinement, Dzhokhar Dudayev or something else' (2006b).

And who is Dzhokhar Dudayev?

Dudayev was the commander of the nuclear bomber aircraft division at the Tartu air base during the perestroika years. He became a popular figure in Estonia after refusing the Kremlin's orders to block the television and parliament buildings, and to suppress the local bid for independence. This decision, and his open support for Boris Yeltsin (later his main adversary), was meant to be the end of Dudayev's military career in the Soviet army. In 1991, he moved to Grozny and became president of Chechnya, initiating a process of independence that led to several wars against Moscow. He was killed in 1996 by two missiles directed at him after a satellite phone connection was traced. In spite of what occurred, several Baltic cities gave the name of Dudayev to streets and even erected monuments to the Chechen leader. Even so, reactions against this tribute were frequent, as we can see in the letters of protest sent by the neighbours, urging that their streets be renamed, and Russian journalists accusing the Baltic States of 'supporting international terrorism' and 'believing that the warriors of Allah are innocent victims'.[12]

On the façade of the Barclay hotel, in the centre of Tartu, we can find a commemorative plaque remembering Dudayev. Although he lived on Friendship Street (Ulitsa Druzhva; Sõpruse puistee), the Soviet commander had a room in that hotel where he frequently met with local researchers, such as professor Linnart Mall, an orientalist who became the founder of the Unrepresented Nations and Peoples Organisation. In 2012, artist Tanel Rander presented a project advocating to name Friendship Street after the Chechen leader, as well as the Raadi airfield (figure 7.5). In his view, the symbolic value of Raadi relies on the multiple colonial wounds present there (imperialism, occupation, the racism of Baltic Germans, Estonian self-colonisation and social inequality), rather than on any romanticisation of the area as a Disneyland of memory.[13] Rander claims that in order to 'decolonize' Estonia and unlearn being Eastern Europe, we have to acknowledge the problematic traces of the country. As Rander points out:

> The global meaning of Tartu is related to the Raadi military airport that was one of the most important military objects of the western part of the Soviet Union. Nuclear weapons were stored in Akimetsa, near Luunja. All this made us globally important – we were a threat to the civilised and free world. The grandfathers of our today's Western friends were pointing their guns at us. If not, then why were the children of Tartu playing around with broken gas masks that almost every household had?

In front of the Barclay hotel, I carried out 18 informal interviews, asking people why the new building of the ENM is located in the Raadi area. All the interviews were conducted on 10 November 2014. Half of the interviewees were around 20 years old, not unexpected with the social

Fig. 7.5 Tanel Rander project to rename the Raadi area after Dudayev, 2013. Source: Tanel Rander.

composition of this city, with its many students. In 14 interviews the language used was English; with the other four interlocutors (who were over 60 years old) I spoke in Russian. The results surprised me. One-third of the interviewees (six) acknowledged openly that they had no idea about Raadi (Helen: 'I was not born in Tartu'). Among the rest, only one person (Maret) was clearly aware of the project, arguing that: 'Raadi is an important place because the previous museum, during the First Republic, was there. The culture and the brains of this country are in Tartu. I heard that the museum will host not only beautiful art, but also a theatre and a cinema. More tourists will come to Tartu'.

Four interlocutors suspected urban logic behind the selection of the site, from matters of size (Karl: 'there is free space to build a huge complex'; Margo: 'the building is big, so it needs a lot of space'), to logics of speculation (Erki: 'the city hall and some entrepreneurs want to raise the value of that part of the city'). Other answers were more critical, as for instance Ailen: 'It is a political decision. Tradition, Tartu, nostalgia and whatever you might say. Probably it is not a rational decision'. And, of course, there were people who did not remember exactly the details of the project: 'It is a historical area because of a monastery' (Karl). 'A while ago I read about it. Probably because it has historical importance, but I cannot remember why. I even went to the inauguration of the construction works. Why is it? Please, tell me' (Karl). Hence, according to the answers collected in my interviews, the museum also has to work to explain its rationale and decisions, besides reconsidering its profile and priorities.

The new building has a multifunctional ambition as a centre of entertainment, documentation, branding, workshops for children (only in Estonian), a tourist attraction, as well as simultaneously a home for nationalism. This potpourri of activities evidences the paradox of being an overpoliticised institution which is asked however to sustain itself through commercial activities, reminding us that the marketing dimension of museology should not be ignored. The terrain of memory making is becoming increasingly transnational, meant for tourists and infused with capitalist values, which often generates tensions between remembrance and forgetfulness (Martínez 2017c; Schwenkel 2006). ENM might have been created in the sunset of romantic nationalism, but it has to survive financially in a context of neoliberal ideology and austerity policies. As Kaarel Tarand (public relations for the museum) declared, the government believes that it is enough to build the building and it does not provide enough funding to hire the workers needed to allow a full use of the venue.

In our encounter of two hours just before the opening, Kaarel repeated three times that the main aim of the museum was not to tell a final truth, but to show stories about the life of Estonians. As he explained, 'traditional minorities such as the Swedish and the Russian already have their own museum', so this one is about Estonians, 'not genetically Estonians, but culturally Estonians'. The aesthetics of the display are brand new and based on interactive principles, yet grounded in ethnocentric ideals, materialising the political principles of the new historical regime, for instance, by externalising communism from the life of people (Nicolescu 2017; Vukov 2008), and by projecting Estonianness as an untouched reality.

One of the challenges of the new building of ENM has been that different people have diverse expectations about the role of this institution in the twenty-first century. Simultaneously, the institution has to engage with global trends and 'restore and consolidate' an 'ethnically based sense of nationhood', since 'the world was open to them after fifty years of closure, but they still had work to do at home' (Runnel, Tarand and Tamm, 2014, 330).

I realised therefore that, in order to contextualise the new building of the ENM, the discussion on the expected role of this institution is unavoidable; so I asked a few colleagues for their opinion on this matter. For instance, Kai Lobjakas (director of the Estonian Museum of Applied Arts) observes that 'The national museum is one with the widest and therefore hardest concept of its kind. After a hundred years of waiting for ideal conditions it is facing the task of responding to the ideals of a myriad of different target groups. I admit, I can't think of a harder task'. Mart Kalm, Rector of the Estonian Academy of Arts, notes that 'There is a unique conflict between the building and the collections. The collections of folkloric material arose in the nineteenth century as in many other countries, and they are usually exhibited in museums of classical architecture. But since Estonian society was small and poor, and many of the major steps in developing nations were taken late, the house for this material was not ready until now, 100 years after the right time'.

In the nineteenth century, having a museum meant having an identity, since museums were the very physical presence that performed national identity and civic pride (Macdonald 2013). However, as cultural theorist Rein Raud points out in his statement sent to me by email, 'At the 21st century, the museum in its principle is far from what it was in the previous centuries, especially considering those big collections, which have the ambition to be displayed in the building and function to preserve identities. . . . If the ideological normativeness dominates over the open rootedness, the national-cultural museums begin to contradict their first intention and alienate the critically thinking future generations from their roots'. Tiina Kirss, literature scholar at the University of Tartu also remarks that 'Hopefully, visitors' images of who qualifies as an "Estonian" will be challenged'. In this vein, Karsten Brüggeman, historian of Tallinn University points out that 'A "national" museum should not try to fall in the populist trap and repeat the "grand narratives" of the past, the success story of one group only. It should be transnational in providing contexts and object-centred in the stories it tries to tell'. And Maria Mälksoo of the University of Kent claims that the ENM has to enable more diversity: 'The main thing is to avoid the reefs of ossification (which the sites of heritage and memory inevitably have a risk of) and embracing the idea of dynamic Estonianness . . . it should certainly continuously engage with the question of "being Estonian as a state of mind" through its various public outreach activities'.[14]

Memory and the other

The dualism of history and tradition has been explained by Hobsbawm and Ranger (1983) as a product of modernity. In their view, the emergence of the nation-state brought with it 'the invention of traditions', a sought-after resource to embody state values and make people feel in terms of identity. According to Hobsbawm and Ranger, a tradition establishes an epic continuity with the past, seeks to inculcate certain values and norms of behaviour by repetition, and attempts to establish continuity with a suitable historic past. Otherwise, the *Oxford English Dictionary* defines 'tradition' as what is passed down orally from one generation to the next; hence, the transmission process defines tradition, as well as the intergenerational interest in preserving something from the past.

As pointed out by Benedict Anderson (1991), the familiarity of tradition is crucial to articulate imagined communities beyond face-to-face contact. Social constructions, such as the nation and tradition, make people perceive themselves as part of a limited group, sovereign and in contraposition to a figurative 'other'. In contemporary Estonia, that role of the 'other' is played by the category 'Russians'. For instance, Rausing (2004, 35–6) notes how 'Russians' are the primary 'other' and embody a set of characteristics that appear as the opposite of what constitutes 'Estonianness', which is order, quietness and individualism, contrasted with a set of opposite characteristics associated with the Russians and the Soviet Union: disorder, emotionality, brutality and the tendency towards collectivity. We can talk of politically mediated affects and the mobilisation of emotions through the past, as the pre-Soviet past is affectively evoked in order to distribute 'proper sentiments' and produce 'emotional standards' and 'public moods' with consequences in social visibility and participation (Stoler 2004).

Identity is constructed by silencing and neglecting, as much as by sharing and preserving. In multiethnic societies with a troubled history, the task of selecting national symbols from specific pasts is particularly challenging; especially when collective memory was abruptly disrupted, after radical political breaks. In the task of re-narrating the past, some pasts loom especially large, while others are relatively short, in both official and popular memory (Macdonald 2013). An example of this is the re-opened Estonian History Museum in Tallinn, which in the exhibition *My Free Country* about the twentieth century in Estonia only dedicates one of the nine rooms to the four decades of Soviet life, presented also through nuclear masks and discourses of brainwashing and political persecution.

Postsocialist countries share particular ways in which past and present are woven together. The most striking one is the pattern of replacement and restoration, arguably related to wider historical events (wars, occupations and abrupt political ruptures) of the twentieth century. In the case of Estonia, this provoked a succession of radical rejections of everything that came before, instead seeking to restore a distant past

(Martínez 2017c). Another common feature is a commemorative excess and a heritage crusade, due to the later invention of traditions and the active manipulation of folklore in order to reinforce discourses of national identity. In this respect, Deema Kaneff (2004) observes how the codification of the past in Bulgaria gave legitimacy to the state-sponsored 'us', marginalising those in conflict with the state. This was achieved through a 'recontextualisation' of the old, reifying peasant traditions as folklore and later transforming them into an ethnological symbol of identity. However, the socialist states of Eastern Europe were not exactly antitradition, since folkloric elements were often incorporated into socialist rituals to compensate for homogenising processes and to replace 'burgeois nationalism' with a sense of authenticity, agency and folk patriotism (Kaneff 2004; Rausing 2004).

Likewise, practices of borrowing and mixing historical facts have been also common in post-Soviet Russia, the past being used as a raw material for creating local belonging, depth and longevity in the present (Kalinin 2013). Nowadays, the official rejection of perestroika and the Yeltsin years is accompanied by efforts to resurrect imperial symbols, which appear decontextualised and emptied of political meaning, being reduced to a form that creates a sense of connection and a shared emotional experience (Oushakine 2013).

In comparing the Russian and Estonian approaches towards the recent past, we find two almost opposite cases. The main differences are, in the Russian case, the absence of positive ideological construction of the Soviet break-up; the postmodern way of rewriting history practised there; and the final goal. The year 1991 is presented as a great break in both cases: in the Estonian accounts as the landmark of independence, whilst the Kremlin depicts it as a source of chaos (Martínez 2017c). Both societies have articulated new continuities and discontinuities, reactivating the past in order to correlate it with the present: in the case of Estonia, a political restoration and an agenda of Westernisation have been accomplished through museums, monuments, rituals and laws; in the case of Russia, a sort of 'nostalgic modernisation' (Kalinin 2011) is manifested in a quotational way, deconstructing historical discourses and trying to reestablish a higher opinion of the role of the country in the world.

A large rethinking of history was precipitated by the Soviet break-up, showing new forms of convergence between the historical and the political. In her classic *What Was Socialism and What Comes Next?*, Katherine Verdery referred to 'nation' as the name of the relationship that links a state with its subject, historically manifested as a relation known as ethnicity (more frequent in Eastern Europe) or as a citizen relationship, emanating from common political participation (Verdery 1996: 84). In the case of Estonia, the two meanings have been often at odds, to a great extent due to how the restoration ideology produced a discriminatory sense of national purity and in consequence a very strict citizenship policy, depriving nearly a third of the society of citizenship – the immigrants of the Soviet period and their descendants (Tamm 2016).[15] In short, the rewriting of history has been one of the sensitive aspects on which the post-Soviet societies were built, yet what took place was not simply efforts to articulate the collective memory, but also strategies of constructing history and Others, generating divides and hierarchies of belonging.

Concluding considerations

The National Museum still functions as a gatekeeper not only of what is to be considered a legacy, but also as a canon for the unvalued, reorganising different centres of historical representation meant to generate a particular sensibility with respect to the past. The chapter foregrounded, however, that in order to reconcile unity and diversity in Estonia the construction of the national identity has to be more plural by relying on multivocality and involving different past narratives and spaces of memory. Along with this argument, we can also assume that the reconsideration of multiple modernities in Estonia – including the Soviet one – should be a task for the ENM too. As sites where disposal and settlement remain as unfinished business (Hetherington 2004), memory fields facilitate a more plural reading of the past, acknowledging the tension that the articulation of collective memory entails. Memory is thus taken as a work in progress, a conglomerate of stories waiting to be narrated and localised. Hence, instead of understanding Estonian culture as fixed and static over centuries, it should be taken as an ongoing process, embodied, recreated and recalibrated by every new generation.

8
Children of the New East

Generational change enhances paradigm shift

The constitution of Estonian identity and the hegemonic interpretation of the Soviet past is increasingly shaped by late-modern processes and generational change. Global networks are pushing to rearticulate spatial and temporal patterns of behaviour, and with them, the way in which people locate themselves and give meaning to the world in which they live. Young people, in particular, have been open to global influences, changing practices and multiple processes of transition. They grew up in a world which became increasingly globalised, with varied notions of normality, among multiple scales of social action and cultural configuration, having to cope with extensive levels of consumer culture, changing media technologies and labour precariousness. This has produced the diminishing significance of structural factors, in addition to a feeling of personal uncertainty, openness . . . and tiredness.

This chapter discusses the ways in which generational change is turning old categories such as postsocialism or Eastern Europe obsolete in Estonia. It sets up to examine the complex ways in which cultural and political continuities interact with generational changes, drawing on the assumption that young people (those who are between 24 and 30 years old today, who have their own vision of the 1990s) are leaving behind the introspective of the transition period, re-enacting and deterritorialising Soviet forms, and re-shaping traditional ideas of nation, location, and identity. Through informal interviews, literature review, cultural criticism and a study of how young people react upon narrations of the past through artistic interventions, the research considers memory discourses in relation to the generational differences after socialism, aiming at updating the categories used for analysing Eastern European societies.

Fig. 8.1   In a meeting at Ülase 12. Source: Author, 2012.

Fig. 8.2   Event organised by Pinksiklubi. Source: Risto Kozer, 2013.

New generations are bringing new notions of value, ugliness, success, scale, location, and materiality. Different cohorts of people tend to create their own socialising patterns and meanings based on the discourses, events, materiality and technologies surrounding them. On the one hand, historical changes form a consciousness of generation through reflexive engagement with the *Zeitgeist*; on the other, it is this very change of worldview that shapes public practices and fosters social transformations. This leads to the acknowledgement that young people are simultaneously makers and breakers of a status quo, both challenging and effecting social transformations; in short, agents of change and not simply disrupters of the established order (Castells 2004; Comte 1974; Mannheim 1952; Honwana and de Boeck 2005).

A crucial issue in this matter is how the post-postsocialist materialises, or in other words, how new generations are changing the way of conducting the content of politics and to what degree the relationship towards the past is of discovery, change or rejection? Nowadays, a resurgence of civic activism and political involvement seems to be taking place in Estonia, at least according to the most recent Human Development Report. In many cases, young people are behind the new expressions of political criticism and cultural activities (discussing LGBT rights and the condition of refugees and immigrants, promoting vegan values, reappropriating the public sphere and materialising post-postsocialist spaces (figure 8.1 and 8.2), with leading groups such as Linnalabor, Stencibility, Pinksiklubi, Kraam, to name but a few). Likewise, new efforts have been dedicated to neighbourhood communities and milieu developing (such as Telliskivi, the Professor's Village and Nõmme's Public Services Associations, NPSA), rather than engaging with the structure of the society as such. As urbanist Keiti Kljavin observes, neighbourhood associations in Estonia have not been politically reactive, responding to social inequality or marginality, but rather they have focused on creating a sense of belonging and devotion to a milieu. Nonetheless, these movements appear as 'trans-local' – drawing inspiration from local struggles elsewhere (Kljavin 2014, 19).

Generational memories

Frames of memory and the construction of identities are not fixed, but in a situational process of becoming, always reproduced through the multiple interactions emerging in the present. For instance, young people in Estonia have their own memory of the 1990s, which is distinctly different from the other generations. They remember playing in playgrounds next to Volga taxis, wearing clothes that came with Swedish aid packages, seeing the construction of the first shopping malls, eating their first burger at McDonald's, listening to the Scorpions on the radio, watching films on VHS cassettes and MacGyver and Nirvana concerts on TV, imagining that the Annelinn's apartment blocks of Tartu was the skyline of Seattle (Preiman 2017; Rander

2016). In the exhibition *Children of the New East* (Tallinn Art Hall, 2017), curator Siim Preiman invited eight young artists of the region to explore how it would be the leading art of the upcoming era. I took part in the project by providing a text for the exhibition booklet, whereby Preiman wrote:

> I'm exactly young enough to have seen the momentous events of the end of the previous century only in retrospect on a TV screen. All of those moments that were of great importance to the development of the Estonia and the Europe we are currently living in actually didn't really happen as far as I'm concerned. . . . As the scenes of the fall of the wall were broadcast on the same screen as MacGyver and Xena: Warrior Princess, you could have easily imagined those events, for all we know (2017, 2).

Sociologist Marju Lauristin categorised those born just before and after the regained independence as the 'Children of Freedom' (*Vabaduse Lapsed*), referring to the idea of growing up in a free society for the first time and being 'unspoiled' by the Soviet system. 'When "they" arrived with their father at the schoolhouse in 1991, the Republic of Estonia had already been restored' (Lauristin 2003). I argue, however, that this label has turned into a cruel optimism (Berlant 2011) – a positive idea and goodwill becoming a cultural burden, with social costs for Estonian society. On the one hand, the concept disregards the way social bonds have been weakened in the last decades because of both internal and global processes. On the other, it ignores that the cluster of promises put into that generation cannot be made possible, at least as originally expected.

It is an illusion to think that those growing up after the break-up of the USSR would partake of the same understanding of freedom, location and identity as their parents, and a similar assessment of the Soviet past. New generations tend to deploy alternative perspectives on the past as part of their ongoing dialogue with the present. Generational memory is something historical and emergent, accompanied by a reappropriation of the past which nowadays is highly mediated and screened. Reflecting on these matters, Preiman (2017) notes how their identity was felt as divided along the former borders yet consuming global cultural products. Also following the idea of the divided individual, local artist Tanel Rander (2016) explains the effect as a geopolitical subjectivity split in half: the younger people's heads were finally living in the West, yet their bodies remained inevitably bound to the East, making people *dividual*, composed of multiple entities (Laviolette 2017; Strathern 1988). Further, Rander argues (2017) that the magnitude and significance of the transition period prevented local people from fully internalising all the meanings and dimensions involved in the change, and only now are they starting to take it in because a sufficient amount of time has passed: 'For example, I just realised that I should really pay attention to the lyrics of "Wind of Change" by the Scorpions. They were straightforward: "Let your balalaika sing, what my guitar wants to say!" This song could be considered as the hymn of Eastern Europe because it emerged during the most pivotal events and it made the masses whistle along because most people could not speak English back then and those who did, practiced it with no sense of criticism'.

More cosmopolitan, no less local

Contrary to what we might initially think, we do not drop our locality to be global, but settle in both; people may be more cosmopolitan without putting aside the local. To show this we can compare, for instance, Russian and Estonian networks of hip-hop in Tallinn during the 1990s. Even though intertwined through global cultural symbols, the two communities showed unequal features of self-construction due to their 'political states of mind' at the local level, with messages such as 'Russians go back to Russia!' circulating. As noted by designer Ott Kagovere (2015), this had two consequences in Lasnamäe, the neighbourhood where he grew up. The first one is that Russian teenagers became 'white niggas' in Estonia; the second was that their rap was considered more authentic than that of fellow Estonians. Globalisation and national identity are thus to be understood as interlinked processes, playing different roles, showing a variation of scales, instead of conceived in binary terms, as two poles (Edensor 2002).

Globalisation can also be understood as a historical moment of rupture which made obsolete old definitions and imaginaries as a side-effect. A contemporary approach to these phenomena seems to require a more relational and comparative approach, as well as the invention of new terms and categories such as 'children of the new east', 'post-Eastern Europe', and 'geopolitical subjectivity split in half', since the meaning of location, traditions and national identity is being shattered, as well as the self-awareness of *being* Eastern European and the responsibility of the past. Hence, there is an increasing need to analyse the region in relation to the global present, and not as substantively defined based on past geopolitical vocabulary (Dzenovska 2014; Ivancheva forthcoming).

We can even ask if 'Eastern Europe' or 'postsocialism' remain as generative terms to be retained, in which way they are nowadays used by the local population and what new terms are being proposed nowadays to replace it (e.g., 'New East'). As a self-explanatory category, 'Eastern Europe' has been circulating for centuries, presented as the internal other of the continent (Wolff 1994). And yet, nowadays Europe itself is being repositioned and altered 'as a place and as an idea' (Green 2013, 345). There are also new forms of 'crosslocations' (as Sarah Green puts it in the description of her research project), in tune with wider processes that intensify dynamics of relative positioning and changes in relations between places and people, forming hybrid and/or multiple attachments.

Further, we can ask whether this coexistence of positions, knowledges and scales is an incremental or a transformative condition, yet the overlap of spatio-temporal registers and cultural referents is already generating complex configurations and producing various modes of belonging and multi-scalar imaginaries. This process undermines traditional predicaments upon the significance of location – the specificities of language, culture, demography, economy and history – and challenges the hegemony of the nation (and methodological nationalism) as a unit of spatial organisation. Hence, to develop a more relational understanding of Europe, as a place and as an idea, we should pay special attention to how the new generation takes on the concept of Eastern Europe, and perhaps add a 'post' to it, as a mark of skepticism, referencing a critical perspective on this condition and positioning.

Nonetheless, this argument does not imply that national identities are relics from the past, but that they are being reshaped, actively reconciling unity and diversity in new ways. Cosmopolitan orientations are contributing to the construction of locality through a targeted and selective adoption of global symbols into the local context; however, young people still narrate their attachment to places in terms of home and tradition (Pilkington et al. 2002). This means that the lived experience of globalisation does not simply scale up the construction of identity through transnational cultural symbols, but also makes the existing scales more irregular.

Young people engage in global processes in various types of local appropriations (Tsuda, Tapias and Escandell 2014), not always as hybrids but also alongside (Pilkington et al. 2002). After all, globalisation is a part of our every day, locally adjusted and affectively negotiated, not an abstract entity or force. These processes have also affected the way we relate to each other, reconfiguring the imagination and scales of societies. Contemporary technologies make it possible for peoples to live in multiple countries simultaneously, influencing identity making over physical distances. This irregular scaling-up allows for the creation of an identity above a given membership in social groupings and cultural traditions, yet this is conditioned by the group dynamics in which we individually engage. Individuals constantly position themselves on several (social, temporal and spatial) scales and discursive levels of belonging, applying sorting mechanisms. The fact that media technologies transcend national boundaries contributes to the complexity of this relationship, increasing the tension between 'imagined communities' and 'imagined networks' as two different forms of place making (Green, Harvey and Knox 2005).

Young people inhabit more plural worlds, comprised by a wide range of local, regional and global identity discourses, which often leads to new forms of accidental communities forged through shared experiences related to chance, taste and leisure (figure 8.3). For instance, we can notice

Fig. 8.3 Henrik Rakitin, *Heraldry*, 2016; included in the *Children of the New East* show.

Fig. 8.4 'Photo family' of the Vint44 gang in Kanala, 4 August 2014.
Source: Riina Varol.

new ways of forming social connections in the bonds created by practices
such as ping-pong or street art in Estonia. Practitioners of these activities
express cultural models that were not formerly present within local social
structures and they present themselves as being involved in a distinct way
of life, rather than simply showing a different subcultural style. An example of this is Vootele Vaher, one of the most popular table tennis players
in Estonia (figure 8.4). As Vootele says: 'A friend called me post-hipster.
I consider myself more of a representative of the "subculture" of hands-on
people – a supporter of a sustainable way of life'.[1]

In 2014, there was an exhibition about the genealogy of graffiti and
street art in Tartu. As the curator Marika Agu explained, the show reflected
on the way in which local culture was shaped 'following examples from
abroad, combining foreign behavioural principles and exemplars with personal ambitions and soul-searchings' (2014, 8). Paradoxically, the emer-

Fig. 8.5   Streets of Tartu; an anonymous work and MinaJaLydia's harajuku twins. Source: Sirla, 2015.

Fig. 8.6   Anonymous picture of the Typical Individuals included at the corresponding exhibition.

gence of local graffiti was depicted as strongly imitative of a vague notion of 'typical Westerner' (figure 8.5. and 8.6): an imitation of the imitation; a form without a clearly delineated content that was reappropriated generation after generation.[2] In this sense, Estonian street art remained influenced by both local policies and global referents simultaneously. Another feature is that, in their secrecy and individualism, graffiti writers form a community of individuals that share strong codes and ethics and show respect for their tradition. These youth practices denote intergroup ties that generate collective meanings to individual lives and have the potential to evoke solidarities and affects that cut across mainstream divides (Martínez 2015a; Pilkington and Omel'chenko 2013).

As Bach, a local artist, acknowledged in the documentary prepared for the exhibition: 'We got our ideas from rap videos where the walls were colourful. We did not want to copy anyone, but we still mimicked the guys in the rap videos'. Also, Barthol Lo Mejor remarked on the significance of the Internet in the search for individual emancipation: 'It was escapist in a way, because you do not identify with the world around you, and your stuff is not organically tied to it. . . . So they imported that whole world . . . a world within a world'. Another important point they shared was the play with identities, felt by MinaJaLydia as 'a magic world where I escape from this reality'.

The memory of Sisyphus

Generations are socially constituted by sharing experiences and cultural referents, in turn formulating particular relations of solidarity and temporal paradigms. The 'Children of Freedom' grew up in a society that increasingly encouraged competition, filled with abundant choices, surrounded by discourses of neoliberal success – a context in which instability turned into its own form of stability. Yet young people acquired a practical and even utilitarian aptitude preparing them to cope with and manage the diversity of life changes, showing different ideals and political goals for which they would like to fight (Kalm 2015; Martínez 2015b). They seem to master global patterns, ubiquitous mediatisation and market economy better than their parents because they had to learn to integrate instability and indefinability into their everyday lives (Markowitz 2000). We can notice indeed that playfulness, novelty and stimulation have become as important as security for young people, who show also more individualistic values and less will to follow the rules (Lilleoja and Raudsepp 2016).

As emotional archaeologists or *retrovators*, young people in Estonia show a curiosity about looking back, inventing their own precursors and uncovering the uneven discourses about the Soviet world. One of the things they detect is that their parents' memories of the socialist experience still inform the current social conditions. The riddle here is to figure out how present-day expectations and experiences might invest the past with novel meaning. Different generations hold different aspects of the past as important, according to narrative principles of how the old was and what is the new. The increasing popularity of seemingly past material culture and Soviet design may be indeed understood as a reflexive step back among young people, who explore the basic layers of collective emotions by acknowledging the evidence of a different value system (taste, money, time) that still remains within contemporary societies. This interest suggests a fundamental shift in the popular relationship with the past, ironic and half-longing, which makes Elizabeth Guffey argue that this unsentimental nostalgia is nothing more than an empty stylistic gesture, a retro pillage of history 'with little regard for moral imperatives or nuanced implications' (2006, 163).

Generations have the memory of Sisyphus, the mythological figure condemned to rolling a rock to the top of a mountain, whence the stone would fall again and again. The appetite of young people for historical forms and emotions reveals also a shift from 'hot' to 'cold' memory (Weeks 2010), as the approach towards the past is characterised by distance and detachment. In contrast to the earlier emphasis on the traumatising consequences of the Soviet regime and the imprint of the identity of the Other within Europe, the engagement of the new generation focuses on material culture, functioning indeed as an instrument of critique of the contemporary that drifts through the ironic and melancholic (Astahovska 2015).

I recall, for instance, the discussion between Marika, my partner, and Luule, her mother, about the furniture to be bought for our apartment in Mustamäe. Marika suggested a retro-style lamp because it was practical and cheap, yet Luule disliked it because it looked Soviet. This lamp, formerly discarded, becomes newly valuable, revealing how wasted legacies can be economically dynamic. It is quite a paradox, if comparing the turnaround of value of these items and their capacity to convey affective messages: from trash to retro-styled brands, not only ceasing to be objects of waste but also becoming precious commodities. Eventually, it shows that something might be 'new' and 'old' simultaneously, interrupting the ongoing assumptions of a single chronology, demonstrating that the recovery of past things does not simply lead to reproduction, but rather to revival, giving new life to those things without erasing their previous lives.

The actual recovery of past things can be also understood as a retro-resistance to social acceleration and the imperative of change, a reaction manifested in the actual search for attachments and a sense of permanence and slow time that seems to be missing in Western societies (Martínez 2015c). Unlike their parents, who still believed in the future as a safe and promising location, contemporary youth tends to locate their anxieties in the future and so search for shelters in the past (Bauman 2017). Certainly, it is high time to discuss the generational differences after socialism and to update the categories used for analysing contemporary youth in Estonia, since young people blur the strict delineation between past, present and future, approaching them in a more porous and situational way.

Children of freedom, cruel optimism

No domination seems to be as natural as the rapport between child and tutor. People perceived as political infants offer an almost perfect argument for control and subjecting order. In a brief period of time, those societies that provoked democratic revolutions assumed the role of being premature and infants of democracy, internalising as normal the need to learn from the old Western brothers how to use what they themselves had conquered. This logic presented by Boris Buden in his article 'Children of Postcommunism' (2010) can also be extended to discourses about 'Children of Freedom' in Estonia. There, young generations have been likewise presented as untroubled by the past and enjoying freedom in a carefree way, exempting them of any responsibility in the current state of affairs and in turn limiting their power of emancipation. In these discursive terms, young people remain childish in the political struggle, continually lacking something that adults have or know (Martínez 2014).

National identities are most often constructed with narratives, rituals and traditions that establish a connection with the past and enhance a sense of belonging to a community (see chapter 7). In Estonia such a process entailed strong generational connotations, since the memory of Soviet time is the basis for how the past is remembered, becoming a 'meaning-making apparatus' (Nugin 2010, 356). One of the complications is that, although young people do not have any personal memories of living in the Soviet Union or about the Singing Revolution of 1991, their identity is directly shaped by stories told by their relatives, school teachers and politicians – thanks to the highly affective character of this memory (Maruste 2014).

In Estonia, the 1990s were a time of self-discovery and self-examination, in which not only the political regime's understanding of the past changed (Vihalemm, Lauristin and Tallo 1997), but also the negative past was juxtaposed with a positive vision identified with those born during the final years of socialism and after the break-up of the USSR (Nugin 2015). These young people were later accused of 'lacking memory', not appreciating their 'given' freedom, ignoring patriotic feelings, or even betraying the nationhood for being critical with the status quo (Maruste 2014; Nugin 2010; Preiman 2017). But why are the older generations in Estonia making such a complaint? As shown by Nugin, there was in Estonia a generation that became the arbiter of taste, establishing what is transient and giving a name to the durable, the 'winners generation': 'they are the ones who participated in creating narratives in discursive fields, influencing the understanding of the period of change', and assessing social 'others' from their perspective (Nugin 2011, 7).

Paradoxically, if a generation in which one has invested the hegemonic idea of a good life does not follow your expectations or does not fulfil the hopes put on them, the very grounds and coherence of social organisation is endangered, since it is this very optimism that maintains people's attachment to the institution that sustains the idea of a good life. In this sense, Estonian society might suffer from what Lauren Berlant calls a 'cruel optimism' (2011), referring to the costs of an illusion. In her view, the effects are 'cruel' because it is the very fantasy of what is 'good' that denies the subject in question all that was initially promised and even the capacity for emancipation. In this sense, it is the very label 'Children of Freedom' which contributes to a 'cruel optimism' by creating a hierarchical bond between generations and by exaggerating the monolithic composition of actual Estonian society, reifying as a consequence a continuity of cultural and political consciousness.

Nowadays, young people are caught by deeply contradictory (cultural and economic) demands which are incompatible with the fixed identity and ordered living expected by older generations. The so-called Children of Freedom are first of all characterised by the need to choose their career and locating options in a global playground (Maruste 2014). Young people appear increasingly open to new horizons and mobilities, yet feeling a certain loss of 'place' and more oriented towards cosmopolitan memories. They also show a tendency to mistrust institutions (rather than simply politics), manifesting ecological concerns and being impelled to cope with a rapid pace of change and media innovations. As noticed by young anthropologist Gustav Kalm in an opinion essay (2015), contemporary Estonian youth thinks less in terms of grand notions and more about specific episodes and with less straightforward categorisations, which makes nationalistic ideals less affecting for youngsters than they are for older generations. As a consequence, this is leading to a depolitisation of history and of the remnants from the Soviet past, along with a repolitisation of everyday life (e.g., ecological, gender and economic issues). In the medium term, generational change might provoke the breaking apart of the revanchist paradigm stemming from the regaining of independence, especially once those who are stuck in reading only the present through the links to the past (relying on the power relations formed accordingly) disappear from the political scene.

An example of this is the radically different attitude towards migration, mobility and civic participation, as well as their diverse strategies for making a living (in an era in which permanent jobs, as well as a career pattern and clear-cut occupational assignments, are increasingly rare). Not long ago, however, the director of the ENM Tõnis Lukas proposed that Estonians should consider those who have emigrated from the country in the past years as 'refugees of comfort' and 'lazy', instructing the younger generation about the difficult path of the nation.[3] In his essay, Gustav Kalm responded to this controversial statement: 'With salaries in neighbouring Finland and Sweden amongst the highest in the European Union and a couple times higher than in Estonia, it is easy to understand why many Estonians choose to emigrate to work in these countries' (2015, 92). Yet, Kalm pointed out further that what the controversy reveals is:

> an intergenerational shift in attitudes. For Tõnis Lukas and his generation, the most important goal they fought for . . . was Estonian independence. . . . In this patriotic instrumentalist vision of labour, work done abroad with the sole goal of personal enrichment does not really count as proper work. Unlike for Lukas's generation, who were born and raised in an Estonia under Soviet rule, contemporary youth in Estonia grew up in an independent country. Even though they might be aware of the battles that were fought, Estonian independence has been for them a given – a reality in which to build one's life and live out its everyday material struggles. (Kalm 2015, 92)

In nationalist constructions of identity, migrant workers are depicted as impure – formless, out of place, to be brushed away, accused of being a foreign contaminant. As shown by Douglas, classifications of dirt and impurity do not only refer to hygiene, but also tell about social order and the reinforcement of internal structures, invoked as a source of power and maintained through rituals and normative codes. In recent years, new accounts against migration have emerged in Estonia; they even used racist discourses to present diversity as dangerous, polluting something supposedly pure, threatening good order and fertility.[4] This affirmation of identity through closure towards others and as a negative representation of the past (justifying hegemonies and political configurations) is delusional and turns into a burden for some groups, validating temporal and social inequality and emphasising a hierarchy of generations, rather than advancing social integration.

Harry Potter, Bob Marley, Che Guevara

The global is being integrated inside the national intensively, reshaping the inherited, destabilising older hierarchies and scales. Further, young people in Estonia seem to be more capable of creating their own social and cultural worlds than the previous generations, shaping and sharing their own lives differently. In the booklet of the exhibition *Third Way* (Tallinn Art Hall, 2016), Tanel Rander reflected on an episode he lived through in the conference 'Communist Nostalgia' (University of Glasgow, 2015), whereby an American lady disclaimed as bizarre to be born in Eastern Europe and feel nostalgia for Kurt Cobain. Trying to understand this generational phenomenon and to depict the varied temporal regimes and attitudes towards the past coexisting in Estonia, I talked to young informants in places that would be familiar to them. Hence I carried out a simple open-ended inquiry based on 25 informal interviews in three prominent bars for young people in Tallinn (Protest), Tartu (Arhiiv), and Narva (Ro-ro), all of them taking place between 19:00 and 22:00. Interviews were carried out in English and Russian, and all of my informants were surprisingly accessible and receptive to discuss these matters. The category 'Children of Freedom' was familiar to them, yet they did not use it in their everyday life. Just two questions were asked: 'Which is your main cultural referent?' and 'Do you see yourself as a child of freedom, growing up in a free society?' With respect to cultural referents, I got answers such as Manchester United, David Beckham, Harry Potter, Buddhism, punk, hippie and surrealist cultures, Kurt Vonnegut, Bob Marley, Michael Jackson, Che Guevara, Versace, Hemingway and Almodóvar.

About the self-identification as Children of Freedom, my informants commented:

> I feel like a Child of Freedom because we can travel to Europe and plan our lives more freely. (Maria, 26)

I feel free, but I'm Russian, not an Estonian Child of Freedom. (Vassif, 25)

I'm in the Estonian Defence Force, so I'm particularly aware of freedom and politics. For me Children of Freedom means that we have the chance to enjoy freedom. (Magnus, 22)

I see myself as a Child of Freedom. I don't have the same guilt as my parents. I don't have a direct connection with the communist past. I was born as part of the West already. (Siim, 23)

I'm a Child of Freedom because I have the freedom to travel all over the world. But there are still too many Russians in Estonia. (Grete, 25)

I'm a Child of Freedom because I can choose the information I read. We don't talk about Communism and my parents don't want to describe it. They just say it was bad. So we don't quite understand it. We kind of feel nostalgia for something we don't understand, for a myth. (Raine, 24)

I feel like a Child of Freedom. I have freedom of choice. I can travel wherever I want in Europe. I can study what I want. I can be who I want. But I don't judge what it was before. According to my parents, Communism was good. Probably it would be good to have a more equal and balanced society. (Lina, 19)

In some ways we are, but we haven't had the experience of not being free. Personally, I see other oppressing forces, not that formal or evil. For instance, the way we are surveilled through the Internet. (Paula, 23)

The so-called Children of Freedom gained access to global cultural referents, diverse values and multiple forms of knowledge, which contributed to form their identity, place-making and assessment of the past. I asked my partner, Marika (28), about her cultural referents and she named the American WFMU radio as her main inspiration nowadays. And as she put it, 'I'm a Child of Freedom because I grew up in the 90s, a very intense and chaotic period in Estonia; also because of seeing how modernist architecture that was familiar to me, somehow part of my identity, has been progressively disappearing; particularly in Tallinn, where I was born'. In her teenage period, she knew by heart songs by Dr. Dre and Tupac; whilst the emotional education of her mother, Luule (56), for instance, was rather shaped by Jaak Joala and Anne Veski, Soviet Estonian singers that she still likes very much. Some of Marika's recent cultural passions are the American artist Miranda July, German Kraut-rock, the Kiwi Connan Mockasin, the Brazilian bossa-psychedelia of Os Mutantes, the desert blues of Ali Farka Touré and Chinawoman, born in Toronto to Russian immigrants and currently living in Berlin. These referents are not just diverse geographically, but also come from different cultural periods.

Young people in Estonia are making the relationship between past, present and future less unidirectional and ordered than the previous generations. Yet in this multiplicity of revivals, endings and new beginnings, what kind of responsibility might the younger generations have to the past? Every generation asks anew how we should orientate in time and space, and are reconstructed by their distinction from preceding cohorts, which entails thus a reappropriation of the past and new temporal experiences. In her ethnography of multiple youths in postwar Bosnia, Monika Palmberger (2016) argues that in order to understand the way present actors give meaning to the past and reshape frames of memory, it is crucial to account of distinct 'generational positionings', paying attention specifically to the way they distance themselves from the experience and memories of their families and narrow past narratives.

The new generation is already bringing with it new stances and imprints, thus reshaping traditional ideas of nation and identity. An example of this is the rapid impact of rapper Stuf (Evgeny Lyapin, 26 years old, born in Narva), who in January 2017 posted on YouTube a song entitled 'Olen Venelane' (I am Russian) which reached over 150,000 views in four months. The song begins with the statement 'I'm Russian, but I love Estonia', and continues saying, 'All are dissatisfied with this State, they dream of a far-off kingdom'. The video was recorded on the border between Estonia and Russia and, with a bilingual composition, he echoes the frustrations of the Russian-speaking community in Estonia; even so, Stuf claims not to be interested in politics.

Another example is the global popularity of Tommy Cash (Tomas Tammemets, 26 years old), making what he dubs 'post-Soviet rap', which combines influences from Kanye West, Eminem and Die Antwoord with Alla Pugacheva, Enya and Russian Orthodox church music. 'I get all my inspiration from my childhood and directly from the place where I grew up [the Kopli and Lasnamäe neighbourhoods of Tallinn]. I don't try to be American, I don't try to sound like no one else', says Tommy Cash.[5] In his videos, Cash features clad in Adidas, with a Dalí moustache and black boots, merging pop culture references with religious, military, Soviet kitsch and ghetto elements. Cash claims that 'Now, post-Soviet aesthetics has become ubiquitous, but when I started working with it, in 2013,

Fig. 8.7 Shop in the old town of Tallinn. Source: Siobhan Kattago, November 2017.

there was no such trend. We got ahead of it.'[6] Nowadays, Gucci and H&M are releasing menswear collections with the lines 'Back in the USSR' and 'What would you wear if you were to time travel to Moscow in 1994?' And if one takes a walk in the old town of Tallinn, one can face advertisements promoting post-Soviet fashion style for the winter season of 2017 (figure 8.7). Not surprisingly, *Vogue* recently published an article asking: 'Has the commercialisation of Russian and Eastern European fashion gone too far?'[7]

Young people are reenacting and deterritorialising Soviet symbols and past forms, in a playful way that serves nonetheless as a trigger for self-assessment. One of the side effects, for instance, is the way an *ersatz* antiquity has been designed into many cafés, shops and restaurants of Tallinn, such as Must Puudel, Sveta or Tops, to name just a few (figure 8.5). Another interesting example of how young people bring with them a new understanding of space, materiality and tradition is Konstanet, a nonprofit gallery that organises both virtual and physical (scaled 1:5) exhibitions of young artists willing to merge the online and offline realm. In a way, this post-internet gallery echos the e-Residency strategy developed by the government, which challenges traditional notions of citizenship by expanding a residency code to foreigners who are not geographically but digitally present in the country.

Concluding considerations

This chapter has discussed place-making experiences of young people in Estonia while also showing ways in which global phenomena have been locally translated and grounded. Representations of the past, social transformations, material culture and systems of valuation are connected and constructed in an ongoing dialectic. They shape each other both simultaneously and sequentially. In Estonia, young people are returning to and revaluating the past and their location anew, not as a straightforward engagement with collective memory or political categories, but rather as part of a wider process of consumption, reuse and rediscovery, which might lead nonetheless to the development of new narratives and epistemic possibilities, and a revaluation of old things that have been already remembered and forgotten and disposed.

Generational change is here presented as an exploratory variable of the social transformations to come. A new generation that does not remember the Soviet time has grown up in Estonia. Their practices appear globally routed and do not search for justification in the past. Therefore, Soviet memory in people's conventional values is losing its effective impact in the course of generational change. Young people inherited the specific historical representations, categories and frames of the previous generations, yet they in turn are increasingly recalibrating the narrative and experience of it.[8] This reinforces Caroline Humphrey's conviction that 'as the generations brought up under socialist regimes disappear from the political scene, the category of postsocialism is likely to break apart and disappear' (2002b, 13); but there is a political act to be accomplished too – the actualisation of past narratives, temporal belonging and obsolete categories.

Conclusion: The past is not what it used to be

Pastness is not an intrinsic quality of things, but a contested social practice, and something from which power relations might be generated. The past becomes something present in the body's memories, allowing us to feel familiar in the world. It is through anniversaries, monuments, museums and storytelling about the past that a community transmits a meaning of collective life to the next generations. Yet we should not ignore that processes of identity construction are directly influenced by coeval events and the materialities and technologies surrounding us when we are growing up; or that people's remembering is not simply past-oriented but points towards the future.

Change and past appear as mutually constitutive, shaping each other and being always tied to the question of 'what next?', entailing different dynamics of deconstruction, reconstruction and replacement. As memory, past changes constantly, being modified through the act of retrieval, becoming a memory of memory, since earlier forms of addressing the past cannot be simply replaced by later ones (Olick 2007). Yet nowadays, anything linked to temporality becomes obsolete increasingly quickly, and the formation of personal identity as a relational process is less determined by local history and culture than ever before. Moreover, and as seen in chapter 8, collective memories are not generating the same reactions from young people as they used to, since they are showing a more plural and selective approach towards past representations.

The impact of late-modern processes could not be foreseen by previous generations, and makes it more difficult to keep a monolithic identity and single cultural categorisations. In an era that is witnessing the diminishing of the traditional power of identity, individuals engage in new place-bound activities from which they derive new cultural forms of personhood and belonging. The result has been the construction of rather flexible identities, directly influenced by cosmopolitan referents and contingent choices. In this light, a narrow articulation of collective memory can only generate further social division between those supposedly belonging to this time and those who are obsolete (no longer relevant, stuck in the past). As pointed out by Michelle Bastian (2014), reductive conceptions of time restrict the way that identities can be presented, excluding some people from communities for not living, embodying or performing time according to normative models. As a result, the use of time often becomes a symbolic resource related to social capital and power, which conditions the way we participate in a society.

We can also refer to Elizabeth Freeman's (2010) notion of 'synchronisation' to conceptualise the ways in which the family and the state, as institutions, establish their relationship to time and seek to bind a subject's daily routines or life course to their own temporality. Nowadays, nations seem to be less and less parallel communities partaking in a homogeneous time and political memories (Anderson 1991), like conjunctions of groups showing different intensities of relation within and between them, and being affected by the penetration of global temporalities into the local regime. We might even speculate that time itself is increasingly heterogeneous, establishing new forms of simultaneity, coincidence and copresence.

In a context of temporal multiplicity, the past means different things too. Further, the past is multiple not only because of generational change but also due to temporality being increasingly multiple, which might lead to conflicting experiences and visions. The dialectical relation between social dynamics and generations implies that the construction of the past may also vary, being cognitive and contingent, mutually and plurally constituted. Any historical representation is tied to changing social and cultural parameters, yet no matter how distinctive generations are with regard to the past, any process of construction of 'new' memories implies an engagement with old legacies, even if just to refuse them. Hence, even if young people in Estonia show a way of relating to the past different from the one manifested by their parents, both generations are framed still by the official histories (Aarelaid-Tart 2006; Halbwachs 1980).

The present never reproduces the past as it was, but its pastness, its echo and performativity appear in the form of past-presencing strategies (Lowenthal 1985; Macdonald 2013). Sociologists Raili Nugin, Anu Kannike and Maaris Raudsepp conclude that the mapping of different generations in Estonia 'depends mainly on the past rather than on the present' (2016, 25). In this light, the past remains as something crucial to be reckoned with, especially if considering the differences between experience, action and expectation (Koselleck [1979] 2004), and how socialist relations have been alive under postsocialist predicaments.

The temporal and the affective space of post-post socialism

By studying how the Soviet past has been rendered problematic in Estonia, I have outlined how postsocialisms were multiple and entailed ambiguities, incongruities and unexpected outcomes. Indeed, the divergences between and within the former socialist countries have been accentuated over the last decades. From the beginning of the process, postsocialist changes have been underpinned by a tension between continuation and rupture, conservation and change, the old and the new, dismissal and repair, anticontinuity and recuperation (Curro 2016; Martínez and Agu 2016). Further, the preserved disrepair of the socialist inheritance has not simply been organised in the present as a source of legitimisation but also directed towards the future to induce the vanishing of what is left behind and appears as problematic. Accordingly, it is important to pay attention to how the operation of postsocialism might influence what comes next, and explore how it would be possible to localise the post-post-socialist in contemporary Estonia.

I have studied generational change, material culture and temporal regimes after socialism, but not Estonian culture or history as such. Rather, the research brings to light the unresolved aspects of recent experiences of change and of what lies behind, or below, official representation. Ethnographically, I draw attention to how a sense of past is negotiated and actualised in contemporary Estonia by looking at specific continuities and anticontinuities with the Soviet past, as well as the dynamic relationship between discourses of the past and actual political practices.

This fringy anthropology is meant to function as an account of the reappropriation of a previous system legacy, and what has been wasted or made superfluous, but also to participate in the process of social inclusion and contribute to envisioning a common past by fostering a sense of unity in diversity, after drawing on the assumption that the treatment of the inherited is a key discursive and material practice to construct a collective social memory. Thus, the framing of legacies is presented as a process of identity formation and historical representation, deeply entwined in temporal regimes and core social bonds, and yet contingent on and subject to constant change and growing old. Often, the buildings, monuments and physical arrangements constructed to reinforce cultural messages are interpreted by others in ways different from those originally intended (Assmann 1995). Likewise, the representations, categories and structures that have functioned to create a sense of order are being affected by the same spatiotemporal scales that make everything obsolete in an *augenblick*.

While reading past literature on Eastern Europe and postsocialism, I often felt myself visiting a graveyard of dead yet unburied concepts and categories, some of them with potential for revision and some others not. Twenty-five years after regaining independence, having achieved institutional and economic stability, and following a strong generational change within society, Estonia has reached the time when it has to talk about the necessity of repairing the inheritance from the Soviet world as well as to distinguish between the Soviet Union, Russia and socialist ideas; still all three are used indiscriminately within many contemporary discussions. In this light, the ghost of socialism has been often used as an 'ideological antioxidant' for justifying inequality and exclusion, reducing support for redistributive policies and preempting social claims and discussions criticising state policies (Chelcea and Druta 2016).

Specifically, postsocialism emerged to designate the processes that followed the 'collapse' of state socialism (privatisation, marketisation, de-statisation . . .). Over time, this category gained a critical stand too, particularly in regard to neoliberal policies and transition theories. At that point, postsocialism and postcolonial agendas started to converge, though the latter always kept a stronger epistemological base (Chari and Verdery 2009; Morozov 2015). Used as a time period or as a critical instance, postsocialism became the 'gatekeeping concept' (Appadurai 1986) for Eastern Europe, presenting transition or nostalgia as the only legitimate lens through which to view the region and excluding alternative anthropological conceptualisations, especially those which implied peripheral theorisation (Kojanic forthcoming).

During the elaboration of this work, it has been a challenge to avoid a priori negative accounts of the Soviet system. Presumptions of socialist life being 'bad', 'abnormal', 'immoral', 'erroneous' and 'devoid of meaning'[1] have been institutionally disseminated during the last decades, using this terminology to explain the experience of those living in the USSR before the break-up of the system – as if Soviet society were already thinking in those terms, and as if the Soviet world was not a reality as any other. And yet, these terms and conjectures gained prominence among the society only within the context of the vanishing system, in the late eighties (Yurchak 2005). References to the Soviet past demonstrate a paradoxical complexity in the conceptualisation of time regimes. On the one hand, they inscribe a temporal logic that determines the actual existence of states in a causal way. On the other, narratives about the Soviet era often collapse the contemporary and the historical, bringing present elements into the past in an anachronistic way for organising what is received and shared (Rancière 2015).

Aiming to take the socialist experience seriously, Alexei Yurchak suggests approaching the Soviet world beyond binary categories such as repression and freedom, good and bad, or regime versus people, since by reproducing these isolated binaries, Soviet life appears to have no meaning, and people who were part of it to have no agency. An interesting case happened around the celebrations of the 100th anniversary of the Estonian Republic, when I wrote an article describing different examples of 'banal nationalism' in the country (Billig 1995). This phenomenon goes from official ways of flagging nationhood through the ordinary engaging activities (e.g., to install Estonian flags along the roads of the main cities or to lighten public squares with the three colours of the flag) to how private companies, some of them foreign, try to promote their products by making use of the nationalist pathos (e.g., adding Estonian flags to the container of goods, inviting well known figures of the so-called Singing Revolution to advertise products on TV and so on). My article generated interesting feedback. On the one hand, several people wrote to me saying thanks for making this view public and the article published in Sirp (in Estonian) received 10 times more visitors than the average of the journal; on the other hand, the article generated heated public comments, accusing me of being a 'Marxist' for criticising 'the Estonian nation' or being put as an example of how foreigners do not understand why Estonian culture has to be defended.[2]

The future of the past

When political realities change, interpretations of the past are turned into a battlefield, so history can be narrated (rediscovered, recreated) in new ways. By grounding discussions of what 'socialist' means today and the fate of the Soviet world 25 years after the dissolution of the previous order, this book has taken into account how the recent past is presented in Estonia, arguing that social perceptions and memories have been constructed in a perspective determined by the year 1991. Accordingly, young generations and the Russian-speaking community have suffered a denial of coevality – the former exists projected towards the future, the latter towards a troubled past, a condition of domination which leads to their objectification and relatively low institutional power.

This denial of coevality implies a recognition de facto of divisions in relation to past representations within Estonian society. Generational and ethnic differences in Estonia still seem to rely on past narratives which resonate in spatial configurations, strategies of value creation, public discourses and structures of inequality and power. However, by foregrounding the interrelationship of material properties, social change and immaterial values assigned by different generations to the inherited from the Soviet world, this research has shown that remnants contain the capacity to be transformed, to become something else and that wasted legacies could be considered as a means of triggering the process of redefinition of belonging and revaluation of the past.

Through a series of case studies, I have argued that the degradation of the Soviet past arose as ad hoc to the abrupt social transformation and the need to build up the new state. Yet the material also suggested that a generational change is already making the postsocialist antiparadigm obsolete, as young people do not search for justification in the past and show a more plural construction of their identity (yet not necessarily more progressive). By addressing how residues of the past are reworked in the present and the way transformations come about precisely through the continuous emergence of new generations, the book set out to answer larger questions and to achieve a comparative potential, accounting for how one set of values displaces another, the connections between societies and their waste, material geographies of affect, and how societies get rid of things and the role that this plays in creating historical representations.

In the last years, the Estonian government has been promoting an active Nordic orientation, discursively differentiating Estonia from the precarious region of Eastern Europe, thus placing the country in a more stable group of sovereign states. As in the case of Finland, the claim to centrality or of being a vanguard state has paradoxically been supported by attributes derived precisely from a sense of marginality and smallness (Browning and Lehti 2007). Further, in the emerging post-post-socialist Estonia, there seem to be two (interrelated) clashes of collective narratives. One is the generational gap between those who grew up in the Soviet regime and those who were born after the regained independence (more plural, with a wide range of identity discourses). The other gap presents a struggle between the economy and the nation as a cultural dominant, in other words, a struggle for the political hegemony between those who situate at the core of Estonian society discourses of suffering and danger (constantly thinking themselves as victims) and those following a 'start-up mentality' who argue for entrepreneurship, technological innovation, global nation branding and neoliberal policies. So far, they have been able to reach compromises, yet their balance is unstable. An example is the debate around the renaming of the Museum of Occupations in Tallinn to 'Vabamu' (Home of Freedom), willing to replace the tragic shadow of the twentieth century for a presentist affirmation and to increase the number of visitors (Kirss 2017; Weekes 2017). This questioning of reference points and engagement with older forms of normativity is a symptom in a broader chain of transformations (Kurg 2014), prompting a novel sociality and a value system which might lead to a redefinition of the boundary between the old and the new. This reminds us, once again, that to draw cultural boundaries and to form a system of value is a contingent social process, being unstable and subject to change, always depending on a different correlation of forces (and weaknesses).

Epilogue: A global *Subbotnik*

Once upon a time, or more concretely, the 3rd of May 2008, over 50,000 Estonians cleaned up thousands of 'illegal trash' piles across the country. In just five hours, about 10,000 tons of garbage was collected, packed and sorted, making it the largest coordinated civic event in the country since the 'Singing Revolution'. The frontman of the initiative, Rainer Nõlvak, received the 'Volunteer of the Year' award. As the description reads, Nõlvak's team was supported by 'top professionals', 'opinion leaders', NGOs, 'partners', even the president of the country, and the Estonian National Museum encouraged the participants to write about their experience. A free waste-mapping application was created, enabling people to hunt the trash and upload the location using Google Earth. The description of the organisers reads that under normal circumstances it would have taken three years and €22,500,000 to do what this private initiative achieved in five hours. By most accounts, the event was considered a 'success',[1] presenting this exceptional initiative as the ultimate solution for lasting collective problems.

The *Teeme Ära!* (Let's Do It!) initiative referred to 'illegal waste lying around in Estonian nature', as if there were something like untouched nature, which is purely Estonian, endangered by random disposals and not by systematic industrial pollution. This did not, however, prompt a sustained public debate about the importance of maintenance and infrastructure for waste collecting, and the fact that hundreds of municipalities provided free garbage trucks and cleaning teams to help this private action was mostly overlooked. Neoliberal policies were not related to the event either, nor the transfer of the responsibility for waste issues to the nonprofit organisations and households, fostering indeed principles of outsourcing public services and short-term solutions (Pikner and Jauhiainen 2014).

This 'entrepreneur', 'visionary', 'pioneer', 'guru' and 'angel investor', as Nõlvak has been dubbed, started to share his views in universities and TED talks on how to first clean a state, and then the entire planet. Following these lectures, he subsequently established the 'Let's Do It!' global platform, which has grown into a network of 113 countries and the creation of the World Cleanup Day (15 September 2018). The project defines itself as decentralised, apolitical, nonpartisan and not affiliated to any ideology or political party, and emphasises the cyber-guided character of the clean-up. The initiative received the 2017 European Citizen's Prize from the European parliament.

When I learned about the story and project, the Soviet *subbotnik* came to my mind. In the USSR, each year in spring, people gathered on Saturdays (*subbota* in Russian) to clean yards, roads and parks, plant new trees and paint fences. This was all volunteer labour, outside the regular working hours; even so, if one had not joined, one could be expected to face reprimands from the administration. The tradition started on 12 April 1919, when a group of workers at the depot of the Moscow–Kazan Railway decided to stay after the end of their shift in order to repair three more locomotives. Lenin publicly praised the idea and a year later it was extended to the whole country. After World War II, Stalin introduced six-day working weeks, so *subbotniks* lost part of their meaning until the five-day week was recovered again in the 1970s. The practice almost died out during the difficult economic conditions of the 1990s; however, it has since been resuscitated by some companies.[2]

All countries struggle in one way or another to deal with their own waste, regardless of its being recently produced or inherited. For instance, Estonia invested €105 million in a new waste-to-energy plant at Iru, which can keep running only by importing rubbish from elsewhere. As Raine Pajo, board member of the state-owned energy company Eesti Energia, explained, 'Let's be honest, the handling of foreign garbage pays better'.[3] In 2014, the company won a competition to incinerate the waste produced in the Finnish city of Turku. However, since the waste incineration plant started working, less sorting has taken place in Estonia, and the plant focuses on importing waste from Finland and England.

Discourses of recycling waste have created new moral economies of global displacement and disregard,[4] in which consumer societies of the global North reproduce a form of neocolonialism, dumping on the peoples and environments of developing countries and receiving the 'commodities' back once refinished (Alexander and Reno 2012).[5] Likewise, the contemporary infrastructures that process our waste appear as technologies of governance that do not have as a priority to make waste systems legible (Offenhuber 2017).

Today, less than 30 per cent of waste is being sorted for recycling in Estonia. The enterprise in charge of dealing with the litter went bankrupt in 2011, after having mixed that waste with other litter and dumped both in a former Soviet military base in southern Estonia (Pikner and Jauhiainen 2014, 46). A decade after the clean-up event, disposal has not finished, partly due to the absence of sustainable and effective management in dealing with waste. A report in 2014 also revealed that of the eight districts in Tallinn, trash transport has been legally organised in only two of them, due, among other reasons, to the lack of professional management.[6] The break-up of state socialism meant also the rapid disintegration of the existing systems for the recycling and reuse of consumer goods; recycled utopia produced waste, but also large systems for storage and reuse (Gille 2007).

Notes

Preface

1 These destinations were written in the panel of flights of the airport before the renovation done in 1980 for the Olympic Games. The panel was part of Timo Toots's exhibition *Soodevahe*.

2 Since 2009, the government has handed around €135 million to Estonian Air in capital injections and state aid. The last time the company earned a profit was in 2005.

3 I could refer to the postmodern building designed by the architect Mikhail Piskov and the stylish interior designed by Maile Grünberg in 1980. Likewise, comment on the actual cozy interior design done by Kristiina Voolaid, colourful, with recorded birds' sounds in the restrooms, yet criticized because it looked like a department store. The first passenger terminal was designed by Arthur Jürvetson in 1938, only finished in 1954. The new project was designed by Jean Marie Bonnard, Pia Tasa and Inga Sirkel-Suviste, and received the award of 'Concrete Building of the Year 2008'.

Introduction

1 I also realised that in Greece there is a radical left-wing coalition (Syriza), in Portugal also a left-wing coalition called Geringonça ('contraption'), and Italy has had a social-democrat prime minister Matteo Renzi whose slogan was *rottamazione* (junk trade, demolishing).

2 For instance, instead of 'Soviet collapse', I talk in this work of a 'break-up', trying to avoid any teleological stand (the final outcome ascribing its meaning retroactively to the recent past) and to acknowledge the existence of a society organised around socialist principles.

Chapter 1

1 In 1992, the then Minister of the Interior Lagle Parek arranged for an exorcism before converting the KGB building into an Estonian police station.

2 I do not consider the question of judging the past, but more the use of it as a resource in the present, particularly for the objective of enhancing a sense of belonging through collective memory as well as of establishing a hierarchical integration within the social system.

3 The term *damnatio memoriae* was not used by the ancient Romans. The first appearance of the phrase as such, in Latin, is in a dissertation written in Germany in 1689. Umberto Eco has commented, however, that the *ars oblivionalis* doesn't function through *damnatio memoriae* but through false synonyms, claiming that, 'There are no voluntary devices for forgetting. . . . One forgets not by cancellation but by superimposition, not by producing absence but by

multiplying presences' (Eco 1988, 259). Have we been remembering insufficiently, or rather forgetting wrongly?

4 As he puts it, 'Politics revolves around what is seen and what can be said about it, around who has the ability and the talent to speak, around the properties of spaces and the possibilities of time' (Rancière 2006, 13).

5 Internet and apps such as Skype brought with them new forms of communicating, which created new jobs and opportunities but also rendered obsolete old professions and, in a way, handwriting.

6 In 2009, the Postimaja was sold to Altenberg-Reval AS (a subsidiary company of the Swedish Claes Magnus Åkerborg) for €8.18 million. The chairman of Eesti Post, M. Atonen, stated: "the Estonian Post is not a real estate company; so we contemplate real estate sales in order to finance its core and become more competitive'.

7 H&M has over 3,000 stores in 48 countries. In October 2013, dozens of teenagers slept outdoors Postimaja waiting for the opening of H&M. For them, this was a memorable event in which they wanted to be present. As shown by the Estonian TV in their report about the opening of the shop in Postimaja, the people who passed by the site believed a concert or a rave party was going on there.

8 '[T]heir valves and heat pipes reached like arteries into thousands of apartments in the district, embedding these boiler rooms inside the very entrails of the system, simultaneously providing . . . time, space, and intellectual freedom from its constraints. These were temporal, spatial, and thematic zones of *vnye* par excellence' (Yurchak 2005, 154). Group Kino has been probably the most popular stoker, working in the boiler room 'Kamchatka' between 1982 and 1987.

9 See, for instance, '"Radar": mis oleks, kui võtaksime vabadussambalt klaasi ümbert ära?' *Radar /Postimees*, 28 February 2017: https://kultuur.postimees.ee/4030077/radar-mis-oleks-kui-vot aksime-vabadussambalt-klaasi-umbert-ara?_ga=2.128477004.198545230.1508448042-13173 53178.1492592105.

10 See Hannes Praks, 'Hannes Praks: mida õpetavad noortele Vabadussamba metallribad?' *Pastimes*, 19 October 2017: https://arvamus.postimees.ee/4282385/hannes-praks-mida -opetavad-noortele-vabadussamba-metallribad?_ga=2.24059704.325668012.1507930930 -617229504.1435219512.

11 I agree with Buchli and Lucas: 'The relation between remembrance and forgetfulness is not a linear process but a struggle, a tension – in every memorial, something has been left out or forgotten, in every removal, something is left behind, remembered' (2001b, 80).

12 Lillepõld (2013) has drawn the topographical routes followed by the monuments of Lenin in Tallinn, Tartu and Narva, and the redesigns undertaken once the monument had vanished. The height of the monument was 7.8 m, including a granite pedestal.

13 The text reads: 'After the Republic of Estonia restored its independence, numerous Soviet monuments all over the country were removed, destroyed or simply put somewhere out of sight. The Estonian History Museum aims to collect these monuments as part of the memories of an era and to place these in a new context . . . mostly made by well-known Estonian sculptors. . . . Anything associated with Soviet ideology is painful and thus there are dissenting opinions about preserving the monuments . . . a symbol of one era of Estonia's past'.

14 See Maarjamäe Loss, 'Outdoor Exhibition of Soviet Monuments', http://www.ajaloomuu seum.ee/exhibitions/permanent-exhibitions/noukogude-aegsete-monumentide-valinaitus (reopened in February 2018).

15 They are a new version of the former *byvshie liudí*, those who 'had been' before the Bolshevik revolution but had become dispossessed and unable to adapt to the new situation.

16 Quotes from my field notes, Tallinn, July and August 2012. Real names are maintained, as a way of recognition, and with the consent of the informants.

Chapter 2

1 Nowadays, in the Estonian capital (over 400,000 inhabitants), there are only a few small places where one can repair broken things.

2 As journalist Iryna Vidanava describes, euroremont was the only Europanization that Belarusians could experience: Iryna Vidanava, 'On the Edge of Europe', *Belarus in Focus*,

23 May 2013, http://www.competition2013.belarusinfocus.info/page_on_the_edge_of _europe.

3 Andrew Stuttaford, 'A Soviet Brigadoon: The Strange History of Estonia's Sillamäe', *National Review*, 8 January 2013, http://www.nationalreview.com/article/337077/soviet-briga doon-andrew-stuttaford.

4 Interview, October 2017.

5 Departure and arrival. The last news I heard from Tartu, in December 2017, was that the Estonian Print and Paper Museum had had to move out from the Aparaaditehas due to a sharp increase in rent, and now the curators are searching for a new place, further away from the city centre.

6 This is manifested in the prefix 're-' that 'repair' shares with 'remembrance', etymologically referring to recollection, recall of the past, a memento and the faculty of memory.

Chapter 3

1 This expression was used by Alla, after I had been looking at her candies for three minutes without making a decision. Fieldwork done in February, April and May 2014.

2 A district of panel-block flats in the eastern part of Tallinn built in the 1970s to 1990s. The population is about 119,000, the majority of whom are Russian-speaking.

3 The hierarchy goes like this (from best to worst): European ('Made in Germany' considered the highest certificate of quality), Russian, Turkish and Chinese (referring to anything produced in Asia without distinction).

4 The year when it was opened remains unclear even for the people working on the site. All of them answered that the origin was during perestroika.

5 Article by Andres Puskar, *Delfi.ee*, 4 July 2012, http://www.delfi.ee/archive/andres-puskar -kas-sinu-laps-julgeks-balti-jaama-taga-bussi-oodata?id=64629468.

6 Conversation held at the gallery, Thursday 15 May 2014, at 13:00.

7 A recreational centre located next to the market with over 25,000 m² of cafés, shops, restaurants and a theatre.

8 Nõmme turg, Uus Maailm festival, Kalamaja päevad, Raekoja plats, among others.

9 Kalamaja, a neighbourhood in the north of Tallinn, has been subject to gentrification in the recent years. Rental prices are higher and the tenants' composition has changed with the increasing arrival of expats and an educated middle class.

10 Surpassed only by Norway and Luxembourg. See 'The Promised Land of Shopping Malls', *Baltic Business News*, 25 October 2013, http://shaan.typepad.com/shaanou/2013/10/tallinn -the-promised-land-of-shopping-malls.html.

11 In shopping malls, people are not simply separated from production but also cut off from nonconsumerist logics; the division between the interior of the mall and its exterior is very clearly marked, appearing as 'a disjunctive point on the map, not part of the city' (Bodnár 2005, 159).

12 In a way, we can say that the mall atmospheres kill the atmospheric dimensions of human experience – the acoustic, tactile and olfactory – which provide the basic texture of urban life as maelstroms of affect (being thus as important as fleeting visual encounters).

Chapter 4

1 It is in this sense that Linnahall fits into what Smithson described as 'ruin in reverse' – the opposite of the romantic ruin, since the building did not fall into ruin after it was built, but rather 'rose' into ruin already before it was built, as a 'self-destroying postcard world of failed immortality and oppressive grandeur' (1972, 72).

2 Hydraulic curtains were brought from Finland and the seats were produced in Yugoslavia, which reveals paradoxical connections during the Soviet time and networks of productions.

3 A Grand Prix from the Interarch World Biennale of 1983 in Sofia and a USSR Award in 1984.

4 The Centre for Political Education (Sakala Keskus 1985) and the National Library (1992).

5 These quotes are taken from the great documentary *The Guard of the House* by Ingel Vaikla (2015).

6　Interviewees were randomly recruited; eighteen interviews were done on the roof of the building, one in a café, and six by mail. All the informants were invited to tell me a few words about what Linnahall evokes for them and if they support the demolition of the building. I added the age and primary language of the interviewed (16 people were questioned in English, 8 in Russian and 1 in Spanish). The youngest was 17 years old and the oldest 71 years old. Among them there were 3 tourists, 2 expats and 20 locals (15 Estonian and 5 Russian speakers).

7　A group of three people were praying on Linnahall on 23 October 2012 at 18:30.

8　The new main municipal building is supposed to be constructed nearby Linnahall.

9　The main agreement was supposed to be signed in May 2010.

10　See Merilin Kruuse, 'Delfi Videod ja Fotod: Linnahalli tuleb plaani järgi tõeliselt moodsa tehnikaga saal ja konverentsikeskus, rõhku pannakse ka nostalgiale', *Delfi*, 19 June 2016, http://www.delfi.ee/news/paevauudised/eesti/delfi-videod-ja-fotod-linnahalli-tuleb -plaani-jargi-toeliselt-moodsa-tehnikaga-saal-ja-konverentsikeskus-rohku-pannakse-ka -nostalgiale?id=74845261.

11　Lynch pointed out that human interest in material decay is wilder than the very interactions at these settings because 'ruins retain their evocative, symbolic power. In abandoned places, the release from a sense of immediate human purpose allows freer action, as well as free mental reconstruction' (1990, vii). He described the wasted as attractive and proposed that decline should not always be perceived as a disease. In this sense, Lynch concluded that 'it is as important for planners to help places decline or even die gracefully as it is to promote development and growth'.

12　See Tallinn Culture and Heritage Department, 2007. For more info, see *How Long Is the Life of a Building?*, edited by Tüüne-Kristin Vaikla, 2012.

Chapter 5

1　As described by Mikhail Bakhtin (1981), a chronotope refers to a condition in which time thickens and takes on flesh, and space becomes charged and responsive to the movement of time. Following Einstein's Theory of General Relativity, Bakhtin created the word 'chronotope' to affirm that space and time are two different perspectives on the same underlying reality. Bakhtin combined the words 'chronos' (time as duration) and 'topos' (space in motion, not as a background) to formulate a narrative form in which the sense of time is experienced spatially, including reflections on being and becoming and how they happen in interrelation within a time-space frame. Spatial and temporal indicators appear fused into one concrete whole, whereby they comingle and correspond to one another. In the study of novels, a chronotope functions as a threshold, facilitating critical turning points in the plot.

2　In an interview by Ruudi, architect Vilen Künnapu explained: 'We experimented with everything back then, you know. The old was no longer valid and the new didn't exist yet – it was the time when there was a vacuum: you could try everything. You really can't measure that time with today's ruler, asking why you did things this way or that. It was an adventure, there were no rules. Like people on a gold rush – have at it, get going! Whoever to wherever. It was a wild time for everyone. All of the projects were half non-existent. But I suppose we did what we knew. Any civilised methods came only later.'

3　The volume was thought of as a compilation of snapshots for contextualising a conference and has a kind of reflexive nostalgia. For instance, Laanemets compared the Moscow Olympic Games in 1980 with the Eurovision Song Contest 22 years later, both as prompters of a building boom and as a chance for local artists to do multiple jobs, ranging from city decorations to souvenir handicraft.

4　A typical Tallinn house has a wooden structure with one central stone entrance hall, commonly built from the 1910s to the 1930s. Within the current cityscape, it coexists with varied architectonic forms, due to Tallinn's being the capital of one of the Soviet Republics for half a century, but also because of how it has been developed since the break-up of state socialism: malls, a business district, suburbanisation and gentrification. Neighbourhoods are also subject to change. For instance, architect Siiri Vallner wrote in 2002 that in Kalamaja 'there is a slightly loser-like attitude' and 'underground feeling'. Nowadays, very few people would consider a walk in Kalamaja as anything wild, but as gentrification and hipster culture.

5 'The buildings and distances were so great that the city's structure remained static from the solitary pedestrian's point of view. The city revealed itself only if you sped through it in a car. But this was a peculiarity of all new cities . . .' (Unt 1985, 90).

6 Tallinn is a contraction of Taani Linn ('Danish fortress'). Other names have been Lindanisa, Kolyvan and Reval.

Chapter 6

1 The St George ribbon is a Russian military symbol consisting of black and orange stripes; restored by the Kremlin in 2005 as a World War II memorial.

2 Some of my interviews were held informally in quotidian settings. Consequently, I have used pseudonyms for those informants who were not *au courant* of my purpose.

3 The heading of this section comes from a statement by Tatyana Kozlova; interview conducted by Eléonore de Montesquiou (2010, 221).

4 Around 550 cars (A/B), 120 trucks (C) and eight buses (D) cross the border every day.

5 Between 2008 and 2011, the number of holders of grey passports dropped from 110,000 to 97,800. Yet of the reduction, 48 per cent is due to death. A total of 44 per cent of Narva has Estonian citizenship, 33 per cent Russian citizenship, and the remainder are stateless. Otherwise, the number of ethnic Russians in Estonian prisons is 58 per cent (despite being only 31 per cent of the total population); also the rate of those ethnic Russians infected by HIV or unemployed is double those of ethnic Estonians. Nonetheless, it cannot simply be explained by ethnic discrimination as such, but also by socioeconomic differences driven by postsocialist processes.

6 In 1872, a workers strike took place in Kreenholm; this event was marked as one of the key moments that led to the Soviet Revolution.

7 The current plan of Narva Gate is to construct four twenty-storey buildings, of which three will be residential and one designated for business; 'New Narva Starts Here', *Narva Gate OÜ*, 2013, http://www.narvagate.eu/eng/partplan.html.

8 In Narva, personal resistance to hardships and misfortunes seems to take the form of irony rather than of nostalgia. Here, irony appears as therapeutic, encompassing a certain cognitive detachment or ambiguity.

9 Otto Pius Hippius, of the St. Petersburg Academy of Sciences, was the architect of a church that was meant to host the 5,000 workers that the Kreenholm factory employed at the time.

10 For more on the topic see Mehis Helme, *Estonian Railway Stations* (Tallinn: Tänapäev, 2003), and Norman Rich and M. H. Fisher, eds., *The Holstein Papers*, vol. 3, *Correspondence, 1861–1896* (Cambridge: Cambridge University Press).

11 Narva in Figures 2002. People with different beliefs and ethnicity were buried in Narvian cemeteries, including Russians, Estonians, Germans, Swedish, Danes, Jews, and Muslims; see also: https://www.citypopulation.de/php/estonia-admin.php?adm2id=A0511.

12 'Narva in Figures 2010'. Narva City Government. See also Irina Dankovtseva remembrances of her childhood in Narva right after the war (cf. de Montesquiou 2010, 51).

13 Cf. de Montesquiou (2010, 53).

14 Stated in her talk at the 'Stop and Go' workshop, Tallinn, 20 May 2015.

15 See de Montesquiou (2010, 30).

16 The roundtables were organised under the institutional umbrella of the Estonian Academy of Arts. The first discussion can be found transcribed in 'Discussing Identities and Minorities in an Estonian Border City', *Deep Baltic*, 7 April 2017, https://deepbaltic.com/2017/04/07/identity-minorities-narva-estonia-border/; the second part was video recorded and is available at EKA sisearhitektuur, Facebook, 8 September 2017, https://www.facebook.com/EKAsisearhitektuur/videos/1467984796612028/?hc_ref=ARQr-gYppFYnT2ZCyy1P-yv5O87JL3og4abflEQ731GWrZa3170QGvZplijOl2jCR8I.

17 'Russian Border Crossers Sentenced to Two Months in Prison', *ERR News*, 13 November 2014, http://news.err.ee/v/politics/980d4a4c-cb03-4314-b763-34c3c4c1eb6e.

18 As an example, the emotional thickness of borderlands and the consequences of the break-up of the USSR are well represented in the film *The Borderline Effect* (2012), in which three authors (Kirill Sedukhin, Georgy Molodtsov and Olga Stefanova) tell the stories of a Russo-Ukrainian couple who struggle to get married, a grandmother who has to cross the

border in Narva every week to take care of her grandchildren, and a Georgian mother who goes back to Abkhazia to renovate the graveyard of her father, who had died two decades before.

19 Nonetheless, we should not simply equate inclusion with debordering, and exclusion with bordering. There are different forms of being 'in', and being 'out', as well as situations in which people are 'in' and 'out' simultaneously – connecting and disconnecting at once.

20 Otherwise, Russia is often referred to, not merely as a state, but as a civilisation that has some remains on the Estonian side of the border (Kuus 2007). Also, it is obvious that Russia has not been always the main 'enemy', since the Estonian War of Independence of 1918 was mostly seen as a struggle to be liberated from 700 years of the German yoke (Brüggemann 2006).

Chapter 7

1 Raadi was designated as the site of the new building (33,268 m²), which had a budget of €63.1 million. Unexpectedly, the European Commission refused to contribute to the budget; their representatives argued that the purpose of the project was unclear – either a cultural heritage depository or a tourist attraction. Since the Estonian authorities applied for funding allocated for tourist projects, international experts recommended relocating the building site to Tallinn, accessible thus to a larger number of visitors. That option was strongly rejected by the Estonian government, which, after the negative response from Brussels to contribute to the project, announced that it would itself match the €32 million requested from the EU.

2 One of Nugin's informants, Kristjan, summarises the memory approach of the 'threshold generation' in this way: 'We made these laws and rules and built this state, we have the right to be sometimes creative in remodelling them in our own interest' (2015, 119).

3 See Runnel, Tatsi and Pruulmann-Vengerfeldt 2014.

4 See Runnel, Tarand and Tamm 2014.

5 For more on the topic see http://www.ejection-history.org.uk/project/YEAR_Pages/1991.htm.

6 Runnel, Tarand and Tamm 2014. The soil is contaminated with 1.04 million tons of oil and chemicals.

7 See Karin Bachmann, 'Mental Pollution of a Place: The Case Study of Raadi'a', MA thesis, Tartu University, 2006; and Joseph Enge, Raadi's Airport Is Tartu's White Elephant', *Baltic Times*, 6 January 2000, http://www.baltictimes.com/news/articles/560/#.VGUnKPmUfCs.

8 There were also plans to erect a new museum building in the centre of the city. See Runnel, Tatsi and Pruulmann-Vengerfeldt 2014.

9 'Ja saagu muuseum!', *Postimees*, 31 July 2003 (translated in Runnel, Tatsi and Pruulmann-Vengerfeldt 2014), https://arvamus.postimees.ee/2038563/ja-saagu-muuseum.

10 See M. Aesma, 'Võitjaarhitekt Dan Dorell: Raadist võib saada põnev paik', *Postimees*, 17 January 2006, https://www.postimees.ee/1521781/voitjaarhitekt-dan-dorell-raadist-voib-saada-ponev-paik.

11 The text used to be accessible in this link: http://www.erm.ee/en/about-us/new-building (Retrieved 28.05.2015).

12 A. Nosovich, 'Far Away from Volgograd: Baltic States on the Map of International Extremism', *Rubaltic*, Russia Week News Forum in Riga, 2 January 2014, and 'In Riga, organisers of Dispersed Picket for Renaming Dudaev Street Will Go to Court against Police Actionsc', *Caucasian Knot* (Riga), 30 August 2010, http://eng.kavkaz-uzel.ru/articles/14282/.

13 'Because he [Dudayev] was also them, who became we'. See Tanel Rander, 2014. 'Raadi. Description of the Project'. See http://decolon.blogspot.com.ee/.

14 Statements originally gathered for an article published in Estonian in the cultural journal *Sirp,* 'Paradoksaalne uus algus', http://www.sirp.ee/s1-artiklid/c6-kunst/paradoksaalne-uus-algus/.

15 In his article, Marek Tamm examines how the leadership of the restored Estonian republic consisted, for the most part, of historians, intellectuals and dissidents, who used phrases such as 'to restore truth' and 'the Estonians' control over their past', which had been 'expropriated', and correlated the process of building up a new state with the need of filling in 'the blank spots of the past'.

Chapter 8

1 See 'Sõber on nimetanud mind posthipsteriks, ise pean ennast pigem isetegijate subkultuuri esindajaks – jätkusuutliku eluviisi pooldajaks', *Delfi*, 9 May 2015.
2 Marika notes how the reasons exposed by local street artist Edward von Lõngus to justify his practice (apathy of the consumerist society and visual pollution found in urban spaces) were similar to those argued in New York and Berlin. Yet in this context (Tartu, a university town of 100,000 inhabitants), the pressure of advertising and capital speculation on public spaces is not nearly as acutely manifested as in some big cities.
3 Lukas: 'praegused Eestistlahkujad on mugavus-jalodevuspagulased', *Uudised*, ERR 15 September 2014.
4 See Raimo Poom, 'Estonia and Refugees: Timid and Inept Government Lets Loose a Wave of Rage', *Medium*, 6 September 2015, https://medium.com/@RaimoPoom/estonia-and -refugees-timid-and-inept-government-lets-loose-a-wave-of-rage-644212e1c7ba.
5 See Braudie Blais-Billie, 'The estonian rapper tommy cash wants to be "kanye east"', *Vice* 25 April 2017, https://i-d.vice.com/en_us/article/estonian-rapper-tommy-cash-wants-to-be -kanye-east.
6 See the interview of Tommy Cash with Andrei Nedashkovsky in the journal Flow, 15 June 2017, http://the-flow.ru/features/tommy-cash-interview-2017.
7 See Liana Satenstein, 'Has the Commercialisation of Russia and Eastern European Fashion Gone Too Far?', *Vogue*, 22 March 2017, http://www.vogue.com/article/commercialization -of-russian-and-eastern-european-culture-in-fashion.
8 Socialist experiences and values still have an impact on the present-day life of young people in Estonia, and not simply on their parents' memories; this is happening not only because of state policy, but also because of certain patterns of interfamilial and intergenerational communication of the past.

Conclusion

1 Constructed through expressions such as 'the return to Europe' and 'normality' (Lauristin and Vihalemm 1997), not only in Estonia but also in other Eastern European countries such as Poland (Sztompka 1996), Hungary (Hankiss 1994) and Bulgaria (Kiossev 2008), presenting Soviet life as characterised by failure, humiliating compromises and an existence without dignity.
2 See, for instance, the advertising of Paulig: https://www.youtube.com/watch?v=D4orBO 3ZbVk; and here the articles published in Estonian (Sirp): http://www.sirp.ee/s1-artiklid /c6-kunst/achtung-banaalse-rahvusluse-epideemia-levib-ule-riigi/ and in English (Arter-ritory): http://arterritory.com/en/texts/articles/7300-achtung_an_epidemic_of_banal _nationalism_runs_through_estonia/.

Epilogue

1 'Having scored a success in diminutive Estonia, the software wizards have now set their sights on greater challenges'; AFP, 'Estonian Web Gurus Devise Country Clean-up Plan', May 29, 2008: http://www.teeme2008.ee/?op=body&id=48&prn=1&art=262&cid=.
2 'Thanks to this Soviet-era idiocy, the cleaning around our buildings takes place only once a year'; 'as always, our yards are swept by Tajiks who do the *subbotnik* "for 100 or 200 Rubles"'; see Svetlana Osadchuk, 'Time to Clean, Comrades' *Moscow Times*, 15 April 2008.
3 News from Elsewhere, 'Estonia Imports Rubbish to Keep Power Plant Running', *BBC News*, 5 October 2016: http://www.bbc.com/news/blogs-news-from-elsewhere-37562149.
4 As Alexander and Reno explain, recyclable materials circulate on international markets and are sold as commodities: 'exhortations to recycle become more complicated once we consider where materials go to be revalued and reinserted into mainstream material flows. . . . Risk, danger and pollution are all too often simply displaced to other places and glossed over in feel-good accounts' (2012, 3).

5 A paradox surrounding the official waste dealing is that the import of waste from Finland and England costs Estonian consumers up to €1.7 million a year in public subsidies. In total, 86,000 tons of Turku waste is packaged in drums and delivered to Estonia by vessel. The Iru waste-to-energy plan has been presented as an attempt to make Estonia energetically autonomous; however, its boiler is fuelled by the big neighbours' gas. An alternative to Russian fossil energy is being developed with a public investment of €640 million in a combined oil, shale and biomass power plant in Narva (built by the French company Alstom). Nevertheless, this initiative to exploit the fossil fuel legacy has been criticised by the Estonian Fund for Nature, an NGO for which Rainer Nõlvak is the chairman of the board. The company Nelja Energia was formed in 2012 to produce renewable energy from wind power and biopower. It has been the first one in Eastern Europe to issue a green bond (€50 million at the Oslo stock market).

6 See Andres Reimer, 'Report Reveals Tallinn Trash Business Blunder', *Postimees*, 4 June 2014.

References

Aarelaid-Tart, Aili. 2006. *Cultural Trauma and Life Stories*. Helsinki: Kikimora.

Aarelaid-Tart, Aili. 2016. 'The Soviet Past through the Lenses of Different Memory Communities'. In *Generations in Estonia: Contemporary Perspectives in Turbulent Times*, edited by Raili Nugin, Anu Kannike and Maaris Raudsepp, 106–27. Tartu: University of Tartu Press.

Agamben, Giorgio. 2009. 'What Is the Contemporary?' In *What Is an Apparatus? and Other Essays*, 39–54. Palo Alto, CA: Stanford University Press.

Agu, Marika. 2014. *Typical Individuals: Graffiti and Street Art in Tartu, 1994–2014*. Tartu: Tartu Art Museum.

Aidis, Ruta. 2003. 'Officially Despised Yet Tolerated: Open-Air Markets and Entrepreneurship in Post-Socialist Countries'. *Post-Communist Economies* 15 (3): 461–73.

Aleksievich, Svetlana. 2015. *El fin del 'Homo sovieticus'*. Translated by Jorge Ferrer. Barcelona: Acantilado.

Alexander, Catherine. 2012. 'Remont: Works in Progress'. In *Economies of Recycling: The Global Transformation of Materials, Values and Social Relations*, edited by Catherine Alexander and Joshua Reno, 255–75. London: Zed.

Alexander, Catherine, and Joshua Reno. 2012. 'Introduction'. In *Economies of Recycling: The Global Transformation of Materials, Values and Social Relations*, edited by Catherine Alexander and Joshua Reno, 1–33. London: Zed.

Allik, Allari. 2012. 'How Many Lives Does a Building Have?' In *How Long Is the Life of a Building?*, edited by Tüüne-Kristin Vaikla, 161–5. [Catalogue Estonian National Exhibition at the XIII International Architecture Exhibition – la Biennale di Venezia.] Talinn: Estonian Centre of Architecture.

Anderson, Benedict. (1983) 1991. *Imagined Communities: Reflections on the Origin and Spread of Nationalism*. 2nd ed. London: Verso.

Anderson, Michael C., Robert A. Bjork and Elizabeth L. Bjork. 1994. 'Remembering Can Cause Forgetting: Retrieval Dynamics in Long-Term Memory'. *Journal of Experimental Psychology: Learning, Memory and Cognition* 20:1063–87.

Annist, Aet. 2014. 'Losing the Enterprising Self in Post-Soviet Estonian Villages'. In *Neoliberalism, Personhood, and Postsocialism: Enterprising Selves in Changing Economies*, edited by Nicolette Makovicky, 89–108. Farnham: Ashgate.

Annus, Epp. 2012. 'The Problem of Soviet Colonialism in the Baltics'. *Journal of Baltic Studies* 43 (1): 21–45.

Annus, Epp. 2015. 'Footsteps and Gazes: Mati Unt's Mustamäe'. In *Urban Semiotics: The City as a Cultural-Historical Phenomenon*, edited by Igor Pilshchikov, 65–87. Tallinn: TLU Press.

Appadurai, Arjun, ed. 1986. *The Social Life of Things: Commodities in Cultural Perspective*. Cambridge: Cambridge University Press.

Appadurai, Arjun. 1986. 'Theory in Anthropology: Center and Periphery'. *Comparative Studies in Society and History* 28:356–61.

Arnason, Johann P. 2005. 'Alternating Modernities: The Case of Czechoslovakia'. *European Journal of Social Theory* 8 (4): 435–51.

Assmann, Jan. 1995. 'Collective Memory and Cultural Identity'. *New German Critique* 65:125–33.

Astahovska, Ieva. 2015. 'On Forgetting and Remembering: Relations to the Past in Latvian Art'. In *Revisiting Footnotes: Footprints of the Recent Past in the Post-Socialist Region*, edited by Ieva Astahovksa and Inga Lāce, 113–24. Riga: Latvian Centre of Contemporary Art.

Atarov, Nikolai. 1940. *Dvorets Sovetov*. Moscow: Moskovskii rabochii.

Attia, Kader. 2014. *The Repair from Occident to Extra-Occidental Cultures*. Berlin: Green Box.

Augé, Marc. 1995. *Non-Places: An Introduction to Supermodernity*. Translated by John Howe. London: Verso.

Bach, Jonathan. 2017. *What Remains: Everyday Encounters with the Socialist Past in Germany*. New York: Columbia University Press.

Bakhtin, Mikhail M. 1981. 'Forms of Time and of the Chronotope in the Novel: Notes toward a Historical Poetics'. In *The Dialogic Imagination: Four Essays*, edited by Michael Holquist, 84–258. Austin: University of Texas Press.

Bal, Mieke. 1996. *Double Exposures: The Subject of Cultural Analysis*. London: Routledge.

Balibar, Etienne. 2004. *We, the People of Europe? Reflections on Transnational Citizenship*. Princeton, NJ: Princeton University Press.

Bastian, Michele. 2014. 'Time and Community: A Scoping Study'. *Time and Society* 23 (2): 137–66.

Bataille, George. 1989. *The Accursed Share*. Translated by Robert Hurley. New York: Zone.

Bauman, Zygmunt. 1991. *Modernity and Ambivalence*. Cambridge: Polity.

Bauman, Zygmunt. 1998. *Work, Consumerism and the New Poor*. Milton Keynes: Open University Press.

Bauman, Zygmunt. 2004. *Wasted Lives: Modernity and Its Outcasts*. London: Polity.

Bauman, Zygmunt. 2015. *Retrotopia*. London: Polity.

Benjamin, Walter. 1968. 'Theses on the Philosophy of History'. In *Illuminations: Essays and Reflections*, 253–64. Edited by Hannah Arendt. Translated by Harry Zohn. New York: Schocken.

Benjamin, Walter. 1986. *Moscow Diary*. Edited by Gary Smith. Translated by Richard Sieburh. Cambridge, MA: Harvard University Press.

Benjamin, Walter. 1998. *The Origin of German Tragic Drama*. Translated by John Osborne. London: Verso.

Benjamin, Walter. 1999. *The Arcades Project*. Translated by Howard Eiland. Cambridge, MA: Belknap Press for Harvard University Press.

Berdahl, Daphne. 1999. *Where the World Ended: Re-Unification and Identity in the German Borderland*. Berkeley: University of California Press.

Berdahl, Daphne. 2000. 'Introduction: An Anthropology of Postsocialism'. In *Altering States: Ethnographies of Transition in Eastern Europe and the Former Soviet Union*, edited by Daphne Berdahl, Matti Bunzl and Martha Lampland, 1–13. Ann Arbor: University of Michigan Press.

Berdahl, Daphne. 2001. 'Go, Trabi, Go! Reflection on a Car and Its Symbolization over Time'. *Anthropology and Humanism* 25 (2): 131–41.

Berlant, Lauren. 2007. 'Slow Death (Sovereignty, Obesity, Lateral Agency)'. *Critical Inquiry* 33:754–80.

Berlant, Lauren. 2011. *Cruel Optimism*. Durham, NC: Duke University Press.

Bevan, Robert. 2006. *The Destruction of Memory: Architecture at War*. London: Reaktion.

Bhabha, Homi K. 1994. *The Location of Culture*. London: Routledge.

Billig, Michael. 1995. *Banal Nationalism*. London: Sage.

Bjerregaard, Peter. 2015. 'Disconnecting Relations'. In *Objects and Imagination: Perspectives on Materialization and Meaning*, edited by Øivind Fuglerud and Leon Wainwright, 45–64. Oxford: Berghahn.

Black, Jeremy. 2008. 'Contesting the Past'. *History* 93 (310): 224–54.

Bodnár, Judit. 2000. *Fin de Millénaire Budapest: Metamorphoses of Urban Life*. Minneapolis: University of Minnesota Press.

Bodnár, Judit. 2005. 'Mean Streets, Neat Malls, and Market Halls: Commercialization and Public Space in the Age of Globalization'. In *Vásárcsarnok: Minőségét Korlátlan Ideig Megőrzi*, edited by Allan Siegel and Gabriella Uhl, 159–61. Budapest: Ernst Múzeum.

Boltanski, Luc, and Laurent Thévenot. 2006. *On Justification: Economies of Worth*. Translated by Catherine Porter. Princeton, NJ: Princeton University Press.

Bös, Mathias, and Kerstin Zimmer. 2006. 'Wenn Grenzen wandern: Zur Dynamik von Grenzver-schiebungen im Osten Europas'. In *Grenzsoziologie: Die politische Strukturierung des Raumes*, edited by Monika Eigmüller and Georg Vobruba, 157–84. Wiesbaden: Verlag für Sozialwissen-schaften.

Boyer, Dominic, and Alexei Yurchak. 2008. 'Postsocialist Studies, Cultures of Parody and American Stiob'. *Anthropology News* 49 (8): 9–10.

Boym, Svetlana. 1994. *Common Places: Mythologies of Everyday Life in Russia*. Cambridge, MA: Harvard University Press.

Boym, Svetlana. 2001. *The Future of Nostalgia*. New York: Basic Books.

Boym, Svetlana. 2007. 'Nostalgia and Its Discontents'. *Hedgehog Review* 9 (2): 7–18.

Brand, Stewart. (1994) 2014. *How Buildings Learn: What Happens after They're Built*. New York: Viking Penguin.

Brand, Stewart. 2012. 'Preservation without Permission: the Paris Urban eXperiment'. *Introduction to the Long Now Seminar*, November 13. http://longnow.org/seminars/02012/nov/13/preservation-without-permission-paris-urban-experiment.

Brandstädter, Susanne. 2007. 'Transitional Spaces: Postsocialism as a Cultural Process'. *Critique of Anthropology* 27 (2): 131–45.

Brednikova, Olga. 2007. '"Windows" Project ad Marginem or the "Divided History" of Divided Cities? A Case Study of the Russian–Estonian Borderland'. In *Representations on the Margins of Europe: Politics and Identities in the Baltic and South Caucasian States*, edited by Tsypylma Darieva and Wolfgang Kaschuba, 43–64. Frankfurt am Main: Campus Verlag.

Brednikova, Olga, and Viktor Voronkov. 1999. 'Border and Social Space Restructuring (the Case of Narva-Ivangorod)'. In *Nomadic Borders: Proceedings of the Seminar Held in Narva (12–16 November 1998)*, edited by Olga Brednikova and Viktor Voronkov, 104–9. St. Petersburg: CISR.

Brennan, Teresa. 2004. *The Transmission of Affect*. Ithaca, NY: Cornell University Press.

Brown, Kate. 2013. *Plutopia: Nuclear Families, Atomic Cities, and the Great Soviet and American Plutonium Disasters*. Oxford: Oxford University Press.

Browning, Christopher, and Marko Lehti. 2007. 'Beyond East-West: Marginality and National Dignity in Finnish Identity Construction'. *Nationalities Papers*, 35 (4): 691–716.

Brüggemann, Karsten. 2004. 'Der Wiederaufbau Narvas nach 1944 und die Utopie der "sozialistischen Stadt"'. In *Narva und die Ostseeregion / Narva and the Baltic Sea Region*, edited by Karsten Brüggemann, 81–103. Narva: Narva Kolledz.

Brüggemann, Karsten. 2006. '"Foreign Rule" during the Estonian War of Independence 1918–1920: The Bolshevik Experiment of the "Estonian Worker's Commune"'. *Journal of Baltic Studies* 37 (2): 210–26.

Brüggemann, Karsten, and Andres Kasekamp. 2008. 'The Politics of History and the "War of Monuments" in Estonia'. *Nationalities Papers* 36 (3): 425–48.

Bruns, Dmitri. 2006. 'Linnahall, teenimatult lohakil'. *Ehitaja* 3:29–31.

Buchli, Victor. 1999. *An Archaeology of Socialism*. Oxford: Berg.

Buchli, Victor. 2002. 'Introduction'. In *The Material Culture Reader*, edited by Victor Buchli, 1–22. Oxford: Berg.

Buchli, Victor. 2007. 'Astana: Materiality and the City'. In *Urban Life in Post-Soviet Asia*, edited by Catherine Alexander, Victor Buchli, and Caroline Humphrey, 40–69. London: UCL Press.

Buchli, Victor, and Gavin Lucas. 2001a. 'The Absent Present: Archaeologies of the Contemporary Past'. In *Archaeologies of the Contemporary Past*, edited by Victor Buchli and Gavin Lucas, 3–18. London: Routledge.

Buchli, Victor, and Gavin Lucas. 2001b. 'Between Remembering and Forgetting'. In *Archaeologies of the Contemporary Past*, edited by Victor Buchli and Gavin Lucas, 79–83. London: Routledge.

Buchowski, Michał. 2006. 'The Specter of Orientalism in Europe: From Exotic Other to Stigmatized Brother'. *Anthropological Quarterly* 79 (3): 463–82.

Buck-Morss, Susan. 2000. *Dreamworld and Catastrophe: The Passing of Mass Utopia in East and West*. Cambridge, MA: MIT Press.

Buden, Boris. 2010. 'Children of Postcommunism'. *Radical Philosophy* 159:18–25.

Burch, Stuart, and David J. Smith. 2007. 'Empty Spaces and the Value of Symbols: Estonia's "War of Monuments" from Another Angle'. *Europe-Asia Studies* 59 (6): 913–36.

Caldwell, Melissa L. 2005. 'Newness and Loss in Moscow: Rethinking Transformation in the Postsocialist Field'. *Journal of the Society for the Anthropology of Europe* 5 (1): 2–7.

Calvino, Italo. 1974. *Invisible Cities*. Translated by William Weaver. New York: Harcourt Brace.

Castells, Manuel. 2004. *The Information Age: Economy, Society and Culture*, vol. 2, *The Power of Identity*. 2nd ed. Oxford: Blackwell.

Chapman, Jonathan. 2016. 'Subject/Object Relationship and Emotionally Durable Design'. In *Longer Lasting Products: Alternatives to the Throwaway Society*, edited by Tim Cooper, 61–76. London: Routledge.

Chari, Sharad, and Katherine Verdery. 2009. 'Thinking between the Posts: Postcolonialism, Postsocialism, and Ethnography after the Cold War'. *Comparative Studies in Society and History* 51 (1): 6–34.

Chelcea, Liviu. 2015. 'Post-Socialist Acceleration: Fantasy Time in a Multinational Bank'. *Time and Society* 24 (3): 348–66.

Chelcea, Liviu, and O. Druţă. 2016. 'Zombie Socialism and the Rise of Neoliberalism in Post-Socialist Central and Eastern Europe'. *Eurasian Geography and Economics* 57 (4–5): 521–44.

Cherrier, Hélène, and Tresa Ponnor. 2010. 'A Study of Hoarding Behavior and Attachment to Material Possessions'. *Qualitative Market Research* 13 (1): 8–23.

Chu, Julie. 2014. 'When Infrastructures Attack: The Workings of Disrepair in China'. *American Ethnologist* 14 (2): 351–67.

Collier, Stephen J. 2011. *Post-Soviet Social*. Princeton, NJ: Princeton University Press.

Comte, August. (1853) 1974. *The Positive Philosophy of Auguste Comte*. Translated by Harriet Martineau. New York: AMS Press.

Connerton, Paul. 2009. *How Modernity Forgets*. Cambridge: Cambridge University Press.

Craciun, Magdalena. 2013. *Material Culture and Authenticity: Fake Branded Fashion in Europe*. London: Bloomsbury.

Cresswell, Tim. 1996. *In Place/Out of Place: Geography, Ideology and Transgression*. Minneapolis: University of Minnesota Press.

Crowley, David, and Susan E. Reid, eds. 2002. *Socialist Spaces: Sites of Everyday Life in the Eastern Bloc*. Oxford: Berg.

Curro, Costanza. 2016. 'Hospitality Bricolage in Times of Change'. In *Aesthetics of Repair in Contemporary Georgia*, edited by Francisco Martínez and Marika Agu, 198–205. Tartu: Tartu Art Museum.

Czepczynski, Mariusz. 2008. *Cultural Landscapes of Post-Socialist Cities*. Farnham: Ashgate.

Dant, Tim. 2009. *The Work of Repair: Gesture, Emotion and Sensual Knowledge*. Lancaster: Lancaster University Press.

De Boeck, Filip. 2015. '"Divining" the City: Rhythm, Amalgamation and Knotting as Forms of "Urbanity"'. *Social Dynamics* 41 (1): 47–58.

De Boeck, Filip, and Sammy Baloji. 2016. *Suturing the City: Living Together in Congo's Urban Worlds*. London: Autograph ABP.

Delaplace, Grégory. 2012. 'A Slightly Complicated Door: The Ethnography and Conceptualisation of North Asian Borders'. In *Frontier Encounters*, edited by Franck Billé, Grégory Delaplace and Caroline Humphrey, 1–17. Cambridge: Open Books.

Della Dora, Veronica, and Helen Sooväli. 2009. 'Sacred Space and Uncomfortable Memories: The Alexander Nevski Russian Orthodox Cathedral in Tallinn, Estonia'. In *Heritage, Images, Memory of European Landscapes / Patrimoine, images, mémoire des paysages européens*, 215–39. Paris: L'Harmattan.

de Montesquiou, Eléonore. 2006. *Atom Cities Sillamäe*. Tallinn: Linnagaleriis.

de Montesquiou, Eléonore. 2010. *Narva/Ivangorod*. Berlin: Argo.

Denis, Jérôme, and David Pontille. 2015. 'Material Ordering and the Care of Things'. *Science, Technology and Human Values* 40 (3): 338–67.

DeSilvey, Caitlin. 2006. 'Observed Decay: Telling Stories with Mutable Things'. *Journal of Material Culture* 11 (3): 318–38.

DeSilvey, Caitlin. 2017. *Curated Decay: Heritage beyond Saving*. Minneapolis: University of Minnesota Press.

Donnan, Hastings, and Thomas M. Wilson. 1999. *Borders: Frontiers of Identity, Nation and State*. Oxford: Berg.

Douglas, Mary. 1966. *Purity and Danger: An Analysis of the Concepts of Pollution and Taboo*. London: Routledge and Kegan Paul.

Douglas, Mary, and Baron Isherwood. 1979. *The World of Goods*. London: Routledge and Kegan Paul.

Drazin, Adam. 2002. 'Chasing Moth'. In *Markets and Moralities*, edited by Ruth Mandel and Caroline Humphrey, 101–25. Oxford: Berg.

Dwyer, Owen J., and Derek H. Alderman. 2008. 'Memorial Landscapes: Analytic Questions and Metaphors'. *GeoJournal* 73 (3): 165–78.

Dzenovska, Daze. 2014. 'Bordering Encounters, Sociality, and Distribution of the Ability to Live a Normal Life'. *Social Anthropology* 22 (3): 271–87.

Eco, Umberto. 1988. 'An Ars Oblivionalis? Forget It!'. *PMLA* 103 (3): 254–61.

Edensor, Tim. 2002. *National Identity, Popular Culture and Everyday Life*. Oxford: Berg.

Edensor, Tim. 2005. *Industrial Ruins: Space, Aesthetics and Materiality*. Oxford: Berg.

Eesti Entsüklopeedia. 1994. 'Kreenholm'. Tallinn: Eesti Entsüklopeediakirjastus.

ENM. 2006. 'General Committee's Remarks Concerning the Winning Entries'. In *Estonian National Museum Open International Architecture Competition*, edited by Agnes Aljas, 25. Tartu: Estonian National Museum.

Eriksen, Thomas Hylland. 2016. *Overheating: An Anthropology of Accelerated Change*. London: Pluto.

Errázuriz, Tomas. Forthcoming. 'When New Is Not Better. The Making of Home through Holding on to Objects'. In *Ethnographies of Brokenness and Repair*, edited by Francisco Martínez and Patrick Laviolette. Oxford: Berghahn.

Estalella, Adolfo, and Tomás Sánchez Criado. Forthcoming. 'DIY Anthropology: A Peripheral Discipline'. In *Common Grounds? Locating, Contesting and (Not) Defining Euro-anthropologies*, edited by Francisco Martínez and Damián Omar Martínez. Oxford: Berghahn.

Fabian, Johannes. 1983. *Time and the Other: How Anthropology Makes Its Object*. New York: Columbia University Press.

Färber, Alexa, and Cordula Gdaniec. 2004. 'Shopping Malls and Shishas: Urban Space and Material Culture as Approaches to Transformation in Berlin and Moscow'. *Ethnologia Europaea* 34 (2): 113–28.

Farías, Ignacio. 2011. 'The Politics of Urban Assemblages'. *City* 15 (3–4): 365–74.

Fehérváry, Krisztina. 2009. 'Goods and States: The Political Logic of State-Socialist Material Culture'. *Comparative Studies in Society and History* 51 (2): 426–59.

Fehérváry, Krisztina. 2013. *Politics in Color and Concrete: Socialist Materialities and the Middle Class in Hungary*. Bloomington: Indiana University Press.

Feldman, Merje. 2000. 'Urban Waterfront Regeneration and Local Governance in Tallinn'. *Europe-Asia Studies* 52 (5): 829–50.

Feldman, Merje. 2001. 'European Integration and the Discourse of National Identity in Estonia'. *National Identities* 3 (1): 5–21.

Ferguson, James. 1999. *Expectations of Modernity: Myths and Meanings of Urban Life on the Zambian Copperbelt*. Berkeley: University of California Press.

Flower, Harriet I. 2006. *The Art of Forgetting: Disgrace and Oblivion in Roman Political Culture*. Chapel Hill: University of North Carolina Press.

Forty, Adrian. 1999. 'Introduction'. In *The Art of Forgetting*, edited by Adrian Forty and Susanne Küchler, 1–18. Oxford: Berg.

Forty, Adrian, and Susanne Küchler, eds. 1999. *The Art of Forgetting*. Oxford: Berg.

Foucault, Michel. 1975. *Discipline and Punish: The Birth of the Prison*. Translated by Alan Sheridan. New York: Random House.

Frederiksen, Martin. 2013. *Young Men, Time, and Boredom in the Republic of Georgia*. Philadelphia: Temple University Press.

Frederiksen, Martin. 2016. 'Material Dys-appearance: Decaying Futures and Contested Temporal Passage'. In *Materialities of Passing: Transformation, Transition and Transcience*, edited by Peter Bjerregaard, Anders Emil Rasmussen, and Tim Flohr Sørensen, 49–64. Abingdon: Routledge.

Freeman, Elizabeth. 2010. *Time Binds: Queer Temporalities, Queer Histories*. Durham, NC: Duke University Press.

Freitas, Ricardo. 1996. *Centres commerciaux: Îles urbaines de la post-modernité*. Paris: L'Harmattan.

Garb, Yaakov, and Tomasz Dybicz. 2006. 'The Retail Revolution in Post-Socialist Central Europe and Its Lessons'. In *The Urban Mosaic of Post-Socialist Europe*, edited by Sasha Tsenkova and Zorica Nedović-Budić, 231–52. Heidelberg: Physica.

Gell, Alfred. 1998. *Art and Agency: An Anthropological Theory*. Oxford: Oxford University Press.

Gerasimova, Ekaterina, and Sof'ia Chuikina. 2009. 'The Repair Society'. *Russian Studies in History* 48 (1): 58–74.

Gille, Zsuzsa. 2007. *From the Cult of Waste to the Trash Heap of History*. Bloomington: Indiana University Press.

Gille, Zsuzsa. 2010. 'Is There a Global Postsocialist Condition?' *Global Society* 24 (1): 9–30.

Gitt, Aala, ed. 2015. *Как Молоды Мы были . . .* [How young we were . . .]. Sillamäe: Sillamäe Museum.

Gordillo, Gastón R. 2014. *Rubble: The Afterlife of Destruction*. Durham, NC: Duke University Press.

Goss, Jon. 1993. '"The Magic of the Mall": An Analysis of Form, Function, and Meaning in the Contemporary Retail Built Environment'. *Annals of the Association of American Geographers* 83 (1): 18–47.

Graham, Stephen, and Nigel Thrift. 2007. 'Out of Order: Understanding Repair and Maintenance'. *Theory, Culture and Society* 24 (3): 1–25.

Grant, Bruce. 2001. 'New Moscow Monuments, or, States of Innocence'. *American Ethnologist* 28 (2): 332–62.

Green, Sarah. 2013. 'Borders and the Relocation of Europe'. *Annual Review of Anthropology* 42:345–61.

Green, Sarah. 2015. 'Making Grey Zones at the European Peripheries'. In *Ethnographies of Grey Zones in Eastern Europe*, edited by Ida Harboe Knudsen and Martin Demant Frederiksen, 173–86. London: Anthem.

Green, Sarah, Penny Harvey and Hannah Knox. 2005. 'Scales of Place and Networks: An Ethnography of the Imperative to Connect through Information and Communications Technologies'. *Current Anthropology* 46 (5): 805–26.

Gregson, Nicky. 2007. *Living with Things: Ridding, Accommodation, Dwelling*. Wantage: Sean Kingston.

Gregson, Nicky, and Louise Crewe. 2003. *Second-Hand Cultures*. Oxford: Berg.

Gregson, Nicky, Alan Metcalfe and Louise Crewe. 2007. 'Moving Things Along: The Conduits and Practices of Divestment in Consumption'. *Transactions of the Institute of British Geographers* 32 (2): 187–200.

Guffey, Elizabeth. 2006. *Retro: The Culture of Revival*. London: Reaktion.

Guyer, Jane I. 2017. 'Aftermaths and Recuperation in Anthropology'. *Hau: Journal of Ethnographic Theory* 7 (1): 81–103

Halbwachs, Maurice. 1980. *The Collective Memory*. New York: Harper and Row Colophon.

Hallas-Murula, Karin. 2006. 'Võidutöö tekistas masendust'. *Postimees*, 17 January.

Hallik, Klara. 2002. 'Nationalising Policies and Integration Challenges'. In *The Challenge of the Russian Minority: Emerging Multicultural Democracy in Estonia*, edited by Marju Lauristin and Mati Heidmets, 65–88. Tartu: Tartu University Press.

Hankiss, Elemér. 1994. 'European Paradigms: East and West, 1945–94'. *Daedalus* 123 (3): 115–26.

Haraway, Donna. 1984. 'Teddy Bear Patriarchy: Taxidermy in the Garden of Eden, 1908–1936'. *Social Text* 11 (Winter): 20–64.

Harris, Neil. 1999. *Building Lives: Constructing Rites and Passages*. New Haven, CT: Yale University Press.

Hartley, L. P. 1953. *The Go-Between*. London: Hamish Hamilton.

Hartog, Fransh Hamilton. *Regimes Dransh Hamilt*. Paris: Seuil.

Harvey, David. 1990. *The Condition of Postmodernity: An Enquiry into the Origins of Cultural Change*. Oxford: Blackwell.

Hetherington, Kevin. 2001. 'Phantasmagoria/Phantasm Agora: Materialities, Spatialities and Ghosts'. In 'Spatial Hauntings', edited by Kevin Hetherington and Monica Degen. Special issue, *Space and Culture* 11–12:24–41.

Hetherington, Kevin. 2004. 'Secondhandedness: Consumption, Disposal, and Absent Presence'. *Environment and Planning D: Society and Space* 22 (1): 157–73.

Hirt, Sonia. 2012. *Iron Curtains: Gates, Suburbs and Privatization of Space in the Post-Socialist City*. Chichester: Wiley-Blackwell.

Hirt, Sonia. 2013. 'Whatever Happened to the (Post)socialist City?' *Cities* 32 (1): 29–38.

Hirt, Sonia, Slavomíra Ferenčuhová and Tauri Tuvikene 2016. 'Conceptual Forum: The "Post-Socialist" City'. *Eurasian Geography and Economics* 57 (4–5): 497–520.

Hobsbawm, Eric, and Terence Ranger, eds. 1983. *The Invention of Tradition*. New York: Cambridge University Press.

Hodgkin, Katharine, and Susannah Radstone. 2003. 'Patterning the National Past: Introduction'. In *Contested Pasts: The Politics of Memory*, edited by Katharine Hodgkin and Susannah Radstone, 169–74. London: Routledge.

Hollander, John. 1998. 'The Waste Remains and Kills'. *Social Research* 65 (1): 3–8.

Hommels, Anique. 2005. *Unbuilding Cities: Obduracy in Urban Sociotechnical Change*. Cambridge, MA: MIT Press.

Honwana, Alcinda, and Filip de Boeck, eds. 2005. *Makers and Breakers: Children and Youth in Postcolonial Africa*. Oxford: James Currey.

Hoskins, Janet. 1998. *Biographical Objects: How Things Tell the Stories of People's Lives*. London: Routledge.

Hroch, Miroslav. 1985. *Social Preconditions of National Revival in Europe*. Cambridge: Cambridge University Press.

Humphrey, Caroline. 2002a. 'Does the Category "Postsocialist" Still Make Sense?' In *Postsocialism: Ideals, Ideologies and Practices in Eurasia*, edited by C. M. Hann, 12–15. London: Routledge.

Humphrey, Caroline. 2002b. *The Unmaking of Soviet Life: Everyday Economies after Socialism*. Ithaca, NY: Cornell University Press.

Humphrey, Caroline. 2005. 'Ideology in Infrastructure: Architecture and Soviet Imagination'. *Journal of the Royal Anthropological Institute* 11 (1): 39–58.

Humphrey, Caroline. 2008. 'Reassembling Individual Subject: Events and Decisions in Troubled Times'. *Anthropological Theory* 8 (4): 357–80.

Hüwelmeier, Gertrud. 2013. 'Post-Socialist Bazaars: Diversity, Solidarity, and Conflict in the Marketplace'. *Laboratorium: Russian Review of Social Science* 5 (1): 52–72.

Huyssen, Andreas. 2003. *Present Pasts: Urban Palimpsests and the Politics of Memory*. Palo Alto, CA: Stanford University Press.

Ivancheva, Mariya. Forthcoming. 'Transgressing Core-periphery Relations in European Anthropology: An (Auto)ethnographic Reflection of Disciplinary and Job Market Boundaries'. In *Common Grounds? Locating, Contesting and (Not) Defining Euro-anthropologies*, edited by Francisco Martínez and Damián Omar Martínez. Oxford: Berghahn.

Jackson, Steven J. 2014. 'Rethinking Repair'. In *Media Technologies: Essays on Communication, Materiality, and Society*, edited by Tarleton Gillespie, Pablo J. Boczkowski and Kirsten A. Foot, 221–39. Cambridge, MA: MIT Press.

Jacobs, Jane M., and Stephen Cairns. 2011. 'Ecologies of Dwelling: Maintaining High-Rise Housing in Singapore'. In *The New Companion to the City*, edited by Gary Bridge and Sophie Watson, 79–95. Oxford: Blackwell.

Jagodin, Karen. 2012. *Walking Tours of Tallinn*. Tallinn: Solnessi Arhitektuurikirjastus.

Jarillo de la Torre, Sergio. 2013. 'Art and Anthropology beyond Beautiful Representations: The Material Hyperreality of Artistic Ethnography'. *Laboratorium: Russian Review of Social Research* (2): 128–48.

Jauhiainen, Jussi S., and Tarmo Pikner. 2009. 'Narva–Ivangorod: Integrating and Disintegrating Transboundary Water Networks and Infrastructure'. *Journal of Baltic Studies* 40 (3): 415–36.

Johnson, Juliet. 2001. 'Path Contingency in Postcommunist Transformations'. *Comparative Politics* 33 (3): 253–74.

Jones, Phil. 2012. 'Sensory Indiscipline and Affect: A Study of Commuter Cycling'. *Social and Cultural Geography* 13 (6): 645–58.

Judt, Tony. 2005. *Postwar: A History of Europe since 1945*. London: Heinemann.

Kagovere, Ott. 2015. 'Shifting Identities in Estonian Punk and Hip-hop'. In *Hopeless Youth!* edited by Francisco Martínez and Pille Runnel, 78–83. Tartu: ENM.

Kaiser, Robert, and Elena Nikiforova. 2008. 'The Performativity of Scale: The Social Construction of Scale Effects in Narva, Estonia'. *Environment and Planning D: Society and Space* 26 (3): 537–62.

Kalinin, Ilya. 2011. 'Nostalgic Modernization: The Soviet Past as a Historical Horizon'. *Slavonica* 17 (2): 156–66.

Kalinin, Ilya. 2013. 'The Struggle for History: The Past as a Limited Resource'. In *Memory and Theory in Eastern Europe*, edited by Uilleam Blacker, Alexander Etkind and Julie Fedor, 255–65. New York: Palgrave Macmillan.

Kalm, Gustav. 2015. 'The Age of Comfort Migrants'. In *Hopeless Youth!* edited by Francisco Martínez and Pille Runnel, 91–4. Tartu: ENM.

Kalm, Mart. 2001. *Eesti 20. sajandi arhitektuur* [Twentieth-century Estonian architecture]. Tallinn: Prisma Prindi Kirjastus.

Kaneff, Deema. 2002. 'The Shame and Pride of Market Activity: Morality, Identity and Trading in Postsocialist Bulgaria'. In *Markets and Moralities: Ethnographies of Postsocialism*, edited by Ruth Mandel and Caroline Humphrey, 33–53. Oxford: Berg.

Kaneff, Deema. 2004. *Who Owns the Past? The Politics of Time in a 'Model' Bulgarian Village*. Oxford: Berghahn.

Kasearu, Kairi, and Avo Trumm. 2008. 'Eesti-ja venekeelse elanikkonna aineline olukord ja eluga rahulolu' [Economic situation and life satisfaction of the Estonian- and Russian-speaking population]. In *Eesti Ühiskonna Integratsiooni Monitooring 2008*, edited by Raivo Vetik, 27–53. Tallinn: Integratsiooni Sihtasutus.

Kattago, Siobhan. 2008. 'Commemorating Liberation and Occupation: War Memorials along the Road to Narva'. *Journal of Baltic Studies* 39 (4): 431–49.

Kattago, Siobhan. 2009a. 'Agreeing to Disagree on the Legacies of Recent History: Memory, Pluralism and Europe after 1989'. *European Journal of Social Theory* 12 (3): 375–95.

Kattago, Siobhan. 2009b. 'War Memorials and the Politics of Memory: The Soviet War Memorial in Tallinn'. *Constellations* 16 (1): 150–66.

Kattago, Siobhan. 2012. *Memory and Representation in Contemporary Europe: The Persistence of the Past*. Farnham: Ashgate.

Kattago, Siobhan. 2014. 'All the World's a Stage . . . or a Cage?' In *Playgrounds and Battlefields*, edited by Francisco Martínez and Klemen Slabina, 65–84. Tallinn: Tallinn University Press.

Keller, Margit. 2005. 'Needs, Desires and the Experience of Scarcity'. *Journal of Material Culture* 5 (1): 65–85.

Kesküla, Eeva. 2012. 'Mining Postsocialism: Work, Class and Ethnicity in an Estonian Mine'. PhD diss., Goldsmiths University of London.

Kesküla, Eeva. 2016. 'Temporalities, Time and the Everyday: New Technology as a Marker of Change in an Estonian Mine'. *History and Anthropology* 27 (5): 521–35.

Khalvashi, Tamta. 2015. 'Peripheral Affects: Shame, Publics and Performance on the Margins of the Republic of Georgia'. PhD diss., University of Copenhagen.

Kiaer, Christina. 2005. *Imagine No Possessions: The Socialist Objects of Russian Constructivism*. Cambridge, MA: MIT Press.

Kideckel, David. 2008. *Getting by in Postsocialist Romania: Labor, the Body, and Working-Class Culture*. Bloomington: Indiana University Press.

Kiossev, Alexander. 2008. 'The Oxymoron of Normality'. *Eurozine*, 4 January. http://www .eurozine.com/the-oxymoron-of-normality/.

Kirch, Aksel, ed. 1997. *The Integration of Non-Estonians into the Estonian Society: History, Problems and Trends*. Tallinn: Estonian Academy.

Kirss, Tiina Ann. 2017. 'Those Who Decide About the Fate of the Foreigner'. *Anthropological Journal of European Cultures* 26 (1): 128–33.

Kljavin, Keiti. 2014. 'The Uses of Nostalgia: Neighbourhood Associations in Post-Socialist Estonia'. MA thesis, Estonian Academy of Arts, Tallinn.

Kojanić, Ognjen. Forthcoming. 'Theory from the Peripheries: What Can the Anthropology of Postsocialism Offer to European Anthropology'. In *Common Grounds? Locating, Contesting and (Not) Defining Euro-anthropologies*, edited by Francisco Martínez and Damián Omar Martínez. Oxford: Berghahn.

König, Anna. 2013. 'A Stitch in Time: Changing Cultural Constructions of Craft and Mending'. *Culture Unbound* 5 (4): 569–85.

Kõresaar, Ene. 2005. *Elu ideoloogiad: kollektiivne mälu ja autobiograafiline minevikutõlgendus eestlaste elulugudes'* [Ideologies of life: Collective memory and autobiographical interpretation of the past in Estonians life-stories]. Tartu: ERM.

Koselleck, Reinhart. (1979) 2004. *Futures Past: On the Semantics of Historical Time*. Translated by Keith Tribe. New York: Columbia University Press.

Kracauer, Siegfried. 1969. *History: The Last Things before the Last*. New York: Oxford University Press.

Kristeva, Julia. 1997. *The Portable Kristeva*. New York: Columbia University Press.

Ksenofontov, Andri. 2006. 'The Linnahall Auditorium in the Port of Tallinn'. In *Emotional Architecture 2*, edited by Calin Dan, 4–35. Bucharest: Hand Milked Visions Foundation.

Kurg, Andres. 2006a. 'Estonia: The Remarkable Afterlife of the Linnahall Concert Hall'. In 'The New Europe'. Special issue, *Architectural Design* 76 (3): 46–53.

Kurg, Andres. 2006b. 'Hoolikalt polsterdatud arhitektuurivaidlus' [Deliberately exaggerated architectural contest]. *Eesti Ekspress*, 25 January.

Kurg, Andres. 2007. 'Death in the New Town: Leonhard Lapin's City of the Living – City of the Dead'. *Meno istorija ir kritika / Art History and Criticism* 3:158–66.

Kurg, Andres. 2009a. 'The Bronze Soldier Monument and Its Publics'. In *After-War*, edited by Kristina Norman, 49–65. Tallinn: Centre for Contemporary Arts.

Kurg, Andres. 2009b. 'Social Space and Design: The Case of the Rotermann Quarter'. *Estonian Art* 2:37–40.

Kurg, Andres. 2014. *Boundary Disruptions: Late-Soviet Transformations in Art, Space and Subjectivity in Tallinn in the 1970s*. Tallinn: Estonian Academy of Arts.

Kus, Larissa. 2011. 'Is There a Shared History? The Role of Contextual Factors in the Psychology of Inter-ethnic Relations in Estonia'. PhD diss., Victoria University of Wellington.

Kuuk, Ingel. 2015. *Raadi of Our Dreams*. Tartu: ERM.

Kuus, Merje. 2007. 'Ubiquitous Identities and Elusive Subjects: Puzzles from Central Europe'. *Transactions of the Institute of British Geographers* 32 (1): 90–101.

Kuus, Merje. 2012. 'Banal Huntingtonianism: Civilizational Geopolitics in Estonia'. In *The Return of Geopolitics in Europe? Social Mechanisms and Foreign Policy Identity Crises*, edited by Stefano Guzzini, 174–91. Cambridge: Cambridge University Press.

Laanemets, Mari, and Andres Kurg, eds. 2002. *A User's Guide to Tallinn*. Tallinn: Estonian Academy of Arts.

Lapin, Leonhard. 2015. 'Barbaarsus Tallinna kesklinnas'. *Sirp*, 15 May. http://www.sirp.ee /s1-artiklid/arhitektuur/barbaarsus-tallinna-kesklinnas/.

Laporte, Dominique. 2000. *History of Shit*. Translated by Nadia Benabid and Rodolphe el-Khoury. Cambridge, MA: MIT Press.

Laszczkowski, Mateusz. 2015. 'Scraps, Neighbors, and Committees: Material Things, Place-Making, and the State in an Astana Apartment Block'. *City and Society* 27 (2): 136–59.

Laszczkowski, Mateusz. 2016. *'City of the Future': Built Space, Modernity and Urban Change in Astana*. Oxford: Berghahn.

Latour, Bruno. 1996. *Aramis or the Love of Technology*. Cambridge, MA: Harvard University Press.

Lauristin, Marju. 1997. 'Contexts of Transition'. In *Return to the Western World: Cultural and Political Perspectives on the Estonian Post-Communist Transition*, edited by Marju Lauristin and Peeter Vihalemm, 25–40. Tartu: Tartu University Press.

Lauristin, Marju. 2003. 'Vabaduse Lapsed' [The Children of Freedom]. *Päevaleht*, 16 August.

Lauristin, Marju, and Peeter Vihalemm. 1997. 'Recent Historical Developments in Estonia: Three Stages of Transition (1987–1997)'. In *Return to the Western World: Cultural and Political Perspectives on the Estonian Post-Communist Transition*, edited by Marju Lauristin and Peeter Vihalemm, 73–126. Tartu: Tartu University Press.

Laviolette, Patrick. 2006. 'Ships of Relations: Navigating through Local Cornish Maritime Art'. *International Journal of Heritage Studies* 12 (1): 69–92.

Laviolette, Patrick. 2011. *Extreme Landscapes of Leisure*. Farnham: Ashgate.

Laviolette, Patrick. 2017. 'Riding with Individuals: Hitchhiking as a Total Fiction'. In *Individualism*, edited by Suzana Ignjatović and Aleksandar Bošković, 73–91. Belgrade: Institut Drustvenih Nauka.

Ledeneva, Alena. 2018. *The Global Encyclopaedia of Informality*. London: UCL Press.

Leetmaa, Kadri, and Tiit Tammaru. 2007. 'Suburbanization in Countries in Transition: Destinations of Suburbanizers in the Tallinn Metropolitan Area'. *Geografiska Annaler* 89 (2): 127–46.

Lefebvre, Henri. (1974) 1991. *The Production of Space*. Translated by Donald Nicholson-Smith. Oxford: Blackwell.

Lefebvre, Henri. (1970) 2003. *The Urban Revolution*. Translated by Robert Bononno. Minneapolis: University of Minnesota Press.

Leping, Kristian-Olari, and Ott Toomet. 2008. 'Emerging Ethnic Wage Gap: Estonia during Political and Economic Transition'. *Journal of Comparative Economics* 36 (4): 599–619.

Lilleoja, Laur, and Maaris Raudsepp. 2016. 'Cohort-Specific Value Patterns in the New Millennium'. In *Generations in Estonia: Contemporary Perspectives in Turbulent Times*, edited by Raili Nugin, Anu Kannike and Maaris Raudsepp, 36–69. Tartu: University of Tartu Press.

Lillepõld, Raina. 2014. 'Post-Socialist Movements of Lenin: Travels around Estonia'. In *Futures of the Past, Pasts of the Future: The Politics of the Old in a Contemporary City*, 3–34. Tallinn: Estonian Academy of Arts.

Lobjakas, Kai, and Karin Paulus. 2000. 'Postuumselt rehabiliteeritud? "Asjad minu elus. Nõukogude Eesti tootedisain"' [Posthumously rehabilitated? 'Things in my life. Industrial design of Soviet Estonia']. *Maja* 4:9.

Lotman, Juri. 2005. 'On the Semiosphere'. *Sign Systems Studies* 33 (1): 205–9.

Löw, Martina. 2008. 'The Constitution of Space: The Structuration of Spaces through the Simultaneity of Effects and Perception'. *European Journal of Social Theory* 11 (1): 25–49.

Lowenthal, David. 1985. *The Past is a Foreign Country*. Cambridge: Cambridge University Press.

Lynch, Kevin. 1976. *What Time Is This Place?* Cambridge, MA: MIT Press.

Lynch, Kevin. 1990. *Wasting Away: An Exploration of Waste: What It Is, How It Happens, Why We Fear It, How to Do It Well*. San Francisco: Sierra Club.

Macdonald, Sharon. 1996. 'Introduction'. In *Theorizing Museums: Representing Identity and Diversity in a Changing World*, edited by Sharon Macdonald and Gordon Fyfe, 1–18. Oxford: Blackwell.

Macdonald, Sharon. 2013. *Memorylands: Heritage and Identity in Europe Today*. London: Routledge.

Mälksoo, Maria. 2009. 'Liminality and Contested Europeanness: Conflicting Memory Politics in the Baltic Space'. In *Identity and Foreign Policy: Baltic-Russian Relations and European Integration*, edited by Eiki Berg and Piret Ehin, 65–83. Farnham: Ashgate.

Mälksoo, Maria. 2010. *The Politics of Becoming European: A Study of Polish and Baltic Post–Cold War Security Imaginaries*. London: Routledge.

Mälksoo, Maria. 2014. 'Criminalizing Communism: Transnational Mnemopolitics in Europe'. *International Political Sociology* 8 (1): 82–99.

Mälksoo, Maria. 2015. '"Memory Must Be Defended": Beyond the Politics of Mnemonical Security'. *Security Dialogue* 46 (3): 221–37.

Malve, Martin, Anu Kivirüüt, Raido Roog, Madis Maasing and Sebastian K. T. S. Wärmländer. 2012. 'Archaeological Pilot Study of the Gallows Hill in Tartu'. *Archaeological Fieldwork in Estonia*, 2012:207–16.

Mandel, Ruth, and Caroline Humphrey, eds. 2002. *Markets and Moralities: Ethnographies of Postsocialism*. Oxford: Berg.

Mannheim, Karl. (1927) 1952. 'The Problem of Generations'. In *Essays on the Sociology of Knowledge by Karl Mannheim*, edited by Paul Kecskemeti. London: Routledge and Kegan Paul.

Manzo, John. 2005. 'Social Control and Management of "Personal" Space in Shopping Centers'. *Space and Culture* 8 (1): 83–97.

Marcińczak, Szymon, Michael Gentile and Marcin Stępniak. 2013. 'Paradoxes of (Post)socialist Segregation: Socio-spatial Divisions under Socialism and after in Metropolitan Poland'. *Urban Geography* 34 (3): 327–52.

Marcoux, Jean-Sébastien. 2001. 'The "Casser Maison" Ritual: Constructing the Self by Emptying the Home'. *Journal of Material Culture* 6 (2): 213–35.

Marcus, George. 1995. 'Ethnography in/of the World System: The Emergence of Multi-sited Ethnography'. *Annual Review of Anthropology* 24:95–117.

Marini, Sara, and Giovanni Corbellini, eds. 2016. *Recycled Theory: Illustrated Dictionary*. Macerata: Quodlibet.

Markowitz, Fran. 2000. *Coming of Age in Post-Soviet Russia*. Champaign: University of Illinois Press.

Martínez, Francisco. 2014. 'What Is Your Occupation? Playgrounds and Battlefields of Our Time'. In *Playgrounds and Battlefields*, edited by Francisco Martínez and Klemen Slabina, 21–48. Tallinn: Tallinn University Press.

Martínez, Francisco. 2015a. 'Beautiful Transgressions: Thinking the Flâneur in Late-Modern Societies'. In *Hopeless Youth!* edited by Francisco Martínez and P. Runnel, 403–89. Tartu: ENM.

Martínez, Francisco. 2015b. 'Hopeless, Helpless and Holy Youth'. In *Hopeless Youth!* edited by Francisco Martínez and P. Runnel, 15–41. Tartu: ENM.

Martínez, Francisco. 2015c. 'Old-School Photo Booths and Retro-Modernity in Berlin'. In *Hopeless Youth!* edited by Francisco Martínez and Pille Runnel, 266–91. Tartu: ENM.

Martínez, Francisco. 2017a. 'Que reste-t-il de nos amours? The Expectations of 1989–1991 Revisited'. *Anthropological Journal of European Cultures* 26 (1): 1–16.

Martínez, Francisco. 2017b. '"This Place Has Potential": Trash, Culture and Urban Regeneration in Tallinn, Estonia'. *Suomen Antropologi: Journal of the Finnish Anthropological Society* 42 (3): 4–22.

Martínez, Francisco. 2017c. 'To Whom Does History Belong? Retrofitting the Past in Post-Soviet Russia, Estonia and Georgia'. *Anthropological Journal of European Cultures* 23 (1): 98–127.

Martínez, Francisco. 2017d. 'Waste Is Not the End: For an Anthropology of Care, Maintenance and Repair'. In 'Waste and the Superfluous'. Special section, *Social Anthropology* 25 (3): 346–50.

Martínez, Francisco. Forthcoming. 'Working at, with and through the Margins of European Anthropology'. In *Common Grounds? Locating, Contesting and (Not) Defining Euro-anthropologies*, edited by Francisco Martínez and Damián Omar Martínez. Oxford: Berghahn.

Martínez, Francisco, and Marika Agu. 2016. *Aesthetics of Repair in Contemporary Georgia*. Tartu: Tartu Art Museum.

Martínez, Francisco, and P. Laviolette. 2016. 'Trespass into the Liminal: Urban Exploration in Estonia'. *Anthropological Journal of European Cultures* 25 (2): 1–24.

Martínez, Oscar J. 1994. *Border People: Life and Society in the U.S.–Mexico Borderlands*. Tucson: University of Arizona Press.

Maruste, Madli. 2014. 'From Battlefields to Playgrounds: Ethnic and National Identity of the Children of Freedom'. In *Playgrounds and Battlefields*, edited by Francisco Martínez and Klemen Slabina, 407–25. Tallinn: Tallinn University Press.

Massey, Doreen. 2005. *For Space*. London: Sage.

Materka, Edyta. 2012. 'Hybridizing Postsocialist Trajectories: An Investigation into the Biznes of the U.S. Missile Base in Rędzikowo and Urbanization of Villages in Provincial Poland'. *Anthropology of East Europe Review* 30 (1): 141–83.

McKee, Emily. 2015. 'Trash Talk: Interpreting Morality and Disorder in Negev/Naqab Landscapes'. *Current Anthropology* 56 (5): 733–53.

Medvedev, Sergei. 1999. 'A General Theory of Russian Space: A Gay Science and a Rigorous Science'. In *Beyond the Limits: The Concept of Space in Russian History and Culture*, edited by Jeremy Smith, 15–43. Helsinki: Finnish Historical Society.

Meier, Lars. 2013. 'Encounters with Haunted Industrial Workplaces and Emotions of Loss: Class-Related Senses of Place within the Memories of Metalworkers'. *Cultural Geographies* 20 (4): 467–83.

Melchior, Inge. 2015. 'Guardians of Living History: The Persistence of the Past in Post-Soviet Estonia'. PhD diss., Vrije Universiteit Amsterdam.

Michalski, Sergiusz. 1998. *Public Monuments: Art in Political Bondage, 1870–1997*. London: Reaktion.

Mikelsaar, Raik-Hiio. 2003. 'Rajame Raadile estoloogiakeskuse ja mini-Eesti?' [We are founding an estology center and mini-Estonia in Raadi]. *Tartu Postimees*, 22 May.

Mikula, Maja. 2017. 'Miniature Town Models and Memory: An Example from the European Borderlands'. *Journal of Material Culture* 22 (2): 151–72.

Millar, Kathleen. 2012. 'Trash Ties: Urban Politics, Economic Crisis and Rio de Janeiro's Garbage Dump'. In *Economies of Recycling*, edited by Catherine Alexander and Joshua Reno. London: Zed Books.

Miller, Daniel. 1998. *A Theory of Shopping*. Ithaca, NY: Cornell University Press.

Miller, Daniel. 2005. 'Introduction'. In *Materiality*, edited by Daniel Miller, 1–50. Durham, NC: Duke University Press.

Molnár, Virág. 2013. *Building the State: Architecture, Politics, and State Formation in Post-War Central Europe*. London: Routledge.

Morozov, Viacheslav. 2015. *Russia's Postcolonial Identity: A Subaltern Empire in a Eurocentric World*. New York: Palgrave Macmillan.

Moshenska, Gabriel. 2015 'Curated Ruins and the Endurance of Conflict Heritage'. *Conservation and Management of Archaeological Sites* 17 (1): 77–90.

Murawski, Michał. 2013a. 'Palaeology, or Palace-as-Methodology: Ethnographic Conceptualism, Total Urbanism, and a Stalin Skyscraper in Warsaw'. *Laboratorium: Russian Review of Social Research* 2013 (2): 56–83.

Murawski, Michał. 2013b. 'Warsaw's "Palace Complex": A Stalinist "Social Condenser" in a Capitalist City'. Paper presented at conference, 'Illusions Killed by Life: Afterlives of Soviet Constructivism', Princeton University, 10 May.

Murawski, Michał. 2017a. 'Introduction: Crystallising the Social Condenser'. *Journal of Architecture* 22 (3): 372–86.

Murawski, Michał. 2017b. 'Radical Centres: The Political Morphology of Monumentality in Warsaw and Johannesburg'. *Third Text*, 1–17. https://www.tandfonline.com/doi/full/10.10 80/09528822.2016.1275188.

Murawski, Michał. 2018. 'Actually-Existing Success: Economics, Aesthetics and the Specificity of (Still-)Socialist Urbanism. A Review Essay'. *Comparative Studies in Society and History* 60 (4).

Nabokov, Vladimir. 1952. 'Lance'. *New Yorker* 27: 22.

Napolitano, Valentina. 2015. 'Anthropology and Traces'. *Anthropological Theory* 15 (1): 47–67.

Navaro-Yashin, Yael. 2009. 'Affective Spaces, Melancholic Objects: Ruination and the Production of Anthropological Knowledge'. *Journal of the Royal Anthropological Institute* 15 (1): 1–18.

Navaro-Yashin, Yael. 2012. *The Make-Believe Space*. Durham, NC: Duke University Press.

Navaro-Yashin, Yael. 2017. 'Diversifying Affect'. *Cultural Anthropology* 32 (2): 209–14.

Nicolescu, Gabriela. 2017. 'On Ruination: Piercing the Skin of Communism in 1990s Romania'. In 'Aesthetics, Ethics and Politics'. Special issue, *World Art* 7:283–306.

Nietzsche, Friedrich. (1874) 1980. *On the Advantage and Disadvantage of History for Life*. Translated by Peter Preuss. Indianapolis: Hackett.

Nikiforova, Elena. 2004. 'The Disruption of Social and Geographic Space in Narva'. In *Beyond Post-Soviet Transition: Micro Perspectives on Challenge and Survival in Russia and Estonia*, edited by Risto Alapuro, Ilkka Liikanen and Markku Lonkila, 148–64. Helsinki: Kikimora.

Nora, Pierre. 1989. 'Between Memory and History: Les lieux de mémoire'. *Representations* 26:7–25.

Norman, Kristina, ed. 2009. *After-War*. Tallinn: Centre for Contemporary Arts.

Nugin, Raili. 2010. 'Social Time as the Basis of Generational Consciousness'. *Trames* 14 (4): 342–66.

Nugin, Raili. 2011. 'Coming of Age in Transition: Some Self-Reflexive Social Portraits of the 1970s Cohort'. PhD diss., Tallinn University.

Nugin, Raili. 2015. *The 1970s: Portrait of a Generation at the Doorstep*. Tartu: Tartu University Press.

Nugin, Raili, Anu Kannike, and Maaris Raudsepp, eds. 2016. *Generations in Estonia: Contemporary Perspectives on Turbulent Times*. Tartu: University of Tartu Press.

Offenhuber, Dietmar. 2017. *Waste Is Information: Infrastructure Legibility and Governance*. Cambridge, MA: MIT Press.

Ojari, Triin. 2001. 'On the Threshold of a New Age: The 1990s in Estonian Architecture'. In *Ülbed Üheksakümnendad: Probleemid, Teemad ja Tähendused 1990: Aastate Eesti Kunstis* [Nosy nineties: Problems, themes and meanings in Estonian art in the 1990s], edited by Sirje Helme and Johannes Saar, 265–77. Tallinn: Kaasaegse Kunsti Eesti Keskus.

Ojari, Triin. 2012. 'Nostalgia and the Future of Soviet Architecture's Heritage'. In *How Long is the Life of a Building?*, edited by Tüüne-Kristin Vaikla, 151–6. [Catalogue Estonian National Exhibition at the XIII International Architecture Exhibition – la Biennale di Venezia.] Tallinn: Estonian Centre of Architecture.

Okely, Judith. 1996. *Own or Other Culture*. London: Routledge.

Olick, Jeffrey. 2007. *The Politics of Regret*. London: Routledge.

Olivier, Laurent. 2011. *The Dark Abyss of Time*. Lanham, MD: AltaMira.

Õnnepalu, Tõnu. 2002. 'Essee: Ideaal ja spliin' [Essay: Ideal and spleen]. *Postimees*, 8 November. https://arvamus.postimees.ee/1978415/essee-ideaal-ja-spliin.

Oushakine, Serguei. 2007. '"We're Nostalgic but We're Not Crazy": Retrofitting the Past in Russia'. *Russian Review* 66 (3): 451–82.

Oushakine, Serguei. 2009. *The Patriotism of Despair*. Ithaca, NY: Cornell University Press.

Oushakine, Serguei. 2010. 'New Lives of Old Forms: On Returns and Repetitions'. *Genre* 43 (3–4): 409–57.

Oushakine, Serguei. 2013. 'Remembering in Public: On the Affective Management of History'. *Ab Imperio* 1/2013:269–302.

Oushakine, Serguei. 2014. '"Against the Cult of Things": On Soviet Productivism, Storage Economy, and Commodities with No Destination'. *Russian Review* 73 (2): 198–236.

Paasi, Ansi. 1995. 'Constructing Territories, Boundaries and Regional Identities'. In *Contested Territory: Border Disputes at the Edge of the Former Soviet Empire*, edited by Tuomas Forsberg, 42–61. Aldershot: Edward Elgar.

Pachenkov, Oleg. 2011. 'Every City Has the Flea Market It Deserves: The Phenomenon of Urban Flea Markets in St. Petersburg'. In *Urban Spaces after Socialism: Ethnographies of Public Spaces in Eurasian Cities*, edited by Tsypylma Darieva, Wolfgang Kaschuba and Melanie Krebs, 181–206. Frankfurt am Main: Campus Verlag.

Pae, Kaja, ed. 2011. *Linnafoorumid / Urban Forums*. Tallinn: Estonian Centre of Architecture.

Pallasmaa, Juhani. 2005. *The Eyes of the Skin: Architecture and the Senses*. Chichester: Wiley.

Palmberger, Monika. 2016. *How Generations Remember: Conflicting Histories and Shared Memories in Post-War Bosnia and Herzegovina*. Basingstoke: Palgrave Macmillan.

Paperny, Vladimir. 2002. *Architecture in the Age of Stalin: Culture Two*. Cambridge: Cambridge University Press.

Pardo, José Luis. 2010. *Nunca fue tan hermosa la basura*. Barcelona: Galaxia Gutenber.

Pelkmans, Mathijs. 2003. 'The Social Life of Empty Buildings: Imagining the Transition in Post-Soviet Ajaria'. *Focaal* 41:121–36.

Pétursdóttir, Þóra. 2013. 'Concrete Matters: Ruins of Modernity and the Things Called Heritage'. *Journal of Social Archaeology* 13 (1): 31–53.

Pétursdóttir, Þóra. 2016. 'For Love of Ruins'. In *Elements of Architecture: Assembling Archaeology, Atmosphere and the Performance of Building Spaces*, edited by Mikke Bille and Tim Flohr Sørensen, 365–86. London: Routledge.

Pétursdóttir, Þóra. 2017. 'Drift'. In *Multispecies Archaeology*, edited by Suzanne Pilaar Birch, 85–101. London: Routledge.

Pétursdóttir, Þóra, and Bjørnar Olsen. 2014. 'An Archaeology of Ruins'. In *Ruin Memories: Materialities, Aesthetics and the Archaeology of the Recent Past*, edited by Bjørnar Olsen and Þóra Pétursdóttir, 3–29. London: Routledge.

Pfoser, Alena. 2014. 'Between Russia and Estonia: Narratives of Place in a New Borderland'. *Nationalities Papers* 42 (2): 269–85.

Pfoser, Alena. 2017. 'Nested Peripheralisation: Remaking the East–West Border in the Russian–Estonian Borderland'. *East European Politics and Societies and Cultures* 31 (1): 26–43.

Pikner, Tarmo, and Jussi S. Jauhiainen. 2014. 'Dis/appearing Waste and Afterwards'. *Geoforum* 54:39–48.

Pilkington, Hilary Anne, and Elena Omel'chenko. 2013. 'Regrounding Youth Cultural Theory (in Post-Socialist Youth Cultural Practice)'. *Sociology Compass* 7 (3): 208–24.

Pilkington, Hilary Anne, Elena Omel'chenko, Moya Flynn, Ul'iana Bliudina and Elena Starkova. 2002. *Looking West? Cultural Globalization and Russian Youth Cultures*. Philadelphia: Pennsylvania State University Press.

Pine, Jason. 2016. 'Last Chance Incorporated'. *Cultural Anthropology* 31 (2): 297–318.

Pinney, Christopher. 2005. 'Things Happen: Or, from Which Moment Does That Object Come?' In *Materiality*, edited by Daniel Miller, 256–72. Durham, NC: Duke University Press.

Pop-Eleches, Grigore. 2007. 'Historical Legacies and Post-Communist Regime Change'. *Journal of Politics* 69 (4): 908–26.

Preiman, Siim. 2017. *Children of the New East*. [Catalogue of the exhibition.] Tallinn: Tallinn Art Hall.

Qualls, Karl D. 2009. *From Ruins to Reconstruction: Urban Identity in Soviet Sevastopol after World War II*. Ithaca, NY: Cornell University Press.

Rabinow, Paul. 2007. *Marking Time: On the Anthropology of the Contemporary*. Princeton, NJ: Princeton University Press.

Rancière, Jacques. 2006. *The Politics of Aesthetics*. Translated by Gabriel Rockhill. London: Continuum.

Rancière, Jacques. 2015. 'The Concept of Anachronism and the Historian's Truth'. *In/Print* 3 (1): 21–52.

Rander, Tanel. 2016. *The Power of Nostalgia*. [Catalogue of the exhibition 'Third Way'.] Tallinn: Tallinn Art Hall.

Rander, Tanel. 2017. 'Abiks Idaeurooplase Inkubeerijale' [Help for the Eastern European incubator]. Contribution to the exhibition at the Museum of Contemporary Art of Estonia.

Rathje, William. 1996. 'The Archaeology of Us'. In *Encyclopaedia Britannica's Yearbook of Science and the Future*, 158–77. New York: Encyclopaedia Britannica.

Rausing, Sigrid. 2004. *History, Memory, and Identity in Post-Soviet Estonia: The End of a Collective Farm*. Oxford: Oxford University Press.

Ries, Nancy. 1997. *Russian Talk: Culture and Conversation during Perestroika*. Ithaca, NY: Cornell University Press.

Ringel, Felix. 2013. 'Epistemic Collaborations in Contexts of Change: On Conceptual Fieldwork and the Timing of Anthropological Knowledge'. *Laboratorium: Russian Review of Social Research* 2013 (2): 36–55.

Robinson, Sarah. 2015. 'Boundaries of Skin: John Dewey, Didier Anzieu and Architectural Possibility'. In *Architecture and Empathy*, edited by Philip Tidwell, 42–63. Espoo: Tapio Wirkkala Rut Bryk Foundation.

Rosa, Hartmut. 2013. *Social Acceleration*. New York: Columbia University Press.

Rosner, Daniela K., and Morgan G. Ames. 2014. 'Designing for Repair? Infrastructures and Materialities of Breakdown'. *Proceedings of the 2014 ACM Conference on Computer Supported Cooperative Work*, 319–31. New York: ACM.

Runnel, Pille, Kaarel Tarand and Merike Tamm. 2014. *A Guide to Raadi*. Tartu: ENM.

Runnel, Pille, Taavi Tatsi and Pille Pruulmann-Vengerfeldt. 2014. 'Who Authors the Nation? The Debate Surrounding the Building of the New Estonian National Museum'. In *Democratising the Museum: Reflections on Participatory Technologies*, edited by Pille Runnel and Pille Pruulmann-Vengerfeldt, 19–34. Frankfurt am Main: Peter Lang.

Ruudi, Ingrid. 2015. *Unbuilt: Visions for a New Society, 1986–1994*. Tallinn: Museum of Estonian Architecture.

Saar, Maarja. 2010. 'Reconfiguring Nation and Diaspora: Self-Identifying Estonians in Estonia as a Diaspora'. Master's thesis, University of Wisconsin, Madison.

Sahlins, Marshall. 2013. *What Kinship Is – And Is Not*. Chicago: University of Chicago Press.

Scanlan, John. 2005. *On Garbage*. London: Reaktion.

Schlögel, Karl. 2003. *Im Raume lesen wir die Zeit: Über Zivilisationsgeschichte und Geopolitik*. Munich: Hanser.

Schlögel, Karl. 2012 'Theses on Post-Socialist Urban Transformation Chasing Warsaw'. In *Chasing Warsaw: Socio-Material Dynamics of Urban Change since 1990*, edited by Monika Grubbauer and Joanna Kusiak, 25–32. Frankfurt am Main: Campus Verlag.

Schneider, Arnd, and Christopher Wright. 2010. *Between Art and Anthropology: Contemporary Ethnographic Practice*. Oxford: Berg.

Schofield, John, William Gray Johnson and Colleen M. Beck, eds. 2002. *Matériel Culture: The Archaeology of the Twentieth Century Conflict*. London: Routledge.

Schwenkel, Christina. 2006. 'Recombinant History: Transnational Practices of Memory and Knowledge Production in Contemporary Vietnam'. *Cultural Anthropology* 21 (1): 3–30.

Schwenkel, Christina. 2013. 'Post/Socialist Affect: Ruination and Reconstruction of the Nation in Urban Vietnam'. *Cultural Anthropology* 28 (2): 252–77.

Scott, James C. 1998. *Seeing Like a State: How Certain Schemes to Improve the Human Condition Have Failed*. New Haven, CT: Yale University Press.

Sebald, W. G. 2001. *Austerlitz*. Translated by Anthea Bell. New York: Random House.

Sennett, Richard. 2008. *The Craftsman*. London: Penguin.

Sgibnev, Wladimir. 2015. 'Remont: Housing Adaptation as Meaningful Practice of Space Production in Post-Soviet Tajikistan'. *Europa Regional* 22 (1–2): 53–64.

Shevchenko, Olga. 2009. *Crisis and the Everyday in Postsocialist Moscow*. Bloomington: Indiana University Press.

Silk, Endre, and Claire Wallace. 1999. 'The Development of Open-Air Markets in East-Central Europe'. *International Journal of Urban and Regional Research* 23 (4): 715–37.

Simmel, Georg. 1965. 'The Ruin'. In *Essays on Sociology, Philosophy and Aesthetics*, edited by Kurt H. Wolff, 264–6. New York: Harper and Row.

Simmel, Georg. 1997. *Simmel on Culture*. Edited by David Frisby and Mike Featherstone. London: Sage.

Smith, David J., and Stuart Burch. 2011. 'Enacting Identities in the EU–Russia Borderland: An Ethnography of Place and Public Monuments'. *East European Politics and Societies* 26 (2): 400–24.

Smithson, Robert. 1972. *Robert Smithson: The Collected Writings*, edited by Jack Flam. Berkeley: University of California Press.

Ssorin-Chaikov, Nikolai. 2003. *The Social Life of the State in Subarctic Siberia*. Palo Alto, CA: Stanford University Press.

Ssorin-Chaikov, Nikolai. 2013. 'Ethnographic Conceptualism: An Introduction'. *Laboratorium: Russian Review of Social Research* 2013 (2): 5–18.

Ssorin-Chaikov, Nikolai. 2016. 'Soviet Debris: Failure and the Poetics of Unfinished Construction in Northern Siberia'. *Social Research* 83 (3): 689–721.

Stenning, Alison. 2005. 'Where Is the Post-Socialist Working Class? Working-Class Lives in the Spaces of (Post-)Socialism'. *Sociology* 39 (5): 983–99.

Stenning, Alison. 2010. 'The UK Economy and the Transformation of East Central Europe'. In *The Economic Geography of the UK*, edited by Neil M. Coe and Andrew Jones, 239–52. London: Sage.

Stenning, Alison, and Kathrin Hörschelmann. 2008. 'History, Geography and Difference in the Post-Socialist World: Or, Do We Still Need Post-Socialism?' *Antipode* 40 (2): 312–35.

Stewart, Kathleen. 2007. *Ordinary Affects*. Durham, NC: Duke University Press.

Stewart, Kathleen. 2011. 'Atmospheric Attunements'. *Environment and Planning D: Society and Space* 29 (3): 445–53.

Stewart, Kathleen. 2014. 'Tactile Compositions'. In *Objects and Materials*, edited by Penny Harvey, Eleanor Conlin Casella, Gillian Evans, Hannah Knox, Christine McLean, Elizabeth B. Silva, Nicholas Thoburn and Kath Woodward, 119–27. London: Routledge.

Stoler, Ann Laura. 2004. 'Affective States'. In *A Companion to the Anthropology of Politics*, edited by David Nugent and Joan Vincent, 4–20. Malden, MA: Blackwell.

Stoler, Ann Laura, ed. 2013. *Imperial Debris: On Ruins and Ruination*. Durham, NC: Duke University Press.

Strathern, Marilyn. 1987. 'The Limits of Auto-anthropology'. In *Anthropology at Home,* edited by Anthony Jackson, 59–67. London: Tavistock.

Strathern, Marilyn. 1988. *The Gender of the Gift: Problems with Women and Problems with Society in Melanesia*. Berkeley: University of California Press.

Szelenyi, Ivan. 1996. 'Cities under Socialism—and After'. In *Cities after Socialism: Urban and Regional Change in Conflict in Post-Socialist Societies*, edited by Gregory Andrusz, Michael Harloe and Ivan Szelenyi, 286–317. Oxford: Blackwell.

Sztompka, Piotr. 1996. 'Looking Back: The Year of 1989 as a Cultural and Civilizational Break'. *Communist and Post-Communist Studies* 29 (2): 110–23.

Tamm, Marek. 2005. 'The Status of the ENM within Estonian Culture'. *Maja*. http://web. archive.org/web/20090904112331/http://www.museumcompetition.org/en/museum.

Tamm, Marek. 2013. 'In Search of Lost Time: Memory Politics in Estonia, 1991–2011'. *Nationalities Papers* 41 (4): 651–74.

Tamm, Marek. 2016. 'The Republic of Historians: Historians as Nation-Builders in Estonia (Late 1980s–early 1990s)'. *Rethinking History* 20 (2): 154–71.

Thompson, Michael. 1979. *Rubbish Theory: The Creation and Destruction of Value*. Oxford: Oxford University Press.

Thrift, Nigel. 2004. 'Intensities of Feeling: Towards a Spatial Politics of Affect'. *Geografiska Annaler: Series B, Human Geography* 86 (1): 57–78.

Thrift, Nigel. 2005. 'But Malice Aforethought: Cities and the Natural History of Hatred'. *Transactions of the Institute of British Geographers* 30 (2): 133–50.

Tilley, Christopher. 2011. 'Materializing Identities: An Introduction'. *Journal of Material Culture* 16 (4): 347–57.

Tilley, Christopher. 2017. *Landscape in the Longue Durée*. London: UCL Press.

Tischleder, Babette B., and Sarah Wasserman, eds. 2015. *Cultures of Obsolescence: History, Materiality, and the Digital Age*. New York: Palgrave Macmillan.

Titma, Mikk, ed. 1999. *Kolmekümneaastaste Põlvkonna Sotsiaalne Portree* [The social portrait of the thirty-year-olds]. Tallinn: Teaduste Akadeemia Kirjastus.

Trigg, Dylan. 2009. 'The Place of Trauma: Memory, Hauntings, and the Temporality of Ruins'. *Memory Studies* 2 (1): 87–101.

Tsuda, Tsuda, Maria Tapias and Xavier Escandell. 2014. 'Locating the Global in Transnational. Ethnography'. *Journal of Contemporary Ethnography* 43 (2): 123–47.

Turner, Victor. 1969. *The Ritual Process: Structure and Anti-Structure*. Chicago: Aldine.

Turner, Victor. 1973. 'The Centre out There: Pilgrims' Goal'. *History of Religions* 12 (3): 191–230.

Turner, Victor. 1974. 'Liminal to Liminoid in Play, Flow, and Ritual: An Essay in Comparative Symbology'. *Rice University Studies* 60 (3): 53–92.

Tuvikene, Tauri. 2016. 'Strategies for Comparative Urbanism: Post-Socialism as a De-territorialized Concept'. *International Journal of Urban and Regional Research* 40 (1): 132–46.

Unt, Mati. 1985. *The Autumn Ball: Scenes of City Life*. Translated by Mart Aru. Tallinn: Perioodika.

Văetiși, Șerban. 2011. 'The Material Culture of the Postsocialist City: A Success/Failure Perspective'. *Martor* 16:81–95.

Vaikla, Tüüne-Kristin, ed. 2012. *How Long Is the Life of a Building?* [Catalogue Estonian National Exhibition at the XIII International Architecture Exhibition – la Biennale di Venezia.] Talinn: Estonian Centre of Architecture.

van Dijck, José. 2001. 'Bodyworlds: The Art of Plastinated Cadavers'. *Configurations* 9 (1): 99–126.

Varga-Harris, Christine. 2015. *Stories of House and Home: Soviet Apartment Life during the Khrushchev Years*. Ithaca, NY: Cornell University Press.

Varner, Eric R. 2004. *Mutilation and Transformation: Damnatio Memoriae and Roman Imperial Portraiture*. Leiden: Brill.

Verdery, Katherine. 1996. *What Was Socialism, and What Comes Next?* Princeton, NJ: Princeton University Press.

Verdery, Katherine. 1999. *The Political Lives of Dead Bodies: Reburial and Postsocialist Change.* New York: Columbia University Press.

Verdery, Katherine. 2003. *The Vanishing Hectare: Property and Value in Postsocialist Transylvania.* Ithaca, NY: Cornell University Press.

Vihalemm, Peeter, Marju Lauristin and Ivar Tallo. 1997. 'Development of Political Culture in Estonia'. In *Return to the Western World: Cultural and Political Perspectives on the Estonian Post-Communist Transition*, edited by Marju Lauristin and Peeter Vihalemm, 197–210. Tartu: Tartu University Press.

Viires, Piret. 2003. 'Mustamäe Metamorphoses'. In *Koht ja paik / Place and Location*, edited by Virve Sarapik and Kadri Tüür, 395–403. Tallinn: Eesti Kunstiakadeemia.

Vissak, Tiia. 2014. 'Nonlinear Internationalization in the Context of Nonlinear Economic Development: The Case of Krenholm Group'. *Transformations in Business and Economics* 13 (2A): 431–47.

Voyce, Malcolm. 2006. 'Shopping Malls in Australia: The End of Public Space and the Rise of "Consumerist Citizenship"?' *Journal of Sociology* 42 (3): 269–86.

Vukov, Nikolai. 2008. 'The "Unmemorable" and the "Unforgettable": "Museumizing" the Socialist Past in Post-1989 Bulgaria'. In *Past for the Eyes: East European Representations of Communism in Cinema and Museums after 1989*, edited by Oksana Sarkisova and Péter Apor, 307–34. Budapest: Central European University Press.

Wanner, Catherine. 2016. 'The Return of Czernowitz: Urban Affect, Nostalgia, and the Politics of Place-Making in a European Borderland City'. *City and Society* 28 (2): 123–264.

Weekes, Lorraine. 2017. 'Debating Vabamu: Changing Names and Narratives at Estonia's Museum of Occupations'. *Cultures of History Forum*, 25 April. http://www.cultures-of-history .uni-jena.de/debates/estonia/debating-vabamu-changing-names-and-narratives-at -estonias-museum-of-occupations/.

Weeks, Harry. 2010. 'Re-cognizing the Post-Soviet Condition: The Documentary Turn in Contemporary Art in the Baltic States'. *Studies in Eastern European Cinema* 1 (1): 57–70.

Weiss-Wendt, Anton. 1997. *Must-valge linn: Vana Narva fotoajalugu* [Black-and-white town: A photographic history of old Narva]. Tallinn: Tallinna Raamatutrükikoda.

Weszkalnys, Gisa. 2010. *Berlin, Alexanderplatz: Transforming Place in a Unified Germany.* Oxford: Berghahn.

Williams, Raymond. 1977. *Marxism and Literature.* Oxford: Oxford University Press.

Wittenberg, Jason. 2015. 'Conceptualizing Historical Legacies'. *East European Politics and Societies and Cultures* 20 (2): 366–78.

Wolff, Larry. 1994. *Inventing Eastern Europe.* Palo Alto, CA: Stanford University Press.

Yablon, Nick. 2010. *Untimely Ruins: An Archaeology of American Urban Modernity, 1819–1919.* Chicago: University of Chicago Press.

Yampolsky, Mikhail. 1995. 'In the Shadow of Monuments: Notes on Iconoclasm and Time'. In *Soviet Hieroglyphics: Visual Culture in Late Twentieth-Century Russia*, edited by Nancy Condee, 93–113. Bloomington: Indiana University Press.

Yiftachel, Oren. 2009. 'Theoretical Notes on "Gray Cities": The Coming of Urban Apartheid?' *Planning Theory* 5 (3): 211–22.

Young, James E. 1993. *The Texture of Memory: Holocaust Memorials and Meaning.* New Haven, CT: Yale University Press.

Yurchak, Alexei. 2005. *Everything Was Forever, Until It Was No More: The Last Soviet Generation.* Princeton, NJ: Princeton University Press.

Zhelnina, Anna. 2009. 'From Barakholka to Shopping Mall: Transformation of Retail Spaces in St. Petersburg'. *Anthropology of East Europe* 27 (1): 51–65.

Zhelnina, Anna. 2011. ' "It's Like a Museum Here": The Shopping Mall as Public Space'. *Laboratorium: Russian Review of Social Research* 2011 (2): 48–69.

Index

Page numbers in italics refer to figures.

communities, temporality of, 3–4
construction, demolition and, ix, 27–8
Contemporary Art Museum of Estonia
(EKKM), 34, 36–7, *37*
Cross of Liberty, 40–1, *42*
Culture One and Culture Two dichotomy,
142–3

decay, 128–9
demolition process, ix, 27–8
design, method, x, xiii, 5, 10; architecture, 17,
112, 122, 146, 148, 182; interior, 57, 74,
104; landscape, 40–42, 151; policies, 13
dispossession, 12, 164

Eastern Europe, concept of, 18, 205–6
EKA gallery of Tallinn: 'act of vandalism' at,
100–1; objects on display at, 88–9, *89,*
96–8, *99*; poster of exhibition at, *100*;
selection of objects for, 86, 96, 98–9;
shape and location of, 99; TV broadcast,
99–100; visitors' feedback about, 99,
102
Estonia: attitude towards the past, 6, 22–3,
198, 199–200; as borderland, 177, 181;
celebrations of the 100th anniversary of,
224; citizenship, 160; civic activism, 203,
227; 'cruel optimism' of society, 213;
cultural separation in, 179; currency, 176,
177; destruction of Soviet landmarks, 23,
27–8; emergence of post-post-socialist,
222, 225; emigration from, 214;
e-residency programme, 171, 219;
generational differences, ix, 6, 7, 77, 184,
211–12, 225; historic development of,
168; housing in, 149; income disparity,
160; language policy, 160, 161; legal
continuity of the state, 22; memory
politics, 192; migrant workers, 214–15;
national identity, 178–9, 182, 192–3, 198,
200; NATO military base in, 14; Nordic
orientation of, 225; official and
alternative historical narratives, 22;
post-Soviet transformation of, 13, 22–3,
51–3, 149–50; printing technology in,
72–3; private ownership in, 150; railways,
168; restoration of monuments, 22;
Russia's boundary treaty with, 176; Soviet
cultural legacies, 16–17, 19, 44–5;
Westernisation agenda, 199
Estonian Air, xi
Estonian History Museum in Tallinn: *My Free
Country* exhibition, 198; statues of Lenin
in the backyard of, 45, *46*
Estonian National Museum (ENM):
architectural design, 18, 191–2, 193;
construction of, 182–3; funding of, 196;
main tasks of, 196–7, 200; presentation of
Estonian culture in, 184; public debates

about, 191, 193, 194–6; scholar's views
of, 197
Estonian Print and Paper Museum, 69, 71,
73, *73*
Estonian street art, *209,* 209–10
'Estonian' time, vs. 'the Russian' time, 6
European Union, 11, 17, 65, 156, 170, 214
euroremont, definition of, 60
everyday life, 58, 59
everyday micropowers, 60–3

fakeness, 38, 94, 121
fashion, post-Soviet style, 217–18, *218*
fieldwork, 9, 98–9
Finland, 4, 177, 214, 228
flea markets, 105
forgetting process, 26

Gallery of the Installation, Photography and
Sculpture Departments of the Estonian
Academy of Arts (ISFAG), 37–8, *38, 39,*
39–40
garbage collection initiative, 227
Garbology project, 20–1
generational change, ix, 6, 7, 14–15, 18, 201,
225
'generational habitus', 184
generational memories, 203–5
globalisation, 205
graffiti, 208–10

*Help for the Stoker of the Central Heating
Boiler* (installation-performance), 34,
35, 36–7
heritage: classification of, 24; vs. legacies,
24–5, 26; notion of 'entropic', 128
How Long Is the Life of a Building? (Vaikla),
131
Humphrey, Caroline, 219

identity formation, 24, 70, 192
ideology of restoration, 22
I Looked into the Walls and Saw
(meta-exhibition), 37–8
Iru Power Plant, 228
Ivangorod, 160, 168, 172, 176, *177, 178*

Jaama Turg (Railway market). *See* Baltic street
market

Kinnisvara, Astri, 101
Konstanet (non-profit gallery), 219
Kreenholm factory, 34, 162, *163,* 163–4, *164*
KultuuriKatel (Creative Hub), 34

landscape: acceleration, 140, 150; edgy, 117;
historical, 23; modernist, 152;
monumental, 151; patchwork, 18, 182;
political, 61; urban, 40, 135

9 781787 353541